INFINITE REACH

INFINITE REACH

SPIRITUALITY IN A SCIENTIFIC WORLD

John Biersdorf

RESOURCE *Publications* · Eugene, Oregon

INFINITE REACH
Spirituality in a Scientific World

Resource Publications
An Imprint of Wipf and Stock Publishers
199 W. 8th Ave., Suite 3
Eugene, OR 97401

www.wipfandstock.com

PAPERBACK ISBN 13: 978-1-4982-3865-6
HARDCOVER ISBN 13: 978-1-4982-3867-0

Manufactured in the U.S.A.   06/14/2016

To my wife Ruth who made it possible

Love the questions themselves

- RAINER MARIA RILKE

CONTENTS

Acknowledgements | xi

INTRODUCTION | 1

CHAPTER ONE

SPIRITUAL KNOWING AND SCIENTIFIC KNOWING | 10

    I-Thou, I-It | 11

    Scientific Knowing: Explanation | 17

    Spiritual Knowing: Relationship | 19

    Discovery | 24

    Tradition | 25

    Community Authorization | 26

    Summary | 28

Chapter Two

A BRIEF HISTORY OF SPIRITUAL KNOWING | 30

    Hunting-Gathering Knowing | 32

    Collective Knowing | 34

    The Axial Age | 37

    Declining Violence | 38

    Transforming Sacrifice | 42

    Summary | 44

Chapter Three

AXIAL AGE INSIGHTS | 46

    Unlimited Awareness | 46

    Unconditional Love | 51

    Stages Of Faith | 54

    Summary | 58

Chapter 4

EVOLUTION OF SCIENTIFIC KNOWING | 59

A Brief History Of Scientific Knowing | 59
Scale Of Scientific Knowing | 67
Unintended Consequences | 71
Infinite Reach | 74
Summary | 79

Chapter 5

BRAIN-MIND RESEARCH AND MEDITATION | 80

The Self In Brain-Mind Functioning | 81
The Medial Prefrontal Cortex | 84
Vipassana Meditation | 85
Meditation And The Body | 87
Experiencing Meditation | 90
Personal Growth Methods | 92
Self-Transformation | 93
Integration | 96
Summary | 101

Chapter 6

DIMENSIONS OF PRACTICE: SILENCE, RITUAL, VISION | 102

Silence | 103
Ritual | 108
Vision | 112
Summary | 118

Chapter Seven

COSMOLOGY: THE SELF-ORGANIZING UNIVERSE | 119

Large Versus Small | 121
Fields | 124
Evolution | 128
The Evolution Of Human Life | 130
How Humans Shape Evolution | 133
Is Mathematics Real? | 137
The Challenge | 139
Summary | 142

Chapter Eight

SPIRITUAL KNOWING IN OUR EVOLVING UNIVERSE | 144

Fractals Of Wholeness | 146
Summary | 157

Chapter Nine

MYSTERY | 158

"Dunno" Mind | 158
Facing Death | 160
Responses | 161
The Kingdom Of God | 171
Signs Of The Kingdom | 176
Finding Our Voice | 178
Mystery | 179

Bibliography | 181
Index | 193

ACKNOWLEDGEMENTS

I am grateful for to the communities who shaped and challenged my thinking: the colleague groups in our Doctor of Ministry program in what became the Ecumenical Theological Seminary; the congregation of Point of Vision Presbyterian Church, and Green Gulch and the Soto Zen Buddhist communities founded by Shunryu Suzuki Roshi. I especially am in debt the scientists and mystics whose names appear in these pages, and to those persons who gave essential feedback and helped shaped the manuscript: Alan Green, John Hay, Lois Robbins, Ken Kaibel, and many others, but above all, to my wife Ruth, for her creative suggestions, critical feedback, careful copy editing, and endless typing when my electro-magnetic sensitivities prevented me from using a computer. Special thanks also to the atheists in my family—my brother Bill and my son Mark, for their insights and challenges. And my gratitude to Wipf and Stock publishers for making the book available.

INTRODUCTION

In July 1969 while on vacation in Vermont, we let our oldest son Mark, who was nine years old at the time, stay up late with us one night to watch the first man land on the moon. His grandfather, a child of Swedish immigrants, had run through the streets of Boston one day at the same age of nine to catch a glimpse of the first horseless carriage in the city. In our family history, it had taken us two generations to get from the invention of the automobile to space travel.

For the first time in the history of the world, we live in a situation of continuing and increasing change. The mathematician and philosopher Alfred North Whitehead announced this sea change in world culture in his book *Science and the Modern World* in 1925: "The world is now faced with a self-evolving system it cannot stop." This self-evolving system, he said, is caused by the "novel circumstances of rapid scientific and technological advance."[1] The marriage of science and technology makes this continuing revolution powerful and permanent. New forms of thought have arisen and passed away in times past, but now the results of scientific thought are being permanently actualized in this world through new technology. This irrevocably changes our personal lives, the social order, and the environment, faster and faster, exponentially faster. We are living, to paraphrase Margaret Mead, in a world in which we are immigrants and our children are native-born.[2]

Mark, now in middle age, is a self-professed atheist. In college, he had been evangelized and offended by the fundamentalist Christians he met. As a younger man, Mark once remarked that he didn't believe in anything he could not see. But a few years ago he happened across a form of yoga that

1. (Whitehead 1925)204–5.
2. (Mead 1959)198

involved rigorous breathing and stretching. He was hooked, and has had transcendental experiences including a state of bliss that lasted for three days with residual love and acceptance of those around him. But he insists his yoga is not religion. Like so many of his and younger generations, he does not go to church, and is not "religious."

When I meditate in infinite silence I find the deepest knowing for my life and my world—a knowing as true and necessary as any scientific discovery or new technological gadget, but clearly different.

My lifelong interest and passion has been to discover how these two ways of knowing—spiritual and scientific—intersect. I want to discover a transparent and accessible way to do so, which works for a person rooted both in spirituality and in our contemporary scientific and technological culture. I want it to work for someone like me, and for the increasing numbers of Americans who consider themselves spiritual but not religious. Or spiritual *and* religious. Or "none of the above."

It is a remarkable journey, this evolution of the unique ability of human beings to create mental representations of the world. It suddenly emerged from our hominoid ancestors, as Tattersall describes in Chapter Two. You can see it in the incessant talking of hunting-gathering peoples, waking even during the night to continue the conversation; as Jared Diamond learned, the continuous sharing of mental constructs reassures and binds small bands of people together in the midst of a dangerous and unpredictable natural environment.[3] Schizophrenics can learn to examine their hallucinations to ascertain which ones correspond to actual sensory experience. *A Beautiful Mind* records how John Nash came to realize that the children he saw never changed or grew; hence they were imaginary.[4] Addicts in twelve-step programs confess their inability to resist the pull of representations from brain chemistry through dependence on a higher power, and through a structured program of confessing and meeting with others.[5] New technology in the latest versions of video games can bring us full circle to the unceasing representations of hunting-gathering people—only now relating with fictional representations on a computer instead of talking to others in a threatening environment.

Mental representations diverge into two streams in history. One is the rise of

3. (Diamond 2012)204–205
4. (Nasar 1998)324–327,351
5. (Twelve Steps: A Way Out 1987)

good mental representations or explanations increasingly able to control and predict what we do in the world through ever-advancing science and technology; here it is called *scientific knowing*. The other stream, called *spiritual knowing*, looks through the whole apparatus of mental representations to directly experience the world "so various, so beautiful, so new," as Matthew Arnold put it. There is no apologetic intent here, only the patient determination to find a way to speak the truth I know—that I really know—in a scientific world which "Hath really neither joy, nor love, nor light, nor certitude, nor peace nor help for pain."[6] Spiritual knowing sees directly and clearly through all the mental representations, into the true nature of ourselves and the world. The masthead of the *Christian Century* magazine suggests we can have both streams together: "Thinking critically, living faithfully." This book explores how and to what extent that may be possible. It seems a simple task, but three preliminary considerations are necessary to embark on this journey.

First, we set aside any arbitrary imposition of ideological or institutional authority. In exploring this question, fundamentalists, the Pope speaking *ex-cathedra*, and atheists alike may simply offer an appeal to authority. David Deutsch compares it to a weary parent, worn down by his or her child's endless questions, who just retorts, "because I said so."[7] There is no explanation; the appeal to authority "because I said so" is the entire explanation in itself.

In his play *Cymbeline*, Shakespeare uses the word "seems" in a couple of different ways. In the first place something is false—it seems not what it really is. King Cymbeline thinks his evil queen is "like her seeming" because she is beautiful and flatters him, but "Both her looks and her words deceived."[8]

No carefully tested empirical predictions, no heartfelt confessions, no mystical insights, no admitted flights of speculation and conjecture, no beautiful and profound poetry. That all belongs to Shakespeare's second set of meanings: truth, wonder, beauty, and revelation.[9]

When Cymbeline's daughter Imogene awakens after being drugged and falsely buried, she exclaims:

6. (Arnold 2009)171

7. (Deutsch 2011)311

8. (Garber 2004)820–821

9. (Tippett2010)264 Quoting John Polkinghorne: "A sense of wonder when you see the beautiful structure of the world or the way things work."

"The dream's here still, even when I wake. It is
without me as within me, not imagined, felt"[10]

Buddha famously charged his followers not to accept any teaching on his authority, but to test out everything in their own experience.[11] Christian theology traditionally distinguishes between natural and revealed theology—what you can know by looking around in the world versus what is only revealed in Christ. But revealed theology is not privileged by any authority here. It is simply one of the possible ways of spiritual knowing included in Shakespeare's second sense of seeming—beauty and wonder and truth, "not imagined, felt."

"Because I said so" reasoning is usually accompanied and rationalized by an ideology, a constricted and inflexible belief system, into which all the incredible range and layers of human experience must be jammed. A popular ideology in this time of science and technology is some form of materialism. All reality is reified, or "thingified"—reduced to separate pieces of matter, reminiscent of Alfred North Whitehead's fallacy of misplaced concreteness.[12] Marcus Borg, the New Testament scholar, taught at Oregon State University. A student would come up after class and say, "Professor Borg, I don't believe in God." He would reply, "Tell me about the God you don't believe in." It would turn out that Borg didn't believe in that God either.[13]

As we shall see, tradition and community authorization enter into both spiritual and scientific knowing. But they are interwoven into rich and complex webs of discourse. "Because I said so," standing by itself forbidding critical thinking or any other consideration, is not useful. The Episcopal Church used to have a slogan, "Jesus came to save us from our sins, not our minds."

Second, we need to recognize how difficult it may be to understand each other. The intent of this book is not contained in one academic field or discipline. It has to range over and discover connections among a daunting collection of different areas of study, each with its own traditions, paradigms, methods, and assumptions. And even within what might be thought of as one field, communication may be problematic.

10. (Shakespeare 1997)

11. (K. Armstrong, Buddha 2001)7

12. (Whitehead 1925)52

13. Borg, Marcus, Lecture at First Presbyterian Church, Birmingham, Michigan, (date?)

History records time and again the sheer inability of fellow mathematicians and scientists to grasp something new, complex, and counterintuitive at the time it was first proposed. Subir Sachdev, a physicist at Harvard specializing in condensed matter, thought it might be interesting and mutually beneficial to engage string theorists in conversations about quantum entanglement. He comments on his experience. "I had spent several months reading their papers and books, and I often got bogged down. I was certain I would be dismissed as an ignorant newcomer. For their part, string theorists had difficulty with some of the simplest concepts of my subject. I found myself drawing explanatory pictures that I had only ever used before with beginning graduate students."[14]

In the early centuries of modern science, any fisherman, housewife, shopkeeper, minister, or commentator could pick up stones on a beach, study them, and announce a theory on how they came to be there. But over time the sciences have become highly professionalized. Now you simply cannot come in off the street and run the large Hadron Collider. It takes years of extensive and intensive academic and professional formation and apprenticeship to even enter the field.

In contrast, the study of Christian theology took years of academic and professional formation when modern science was just getting started. In 1835 medical missionary Marcus Whitman journeyed to the Oregon Territory. An elder in the Presbyterian Church, he had been unable due to ill health to complete the four years of college and three years of seminary needed to become an ordained minister. But after sixteen weeks of study at the College of Physicians and Surgeons of the Western District of New York, he had become qualified for a license to practice medicine.[15] The Protestant Reformation, increasing awareness of other religious traditions, and increasing reliance on individual assertion as the ultimate criterion of truth morphed over time into the wild diversity of spirituality in our contemporary culture. And they brought into question the assumptions, doctrines, and traditions of theology. Spirituality and religion became de-professionalized just when science was becoming highly professional and specialized.[16] Now any fisherman, shopkeeper, housewife, or commentator can discourse freely on ultimate questions, from the end of time to literal

14. (Sachdev 2013)46

15. The Whitmans at Whitman Mission National Historic Site (http://www.nps.gov/whmi/newsite

16. (Principe 2006)175

descriptions of life after death, with no other support beyond their individual *imprimatur*, "because I said so." This is not, of course, to diminish the value of original research and thinking.

The conversation about spiritual and scientific knowing, from esoteric Buddhist distinctions to frontiers of quantum physics, has to touch on a wide range of topics with technical terms and specialized knowledge that may require years of preparation and apprenticeship to grasp. Understanding the Higgs field/boson mathematically is as far beyond most of us as the priests in a medieval Cathedral whispering in another language about the forbidden texts of Scripture would have been beyond laypersons in the nave.

Finally, what does it mean to know—what is the process of knowing itself? According to the chemist and philosopher Michael Polanyi, knowing involves a triad. The first partner in the triad is the focus of attention—the pattern or phenomenon the knower wishes to know. The second partner is the "tacit dimension" or "subsidiaries," (Polanyi's terms), through and by which the knower seeks to know the pattern. Polanyi says the tacit dimension or subsidiaries involve my human experience in my whole being—body, mind, spirit, or however one divides up that inseparable whole; as well as in my environment—culture, nature, economic, political systems or again, however one divides up what is "outside" myself. (The distinction between what is "inside" or what is "outside" myself is provisional in spiritual knowing, as we will see later.)

The tacit dimension includes what I know in the depths of my being, conscious and unconscious, in all of these venues. We "indwell" those subsidiaries in the act of focusing on the whole pattern. We look through them, as it were. We assume and depend on them in the act of knowing without paying direct attention or focusing on them. If we were to do so, we would lose our original focus and our intended act of knowing. Subsidiaries can be arranged in levels from literal material to intangible abstract. Each level has its own integrity and structure, and also depends on the intention of the next higher level. For example, the retina, optic nerve, and parts of the cortex that receive visual signals have their own anatomy and physiology. However, they function through skills of sight learned and stored in percepts in the brain at a "higher" level. It is said that when the Tierra del Fuego Indians first encountered a Spanish galleon lying offshore, they could not see it. They had no experience with boats larger than canoes, and so they literally could not see the galleon. Higher level concepts, values, meanings, ideologies, and intentions guide the lower ones.

The third partner is the knower—the singular person who, embodying and using these subsidiaries, focuses on discovering the whole pattern. Not only do we embody and know through our own unique subsidiaries, but we also are responsible for the focus of our attention. We seek to know reality, a specific or universal truth beyond ourselves. We focus on clues, intimations, hints of the partially hidden reality beyond ourselves, so that we might come to know it more clearly and completely. A full account of the act of knowing needs to include this commitment of the knower in the knowing. Polanyi calls this a fiduciary relationship. The knower needs to take responsibility for their own commitment, trust, and confidence in their act of knowing. For Polanyi, "the I-Thou relationship constructs this structure of empathy (which I prefer to call conviviality) which alone can establish a knowledge of other minds—and even of the simplest living beings."[17]

Polanyi called the highest and truest that we know personal knowledge. My commitment to what I know is an essential part of that truth. What I know is deeply personal and true for me, touching the core of my being and my life experience directly and powerfully. But my spiritual knowing is not just an opinion or whimsy. It is meant to be equally universal truth. Hence, it is personal knowledge.

Regardless of our perspective, we all hold our personal knowing with some sort of fiduciary relationship. Much of our personal knowing is nonnegotiable for us, whether it is held consciously or unconsciously in our subsidiaries. It is often not open for change or even examination.

The continuum of pessimistic versus optimistic philosophies illustrates the range of firmly held fiduciary commitments. For example, Jim Holt has examined various philosophical perspectives on why there is something rather than nothing. Schopenhauer concluded that non-existence is better than existence, E. M. Cioran "epigrammatized endlessly about the 'curse' of existence," and Woody Allen concluded that human existence is "brutal, meaningless" with no justice and no reason. He does admit, however, that "I do get a certain amount of solace from whining," and in making films at least in part about whining.[18] On the other end of the continuum, Leibniz was mocked by Voltaire for claiming that we live in the "best of all possible

17. (M. T. Mitchell 2006)130
18. (Holt 2012)213–214

worlds." The contemporary Canadian philosopher John Leslie has created an elegant argument that the "objective value" of goodness creates a world that is "maximally good, infinitely good." Leslie himself seems to be happy, a "temperamentally sunny man."[19]

It is not possible to know exactly how and to what extent pessimistic or optimistic tacit dimensions affect the fiduciary commitments of these philosophies. For Holt, they depend only on logic and reason. As we shall see, those are left brain enterprises and therefore not an inclusive inventory of the human capabilities available to us, which we use whether we are aware of them or not.

The fiduciary relationship can also be quite uncertain. Leslie himself has only "just a little over 50 percent" confidence that his own theories are true.[20] Holt concludes his carefully argued philosophical exploration with a definition from Ambrose Bierce's *The Devil's Dictionary*; "Philosophy: n. A route of many roads leading from nowhere to nothing."[21] Perhaps irony is the default and protective fiduciary relationship of our time.

Given these distinctions, what is the infinite reach and rich interactions of the highest insights of spiritual knowing and the mainstream of current scientific knowing?

Chapter One details the distinctions between I-It explanations in scientific knowing and I-Thou relationships in spiritual knowing. Both scientific and spiritual knowing require individual discovery, connections and breaks with tradition, and community authorization.

Chapter Two is a brief history of knowing and the emergence of spiritual knowing. Spiritual knowing goes back far beyond recorded history. It began with the intimate knowing of hunting-gathering culture. The development of agriculture and city states then introduced spiritual knowing based on collective identity. The Axial Age developed the highest insights of spiritual knowing. Its highest advances happened two thousand years ago and have never been surpassed, although often forgotten or denied.

Chapter Three describes those highest insights in the Axial Age. The decline in violence and transformation of sacrifice led to the fundamental insights of unlimited awareness and unconditional love. Individuals are able to understand them according to different levels or stages of faith.

19. (Holt 2012)200,212–213
20. (Holt 2012)209
21. (Holt 2012)279

Chapter Four reviews the evolution of scientific knowing, which flowered in the Renaissance and advances exponentially faster into the future, in contrast to spiritual knowing. The range in size or scale of scientific knowing is described along with unintended consequences of advances in science and technology. Both scientific and spiritual knowing have infinite reach or aim, mathematically and metaphorically.

Chapter Five describes levels of brain-mind functioning in mindfulness meditation. Integration is the full development of meditation and brain-mind functioning, leading to self-transformation.

Chapter Six describes three dimensions of the practice of spiritual knowing: silence, ritual, and vision. Spiritual knowing does not describe reality, but prescribes how to live, approaching the infinite limit of unlimited awareness and unconditional love.

Chapter Seven explores spiritual knowing in a world described by science. Science and religion both share an interest in cosmology. In scientific cosmology, the universe is an ocean of information-rich, non-material fields within which material interactions arise and pass away. In evolution complex systems emerge, most recently with human beings capable of mental representations. The result is a self-organizing universe.

Chapter Eight describes spiritual knowing in the self-organizing universe of scientific cosmology. Fractals describe self-similar relationships between wholes and parts of the whole. In the Christian tradition we are fractals of ultimate reality, created in the image of God. Ultimate reality is described as the Trinity. Human beings are fractals of that divinity: Creator, Christ, Spirit.

Chapter Nine, "Mystery," concludes these reflections. Facing death is the ultimate challenge to the ego's mistaken quest for certainty and answers, illustrated in levels and examples of religious and spiritual response. The Christian expression of spiritual knowing in the world manifests the kingdom of God. We experience it in worship and finding our own voice. And finally, we jump into mystery.

CHAPTER ONE

SPIRITUAL KNOWING AND SCIENTIFIC KNOWING

Whereof we cannot speak, we must remain silent.

—LUDWIG WITTGENSTEIN[1]

The power of mental representations has multiplied many times over the course of human life on the planet. Intimate communion with ultimate reality among hunting-gathering peoples gave way to collective identifications with deities, mythologies and organized religion in agriculture, city states and empires. Then finally mental representations themselves were transcended in the highest religious insights in the Axial Age two thousand years ago which have not been surpassed, though often neglected or denied. Mental representations that became increasingly effective in addressing everyday realities and manipulating the world around us were originally not separate from religious concerns. But their power exploded in the seventeenth century with the development of the full panoply of resources for scientific methods. The advances of science and technology continue faster and faster into an unlimited future. We humans are confident that, with the power of mental representations, we can create a world to our liking and for our use. In fact, that is what the world *is* for us. As the quantum physicist Erwin Schrödinger wrote, "The world extended in space and time is but our representations (*vorstellung*)."[2] We are not "sufficiently astonished," quantum physicist Louis de Broglie wrote, that "the great wonder in the progress

1. (Goldstein 2005) Proposition 7
2. (Schrödinger 1984) 88

10

of science is that it has revealed to us a certain agreement between our thoughts and things, a certain possibility of grasping, with the assistance of our intelligence and the rules of our reason, the profound relations existing between phenomena."[3]

This book traces the drama of the development, divergence, and interactions of spiritual and scientific knowing. At the extremes, the two ways of knowing are incomprehensible to each other. Spiritual knowing does not even make sense in our common logic and everyday reason. That stark difference is illustrated in my experience studying Rinzai Zen Buddhism under a Korean Zen master. Every morning we would perform 108 profound prostrations, from standing to touching the floor with our forehead, and then returning to standing again. By the second day my legs felt like iron, and about as flexible. Nonetheless we would sit in silence for forty-minute periods, and when a bell rang, jump up to get in line for our private audience with the Sensei. (And when I say "jump," I mean staggering to my feet with my legs about to collapse under me and then struggling toward the line.)

In the private audience Sensei would direct a question or two toward each of us designed to evaluate and encourage our spiritual progress. Fellow student Clay seemed more advanced than some of the rest of us, and received the most challenging questions. One of Sensei's favorite questions involved holding up a bell in one hand and a short staff for ringing it in the other, and demanding, "bell, stick: same or different?" If you ventured to answer "same" he would hit you with the stick. If you tried "different," he would hit you with the stick. Clay had thought hard and long about the question, and when Sensei asked "same or different?" he responded, "My socks are black." Sensei said approvingly, "very good answer." Clay did not accept, reject, or argue Sensei's illusory division of the world into same or different. Since shoes are not worn in the Zendo he simply states what he sees before him, "My socks are black." "Very good answer."

I-THOU, I-IT

Spiritual and scientific knowing, like Sensei's stick and bell, are not simply same or different. Throughout this book we will take successive steps to characterize the rich interwoven differences and similarities between spiritual knowing and scientific knowing. The two ways of knowing have

3. (de Broglie 1984) 117

a complex intertwined history and present interaction. Grammar gives a first cut in distinguishing the difference between the two ways of knowing; between second- and third-person pronouns. Scientific knowing uses third-person pronouns. It involves transactions with third-person "it"s, separate and distinct from the scientist studying them. Spiritual knowing is about relationship. For the mystic or the worshiper, God, nature, and other beings are "You"s, in the second person.

The scholar, poet, and mystic Martin Buber wrote a little book in German in 1923 titled, in the English translation, *I and Thou*.[4] Like most European languages, German uses two different words for the second-person pronoun *you*. When addressing strangers or acquaintances, one uses the formal pronoun *sie*. However, one calls members of the family, loved ones, and dear friends *du*. Buber's book title in the original German is *Ich und Du*—I and you, my loved one, my dearest friend.

Intimate personal relationships happen between I and Thou. The name for that relationship, that *between*, is love. Love creates what happens between I and Thou—love between the whole of who I am, my entire being, and between the whole of reality in any specific instance. Love has no purpose, no meaning beyond the relationship itself. Only in loving do we live fully and completely in this present moment. In that sense, love changes me, makes me whole. It is the only time I am completely whole, completely who I am, relating with all my being to being itself. The truth is that when I relate to any thou, I am in the present, in love, in being itself.

For Buber, I-Thou relationships can happen between human beings, with nature, and with ultimate being—Spirit itself. When I am in love, in I-Thou relationship, I do not know something *about* the other, I *know* the other simply as whole being. The other in that sense is mystery. I do not have information about the consciousness of a tree, for example; I simply know the tree, am in love with the whole of the tree, in my own wholeness. In each single I-Thou relationship, I meet being. In each tree, I can meet wholeness itself.

We can't stay in I-Thou presence all the time. The other quickly passes into the other primary word Buber calls I-it. In I-it transactions I experience or use the other for my own purposes: study photosynthesis in the tree, or cut it down to make furniture. The tree is now a thing, an object, and I no longer live in the present moment. And I am no longer whole; it is a smaller part of me that uses or knows or experiences some aspect of the

4. (Buber 2000)

tree. Only in the present moment do I *meet* the tree and relate to being in I-Thou relationship.

In contrast, I-it transactions abstract, or separate out, some part of that same whole for the use or purposes of the "I." Scientific knowing does that by abstracting and assigning numbers to identical or interchangeable parts or aspects of "it"s. Parts of the whole, or units of "it"s must be identical and interchangeable for numbers to be assigned to them.

Sometimes phenomena are simply regarded as interchangeable in order to assign numbers to them. An example is the Likert scale used in social sciences. Phenomena such as the varying intensity of attitudes are simply assumed to be identical units and so can be added from one to five. The assumption works adequately for many purposes. Sophisticated statistical processes, such as multiple-regression analysis, are often used to discern which numerical units are more important in any complex phenomena. And sometimes scientists just pick a number for "it" that they judge best determines the whole. An example is the land-scattering practiced by medieval English peasants, traditional gardeners in Papua New Guinea, and peasant farmers in the Andes, among others. Each farmer cultivated a number of small plots scattered far apart from each other. Development scientists were appalled at the practice. "The peasant's agricultural inefficiency is so appalling that our amazement is how these people can survive at all," one wrote. They blamed the practice on inheritance and marriage traditions. The obvious scientific solution was to find the plot that had the highest number in average productivity and farm just that one. Fortunately, the peasants ignored the advice—because even if any single field produces much food for several years in a row, if they are followed by a drought, nothing grows, and the peasants starve to death, so it doesn't make much difference. Carol Goland looked for a better number. Since plots varied greatly in their productivity from year to year, the best number was the number of plots in different locations and ecological niches that needed to be farmed so that at least one of them would produce enough food to keep the family alive—around seven.[5]

To summarize and anticipate further refinements in the differences between I-Thou relationships and I-it transactions: I-Thou relationships relate wholes to wholes. I-it transactions need to abstract some aspect or part of the whole in order to use it for some external purpose while I-Thou relationships have no purpose beyond the relationship itself. I-Thou

5. (Diamond 2012)304–5

relationships are expressed in qualitative symbols, which cannot be reduced to simple numbers. I-it transactions intend to do exactly that. I-Thou relationships are unique, with open possibilities for depth and caring to be explored. I-it transactions aim at extension, repeatability, and generalizations. I-Thou relationships are about meeting the other, seeing the other for who they really are. I-it transactions have to do with measuring and controlling the other. I-thou relationships are vulnerable; I-it transactions leave the "I" untouched and distant from "It." I-thou relationships seek life; I-it transactions want to know what works.

Life swings between I-Thou and I-it relationships, between meeting and using, between present moment and past knowledge. I may again meet the tree in I-Thou relationship and then the tree may again become a thing for my use. And so on. And I-it transactions may pretend to be I-thou relationships. For example, when I go to a movie I usually use a parking structure nearby. Following the trends of our time, the attendants have been replaced by machines. When you enter the structure you press a button, and a ticket pops out for you. When you come back for your car, you first go to a machine there, and then insert your ticket and your credit card. The machine deducts what you owe, and returns your ticket for you to use to drive out.

The other day, when the ticket was inserted, the fee for parking registered $10, although the sign said we owed only $1. The person after us was charged $453, which seemed excessive. After driving around the structure for a while, we found a human attendant, who explained that the machine was malfunctioning and that one person had been charged $1,600. The attendant gave us the name and phone number of another actual person who could refund our money.

From the parking garage we went to see *The Best Exotic Marigold Hotel*. The movie began with Judi Dench looking out a window and listening to a voice on the phone saying, "Thank you for your patience. Your call is very important to us. Please wait for the next available operator." After a period of silence, the voice again said, "Thank you for your patience, your call is very important to us. Please wait for the next available operator." After another silence, the voice again repeated the same message.

The New York Times, reporting on new scientific and technological developments that will "change our lives," describes a pet bot—a robot that looks like a cat. Its artificial fur is connected to a computer chip so that when you rub it, the machine—or robot or pet or whatever you wish to call it—emits a sound designed to resemble purring.

These great advances of science and technology depend on the negation of relationship. Science has no personal relationship with the objects it studies. As Martin Buber wrote, those objects are "it"s. They have no personality, no will; are not related to as living beings, and certainly are not persons themselves. They cannot answer back, cannot ask the scientist, "Why do you want to study me?" They are inert "it"s—lifeless objects the scientist manipulates at his or her pleasure, for whatever reason.

In this way the scientists preserve their objectivity. They don't get emotionally involved with the objects of their investigation, so they can just study what is there, without preconceptions, without attachment or any prior assumptions. They are the only actors in their research. Their passive lifeless partners are simply material machines, mindless reactions to be studied at the leisure and the pleasure of the scientist. That's true even when the objects of their investigations are living beings.

Lisa Randall has written a book describing the latest advances in subatomic physics, in which she insists that scientists only study "objects interacting through mechanical causes and their effects."[6] You don't have a relationship with a machine. You may love your new Honda Fit, but it doesn't love you back. It's just a mindless machine.

There is a simple metaphor for this distinction between scientific and spiritual knowing—between it-knowing and thou-knowing. It is stated in a lovely poem written by George Weber, in loving homage to his wife Julie, who was a hospice chaplain:

O, we get asked: How to? What time? How much?
Those questions solved with rulers, clocks and such.
Yes, we get asked to plan, define, replace:
Finite requests resolved in finite space.

But you get asked through teary, hurting eyes
Not simple whens or whats, but awesome whys:
Why now? Why them? Why him, or her, or me?
Why pain? Why death, Why so much tragedy?

6. (Randall 2011) 55

Those questions voiced through feelings of despair
You place like gold in fire within your prayer,
Refining out the need to know or see,
You help the hurting cope with mystery.

The silence of your presence reaches out
To share the quiet tear, the tempting doubt.
Your work is life, in corridors called time.
Your gift is hope—God's hugging hope sublime.[7]

We live mostly in an everyday world, facing everyday problems that can be addressed by: How to? What time? How much? And we have rulers and clocks and such to address those questions. In a way, it feels easier and even more comfortable to address these kinds of problems; they seem to have answers. Even if the answer doesn't work out so well, at least it's sort of familiar and concrete and literal.

But behind and beneath and lurking in the background are often the really important questions. George Weber called them the "awesome whys." You can't solve the awesome whys with rulers, clocks, and such; you may not even be able to solve them in the sense of having an answer that makes them go away, or erases the question so everyone feels better. Those are the questions that get asked with teary, hurting eyes, that are voiced through feelings of sorrow, deep anger, even hopelessness and despair—and sometimes, and even surprisingly often, with joy and a sense of wonder.

If you want to think about what religion is, why people ask the questions of faith, it's because of those big questions, the questions beyond ruler, clocks, and such—the awesome whys. Those questions are so big that even religious people tend to shy away from them, and lose themselves in the easier how-to, what-time, how-much questions—questions of the church budget, heat in the winter, the right way to think and believe, and so on. Regional church organizations tend to do the same, turning awesome whys into legal questions that result in endless discussion, debates, votes, *Robert's Rules of Order,* and so on.

Now, those questions are important, necessary and need to be addressed, but that's not essentially what spiritual relationship knowing is about. We worship; we pray; we meditate; we have quiet intimate conversations spaced with silence, doubts, tears, laughter, and joy, in which the important thing is just our presence with each other, and our presence

7. Weber, George L. , "The Chaplain," permission by Thomas Grady, May 23, 2011

together in the Spirit. That's the way to address the mystery of the big questions, the awesome whys.

Julie Weber began her career as a nun in a cloistered convent, spending her days in silence and in prayer. Later as a chaplain and hospice worker, she had a gift of being with others as they struggled with the big questions. George called it the "silence of your presence."

What we are called to do in spiritual knowing, both in our own individual way and all of us together, is, in George's beautiful words, to place the questions, the doubts, the tragedies, the joys—like gold in fire—within our prayer.

Spiritual knowing expresses our longing, relationship, and oneness with all that is. Spiritual knowing is an end in itself. It creates and participates in a world of powerful symbols that create human community and a vision of the whole of reality. It happens in religion, art, and visioning of the sacred world. It is a world of relationship.

Scientific knowing instrumentally increases our mastery, manipulation, and control over things in the world. Scientific knowing has to do with making our way in the world. It can be called the world of work—what we need to do to survive and thrive. It treats the world and the things in it instrumentally for our own ends. It becomes the seed bed of science and technology.

SCIENTIFIC KNOWING: EXPLANATION

What is scientific about scientific knowing? Essentially, it is self-correcting. A scientific theory explains something in the world. Something doesn't make sense, or some difficulty needs to be overcome. The theory attempts to solve the problem. It needs to be open to, and invite, testing; the theory must be able to make predictions which can be confirmed or falsified by observation or experiment. Confirming the prediction does not necessarily prove the theory to be true, but demonstrating that the prediction is wrong does prove the theory to be incorrect.[8] If the theory is demonstrated to be inadequate, then the search is on to create and test a more inclusive or adequate explanation. This is the continuing cycle of self-correction in science: Conjectures build theories; predictions from theories are tested to see if they are wrong; and theories are criticized and improved. Science depends on it.

8. (Deutsch 2011) 13

Scientific theories can come from anywhere. We may observe something which puzzles us; our ideas about something in the world don't seem right to us, and we reason our way to a potentially better explanation; we may have a dream that reveals a new insight; or we may carry out a carefully designed double-blind experiment, and the results may suggest a better theory. Even our simple observations are theory-laden. When we see something, we see it through a template of neural patterns and prior experiences which shape what we see and how we see it.

Scientific explanations rely on a whole chain of measurements, from direct sensory observation to the final theory or explanation. Every link in the chain (proxy) must be subject to the same criticism and requirement of good explanations that the whole theory does.[9]

David Deutsch calls scientific theories "guesses—bold conjectures."[10] They are creative acts, not only deduced by logic, or induced by observation, or revealed by our dreams alone. We use all of those capabilities, but the theory is a creative act, a "bold conjecture" of the mind. In a later chapter we will review brain mind research that explores neural patterns through which they arise. But the conjecture, the theory itself, is a creative act of the human mind.

Good theories are good explanations in which all the details play a necessary part in the phenomena the theory wants to explain. In that way they are hard to vary, because doing so would lose that close fit. And because of all that, they are often simple, elegant, and beautiful. Beauty is even a criterion in evaluating mathematical ideas.[11]

There is no end to this self-correcting process of conjecture, criticism, improvement. Deutsch calls the process *fallibilism*—all knowledge is subject to continuing improvement.[12] There will always be problems; there will always be testing and criticism; and there will always be new possibilities, sometimes dramatic, of improving what we now know. Deutsch writes, echoing the Roman Catholic theologian Karl Rahner, "our knowledge is tiny and our ignorance vast."[13] That is an optimistic statement, not a pessimistic one. There is no end to the possibilities for creating and testing

9. (Deutsch 2011) 317

10. (Deutsch 2011) 4

11. (Deutsch 2011) 24–25

12. (Deutsch 2011) 9

13. (Deutsch 2011) 449

new knowledge and improving on what we know. The history of science testifies to it.

Most explanations, according to Deutsch, are rules of thumb. That is, they are processes for achieving certain ends that are strictly limited to specific situations; they are parochial in their reach. They use familiar knowledge and depend on certain procedures to be followed. There are usually conflicting theories to explain how and why the rule of thumb works, and experimental testing is designed to resolve or transcend the conflict by a more adequate or inclusive explanation.[14]

Rules of thumb "jump" to universal explanations when they use abstractions which do not depend on descriptions of specific instances.[15] For example, mathematical theorems exist as abstractions, but they explain specific events to which the abstractions can be applied. They do not just explain how to make or do something—they explain why and how they make or do something. The "jump to universality" comes with a sudden increase in function in some area or domain.[16]

DNA is an example of universality. It originally coded for nothing more complex than simple one-celled creatures. But the most complex life forms on earth use the same alphabet of groups of three elements, with only slight variations.[17] Science intends to increase the reach of good explanations, the different situations to which the explanation applies. Often a few abstractions, rigidly tied together so they cannot be varied, make the best explanations, such as the second law of thermodynamics which simply says that "physical processes tend towards ever greater disorder."[18]

There seem to be no theoretical limits to the potential of good explanations; their reach is infinite.[19] Physical matter is finite, but ideas and explanations may not be. They may be the "beginning of infinity" described later.[20]

14. (Deutsch 2011) 14, 16–17

15. (Deutsch 2011) 123

16. (Deutsch 2011) 146

17. (Deutsch 2011) 144

18. (Deutsch 2011) 110

19. (Deutsch 2011) 192–3

20. (Deutsch 2011) 28

SPIRITUAL KNOWING: RELATIONSHIP

Characterizing spiritual knowing is more challenging and takes longer than describing scientific knowing. That is because, as emphasized later, it involves qualitative symbols, connotations, meaning, wholeness, relationship, and all that messy life-giving stuff that scientific knowing wants to be rid of. It is best to proceed by approximation. As mentioned earlier, we will take successive steps through the history of spiritual knowing, its culmination in the enduring insights of the Axial Age, and then up to contemporary interactions with brain mind research and mathematical metaphors for reality. It is like Michelangelo carving his statue of David: He didn't first cut the essential detail of David's right hand, holding the stone that will kill Goliath. First, he had to make rough large cuts to block out David's whole form, and then many smaller cuts until he got to that essential detail.

Spiritual knowing is a fascinating journey covering a vast range of human experience. For transpersonal psychologist Jorge Ferrer, spiritual knowing is a participation in an emergent event or occurrence of mystery. It may happen within a person, a relationship, a community, a collective identity, a place, in any event. We are caught up in ways "that can involve every aspect of human nature, from somatic transfiguration to the awakening of the heart, to erotic communion to visionary co-creation and from contemplative knowing to moral insight."[21]

Spiritual knowing is relational knowing and therefore, personal. It involves aspects of my experience that are personal to me (called "qualia" later on), however one attempts to define that wondrous term "person." "Thou"s do not lend themselves to tidy definitions like "it"s. Spiritual knowing creates relationships; and relationships change, renew, and create the "I"s and "Thou"s involved.

Robert Bellah and others trace the origins of the sacred world back to the emergence of play. Various animals play. But play becomes essential and pronounced in species like ourselves, in which the young are born helpless. That is because the large human brain must pass through the narrow human pelvis long before it reaches full size. An ape is born with forty percent of the size of the adult brain, and reaches eighty percent by the end of the first year. In contrast, the brain of a human baby is twenty-five percent of its full size at birth and fifty percent at the end of the first year. Birth needs to happen before the infant is able to move about and thrive on its own.

---

21. (Ferrer 2002) 12

Mothering is essential for an extended time. The interactions between infant and mother involve what can be called play. The extended nurturing has no purpose beyond itself, although the skills and maturity which are developed become very valuable in the world of work. A "relaxed field" of relationship is created by mother and child apart and safe from the stresses of the world of work.[22]

Improvisation illustrates the creativity of spiritual knowing, how spiritual knowing calls into being. For years the actor Alan Arkin has taught workshops on improvisation. When the participants arrive for the first exercise he tells them the rules: "I don't want to see anything interesting and I don't want to see anything creative." And immediately twenty people's shoulders go down and they breathe a sigh of relief. They play ball with an imaginary ball that keeps changing into a rope, into a suitcase, into a bowl, and so on. After a few minutes people are laughing, enjoying themselves, and being "enormously creative." Then Arkin says, "You failed! The instruction was not to be creative, not to be interesting. . . . Why were you creative?"[23] In the discussion that follows someone replies that "when we leave ourselves alone," flowing without sensing ourselves or pleasing parents or others, "it is our nature to be creative, and that not being creative is the aberration."

I remember the instruction given to me in improvisational dancing that whenever you have an idea about how to move, you throw it away to let the movement come directly from your body moving, not from your left brain thinking about how to move your body.

During the course of Arkin's workshops sooner or later someone takes a big risk, and people begin to move out of what he calls intense devotion: to the craft, to the Spirit, to any relationship at all, really. In their devotion they transcend self-concern, and like athletes enter the zone "where things are flowing and effortless . . . timeless, a place where they can't make mistakes, where everything slows down, where they know."[24]

Mihaly Csikszentmihalyi explored what he called optimal experience—"a sense of *participation* in determining the content of life." It is known as *flow,* the state "in which people are so involved in an activity

22. (Bellah 2011) 77
23. (Ulrich 2012) 16–17
24. (Ulrich 2012) 18

that nothing else seems to matter; the *experience* itself is so enjoyable that people will do it even at great cost, for the sheer sake of doing it."[25]

Composer and artist Robert Fritz realized that creativity happens in relationship with that which does not yet exist, wherever people imagine and then "have the ability" to bring what they imagine into reality."[26] Fritz developed workshops to teach creativity, not only to artists but also to engineers and mechanics, because the process is similar. It includes noting that critical middle stage when all the effort to realize the vision seems to be going nowhere, and one experiences "discomfort, frustration and disappointment."[27] That's when it is so important to face what is there without flinching—feel what you feel, see what you see—and then move on. What you create "will never be truer or deeper than your feeling," as Gertrude Stein remarked.[28]

Annie Dillard, in *The Writing Life*, described writing and art this way: You start with an image, perhaps a few words or a doodle on a napkin during a restaurant conversation. You may not do anything about it for quite a while. But it stays with you, nags at you until finally you take the big risk and put a few words down on paper, or a few brush strokes on canvas. What you have created seems pathetic compared to that bright vision in your mind or sketch on the cocktail napkin. But you keep at it, keep at it until, bit by bit, what is actually there begins to steal your heart away. Finally it stands by itself, it is what it is, the original vision now quite forgotten. And you come to love it, as it is, for itself. Not because you created it, but for itself. That's spiritual knowing, relational knowing, creating. It is an act of love.[29]

The creativity of spiritual knowing has an open-ended depth. Lovers continue to discover nuances and meanings in their loving and in each other. The ultimate I-Thou relationship with the source of all being, God, or however we name it, is about love-creating. In the book of Job in the Hebrew Scriptures, God finally speaks these words to Job (Job 38:1–7):

Then the Lord answered Job out of the whirlwind:

"Who is this that darkens counsel by words without knowledge?

---

25. (Csikszentmihalyi 1990) 4
26. (Fritz 1989) 38
27. (Fritz 1989) 200
28. (Fritz 1989) 236
29. (Dillard 1989) 1–20

Gird up your loins like a man, I will question you, and you shall declare to me.

> "Where were you when I laid the foundation of the earth?
> Tell me, if you have understanding.
> Who determined its measurements—surely you know!
> Or who stretched the line upon it?
> On what where its bases sunk, or who laid its cornerstone
> when the morning stars sang together
> and all the heavenly beings shouted for joy?"[30]

Job has had a tough time. On top of that, he has had false counselors representing the religious authorities of their time assuring him that he was wrong, and that he should repent of his integrity and bow to them. Job is much too stubborn to do anything like that. He has no secret doctrine, no special message given especially to him; he is just this ordinary guy going through a really tough patch, who refuses to compromise or betray who he is.

And then, in the story, God shows up—*really* God, who laid the foundation of the earth, laid its cornerstone when the morning stars sang together and all the heavenly beings shouted for joy. God goes on for four more chapters, making the same point in magnificent poetry. God then asks, "Well, how about you? Who and where are you in all this, Job?"

Job has no answer. He has no special revelation. He says he has no understanding, and so he will not speak. But he also says, "I had heard of you by the hearing of the ear, but now my eye sees you" (Job 42:5). In spiritual knowing Job is just an ordinary guy—who can see God. He does repent of any pretensions he and his false counselors may have had—and what they have spoken that was not right—and in the epilogue God rewards Job mightily. But the heart of the story is right here in this moment, when Job sees God and God sees him. That is spiritual knowing in the ultimate I-Thou. It is relational knowing, participating in some mysterious way in God in the loving act of creating itself.

Time and space came into being at that moment of creation. Augustine taught that time started then, not before creation. Einstein's general theory of relativity, likewise, mathematically described the space-time continuum as beginning at the big bang. There is no "before." One billion people saw one of the works of the Chinese artist Cai Guo-Qiang—a massive display of fireworks at the opening of the Beijing Olympics in 2008. He was motivated

---

30. (The New Oxford Annotated Bible, 3rd Edition (NRSV) 2001) 768

by the thought "that we were all there together at the Big Bang. That every particle in every human being was first given birth when the Big Bang brought matter into being"—all "unified oneness" then.[31]

Spiritual knowing is about reaching down deeply into that centerless center before the world begins, before form and words and specific emotions and images are fixed and material. Spiritual knowing is ultimately about being there in the eternal moment of creation, when the morning stars sing together, and all the heavenly beings shout for joy, as God reminds Job.

Huston Smith writes that the technical language of religion is symbol and the technical language of science is number.[32] Spiritual relational knowing uses the technical language of symbols to discern ultimate meanings of life and reality. Science uses the technical language of numbers to empirically test sensory information about the world.

Number, ideally, is denotation devoid of meaning, metaphor, emotion, attitude, or color. Scientific findings aim toward the universality of denotation. Mathematical demonstrations aim at the universality that number promises. Religious symbols and meanings are connotations, full of all that stuff that denotation avoids. They never entirely can nor want to escape their origin and grounding in personal knowledge. Therefore they can only approach universality in the way great art does—by so resonating with the personal knowledge of others that they transcend a particular personal history and tradition.

That's why specific religious symbols and abstractions may be rich with meaning to those within that history and tradition, and meaningless to those who do not share it. Robertson Davies, in the second volume of his Deptford Trilogy *Manticore,* tells the story of Davey, a Canadian businessman who goes to Zurich for Jungian analysis and is greatly helped by it. He consults Liesl, a wisdom figure who suffers from giantism. They become friends, and he seeks her advice as to whether he should continue for more years in analysis. She explains to him that he will never find his own ultimate truth in the grand theories of Freud, Jung, and Adler. Those theories are all no more and no less that the hard-earned wisdom of their own life journeys and experiences, forged in heroic struggles to raise families, earn a living and develop their career and thought. She ends her consultation thus: "Davey, why don't you go home and shoulder your yoke, and be a hero

31. (Rosenbaum 2013) 29
32. (Smith 2005) 164

too?"[33] Spiritual knowing is relational knowing. It uses qualitative symbols which resonate with those for whom the symbols carry meaning. Thus it is personal knowledge.

DISCOVERY

Spiritual and scientific knowing share rough similarities and connections in at least three ways: individual discovery, relation to tradition, and community acceptance and authorization.

Individual discovery is the foundation of both scientific and spiritual knowing. Individual discovery is built on two legs; call them observation or experience, and insight or explanation.

E. O. Wilson wrote a 330-page textbook describing one species of ants.[34] That's scientific observation! The analogy to observation (or experience) in spiritual knowing is theological seminary for Tibetan monks who supposedly remain secluded in a cave for three years, three months, and three days. The time is spent in meditation. It's not quite correct to just say that one is looking outward to external reality and the other is looking inward to inner reality. Both are observing reality as such, the true nature of things, in different ways.

The second leg of individual discovery, insight or explanation, involves finding an adequate way to describe what has been observed. In scientific knowing, theories are in mathematical formulae and equations; they state what can be confirmed by eventual observations. They are sometimes described in awkward puzzling sentences, but words are no adequate or equivalent substitute for the math—they are simply aids to readily grasp the mathematics. Insight in spiritual knowing is expressed in symbols and thus more dependent on words. The connotations of those symbols need to be unpacked in all possible ways. Ultimately, even words are inadequate to fully express or realize the great insights. Orthodox Christians have icons. Paul, describing his own spiritual experiences, tells us he is not permitted to speak of them (2 Corinthians 12:4).

Some scientists specialize in mathematics; some emphasize observation. Some spiritual teachers only lead meditation; others write theology. But observation and insight are essential to both scientific and spiritual knowing.

33. (Davies 1972) 265–6
34. (Wilson 2012)

TRADITION

Both ways of knowing depend on tradition in different ways. Scientific knowledge is cumulative —it builds on past discoveries. That is why it is so powerful and advances exponentially into the future. Newton said he stood on the shoulders of those who had gone before him. Whenever an observation demonstrates a theory to be inadequate, a more inclusive theory is created that includes what was true in the old one in a larger or different framework. Sometimes the "fine tuning"[35] becomes so unwieldy that the whole theory collapses in what Thomas Kuhn called a paradigm shift.[36] A new theory is born, and the old one goes in the dumpster, of interest only to historians of science, but of no use to advancing science itself.

In contrast, in spiritual knowing sometimes the whole history of a great symbol is needed to fully understand its connotations. From time to time prophets and mystics arise, testifying to new revelations and new ways of observation and insight. And all the ways exist together, sometimes uneasily or in conflict. They are evaluated in light of the great traditions— arising and dying away according to their appeal over time, or living side by side over the centuries as alternate paths to the great realities. Spiritual knowing is not cumulative in the same way as scientific knowing. It must be realized again and again in the lives and experiences of each person on the path.

COMMUNITY AUTHORIZATION

Scientific knowing and spiritual knowing both depend on community authorization—both the authorization of their own subculture, and the longer culture of their time and place. The history of scientific discoveries is littered with the stories of scientists and truths neglected or ridiculed by the mainstream of their profession until recognized later. Georg Cantor was driven to an insane asylum for daring to give a precise mathematical definition of infinity.[37]

Spiritual knowing is all over the place—past and present, heresy and orthodoxy, new revelations and ancient truths, all coexisting, harmoniously, uneasily, in deadly conflict. Some claim all religions are essentially

35. (Randall 2011) 118
36. (Kuhn 1970)
37. (Burger 2005) 163

one, and should recognize each other as such. At the other extreme, some claim their own truth to be absolute and exclusive, rejecting all others, even their own "cousin religions." As just one example, the Wisconsin Lutheran Synod will not allow the Missouri Lutheran Synod to partake in the Eucharist with them.

Spiritual knowing is dependent on the knowing of its larger cultural context. Christianity emerged in the cauldron of Hebrew and Greek culture mixing together. Even fundamentalism is an attempt to imitate science—not the methods, but the presumed certainty that the literal inerrant words of the Bible are as certain and proven as scientific conclusions.

These descriptions and explorations of spiritual and scientific knowing focus on epistemology (how we know), rather than ontology (what is really out there, even beyond our knowing). They do so for several reasons. The question itself is epistemological: Can authentic spiritual knowing thrive in a culture of scientific knowing? It seems to be an important question in our current North American culture. It also lends itself to dialogue. Hopefully this book will contribute to exploring ways that these two ways of knowing can inform, appreciate, and even enrich each other.

Epistemology, the nature and limits of how we know, is more fruitful for this conversation than ontology, the nature of being and existence. That is because we really don't know what is out there beyond our knowing, and because how we know influences what we find. Mark Twain remarked that if the only tool you have is a hammer, everything looks like a nail. If the search is on for good material, mechanical explanations, then relationships are not likely to be found. Theoretical physicist and cosmologist Steven Weinberg wrote, "The more the universe seems comprehensible, the more it also seems pointless."[38] Richard Feynman added that the physical world "has a kind of meaninglessness about it."[39] Given the extraordinary advances of scientific knowing, these are weighty considerations. Nonetheless, if you are looking only for mechanical causes, you are not looking for, or likely to find, spiritual relational knowing.

Ontology is not so hospitable to dialogue. Either you believe that the creator God is really out there, creating all that is, or you believe that everything consists of random interactions of matter. Both are well-attested positions, believed by millions of people, and contradictory. There isn't much that either party can contribute to the other. More fundamentally,

38. (Davies 2007) 16
39. ((Davies 2007) 16

you either hold an instrumentalist or a realist position regarding what is really out there. Realism holds that we can know true descriptions of reality. In instrumentalism, we can only have reasonable explanations that "save the phenomena."[40]

There is no ultimate way to decide which is the case, because all we have is our knowing—not what is out there beyond our knowing. It doesn't make a lot of difference in how we actually go about our knowing. We scientists, mystics, and ordinary people go about our life and work anyway. We are realists in practice, even when not in theory.

We act as if what we do and know is true, even beyond our knowing.[41]

SUMMARY

Spiritual knowing and scientific knowing are both different and similar. In contrast to scientific knowing, in spiritual knowing "I"s meet "Thou"s. In any singular Thou, whole being meets whole being in love, with no purpose beyond the relationship itself. Spiritual knowing uses the language of qualitative symbols, full of connotations, meanings, metaphor, and color.

Scientific knowing abstracts out some aspect or part of the "Thou" for the use of the "I," resulting in I-it transactions. Numbers are assigned to the parts, which are assumed to be identical and interchangeable, and numerical denotations are stripped of qualitative connotations. Scientific knowing aims at good explanations of what is happening in the world, to be continually critiqued and improved.

I-thou relationships can become I-it transactions and back again.

Scientific knowing and spiritual knowing have rough similarities in terms of individual discovery, relation to tradition, and community authorization. The two legs of individual discovery are observation or experiment, and insight or explanation. Scientific knowing is cumulative, building

40. (Principe 2006) 198, 196

41. (Goldstein 2005) 250 Realism, when obsessive, can be dangerous for your health. The mathematician Kurt Goedel and Albert Einstein were great friends at Princeton. They went for long walks together discussing their common aim: to demonstrate that there was an objective knowable reality to the universe outside of our human understandings. As Einstein famously said, "God does not play dice with the universe." Goedel was in no way religious or spiritual, but the intensity of his search finally drove him mad. He refused to eat and starved himself to death because he believed people were trying to poison him.

on past tradition. In spiritual knowing ancient and new insights coexist. They need to be realized anew in personal experience. Both spiritual and scientific knowing depend on community authorization. New scientific insights may be rejected at first by the relevant scientific community. Spiritual knowing uses symbols from the larger culture, sometimes inclusively, sometimes restricted to a particular community.

These distinctions prepare us to explore the fascinating history of spiritual knowing, resulting in the great Axial Age insights, which are not surpassed, though often denied or neglected. After this, we will look at the contrasting history of scientific knowing, which advances exponentially faster into an unknown future.

CHAPTER TWO

A BRIEF HISTORY OF SPIRITUAL KNOWING

This awareness, free from an inside or an outside, is open like the sky
It is penetrating wakefulness, free from limitations or partiality.
Within the vast and open space of this all-embracing mind,
All phenomena of samsara (sensory experience) and nirvana
(ultimate reality) manifest like rainbows in the sky
Within this state of unwavering awareness,
All that appears and exists, like a reflection,
Appears, but is empty, resounds, but is empty.
Its nature is emptiness from the very beginning.

—Tsogdruk Rangdrol, "The Flight of the Garuda"[1]

What is unique about how we humans know, spiritually and scientifically, compared to other living beings? Ian Tattersall is the curator
of the Spitzer Hall of Human Origins at the American Museum of Natural
History. In his research, he asks that same question, beginning with the
hypothetical common ancestry of humans and of other primates living perhaps seven million years ago. Tattersall states that primates are "extremely
complex creatures indeed" but that there is a gap, a chasm, an unprecedented difference between how other primates and even early hominoids knew
and how we know today. The jump came about late in the evolutionary process, and abruptly at that. We have evidence of it in the remarkable cave art
in Ice Age Europe. Those sophisticated images do not just represent what

1. (Rangdrol)

30

the makers saw; they are symbolic—"every image . . . realistic or geometric, is drenched with meaning that goes far beyond its mere form."[2]

Alone among all living beings, and apparently without a gradual evolutionary development, we can create mental maps of the world around us. Other animals deal directly with nature. We alone have a vocabulary of mental representations by which we can create our world.

And the great expression of our amazing capacity is language.[3] We can speak; we alone can hold mental representations of reality in our minds. It's *how* we know. This unique human capability does not deny the abilities of animals and even plants to carry out functions that perhaps could be characterized as learning, adapting, being intelligent, or conceivably even conscious.[4]

All the ways we know, both scientifically and spiritually, are simply developments and variations of that remarkable ability to create mental representations of reality, unprecedented in the history of the universe. In this chapter we will trace the evolution of knowing, from hunting-gathering peoples through the development of agriculture and the emergence of city states, to the great crises and achievements of the Axial Age. After that, scientific knowing and spiritual knowing diverge as described in Chapter Four, along with attempts to reconcile them into the unity of truth.

2. (Tattersall 2012)x, xiv

3. (Tattersall 2012)xi

4. (Pollan 2013) 92 105 Plants, for example, usually move so slowly that you cannot see them do so. To impatient humans, they seem to just be there, immobile, staying exactly where they are planted. But with time-lapse photography, you can see interesting things; a beanpole plant can somehow sense the presence of a pole it needs nearby and infinitesimally slowly, to the unaided eye, stretch and move until it can reach and begin to climb the pole. The mimosa pudica plant has the rare capability of moving so fast that you can actually see it. It closes its leaves when it is threatened, as by toxic insects landing on it, or by being dropped a short distance. One scientist rigged a device to drop some mimosa plants again and again. After just a few such drops, the plants learned that they were safe, even when dropped in this way, and quit closing their leaves when it happened, even twenty-eight days later. Plants seem to be able to literally move toward a desired goal, to learn and remember what they learn, to nurture and support young plants growing from their seeds, and to communicate what they learn to others, even to the next generation. Some scientists, of course, disagree with this. Because plants don't have brains and nerve cells, they can't possibly be conscious or intelligent in any way.

HUNTING-GATHERING KNOWING

The first development of our incredible mental capabilities goes back many thousands of years in hunting-gathering cultures. That knowing is marked by the absence of abstract thought and an intimate communion between humans and nature. Perhaps the oldest known human self-portrait, at Trois Frères in southern France from around 35,000 years ago, is an antlered deer with the face of a human, perhaps a shaman.[5] There may also be a burial sculpture from 19,000 years earlier, near Lascaux, in which a Neanderthal man and a bear's legs have been exchanged with each other and surrounded with pollen.[6] Both of these early symbols express the intimate relationship between animals and humans. Animals were our first mirrors, connecting us to mysterious others who were both like and unlike us. Sacred communion came through "Eating an animal [which] was a sign of profound respect. You absorbed its power, its characteristics . . . The animal was hunted, eaten, worshiped, and above all, used for transformation."[7]

There was no consciousness of an autonomous self, separate from nature. Life was lived in an *intimate relationship* with our natural environment in which human and nature, body, and other were not sharply distinguished. "Men and women took their cues from body feelings and the movements of animals. This was a life governed by shifting moods, rather than the demands of the ego."[8] A contemporary description of hunting by British Columbian Indians attempts to capture this way of being in the world: "Above all they were receptive, prepared for whatever insight or realization may come to them, and ready for whatever stimulus to action might arise. This state of attentive waiting is perhaps as close as people can come to the falcon's suspended flight, when the bird, seemingly motionless, is ready to plummet in decisive action."[9]

Primitive languages are not simpler than ours, but much more complex because of limited mental representations which evolve over the centuries into simpler and more powerful forms. A child growing up in our culture becomes fluent in English by around the age of five or six, no longer making simple mistakes that parents chuckle over. But children speaking Cree,

5. (Wilber 1981)43
6. (Whitney 2010)71
7. (Berman 1989)69
8. (Berman 1989)69
9. (Berman 1989)68–69

a language of Algonquin Indians in northern Canada, struggle to become fluent by the ages of ten to twelve, so complicated is Cree and so complex are the grammatical forms that need to be mastered.[10] In another example, a Polynesian language has a completely different grammatical form for a sentence that is said in the daytime from the same sentence spoken after dark.

Jared Diamond has long years of experience living with and studying hunting-gathering and early farming communities in various parts of the world, especially in Papua New Guinea. He finds much that is admirable in their lifestyle, even superior to how we live, in how "traditional societies raise their children, treat their elderly, remain healthy, talk, spend their leisure time, and settle disputes."[11] He and other researchers are "struck by the emotional security, self-confidence, curiosity, and authority" they demonstrate as adults, and even as children. He is particularly impressed by child-rearing practices: "constant security and stimulation, as a result of the long nursing period, sleeping near parents for several years, far more social models available to children through alloparenting [by the whole community], far more social stimulation through constant physical contact and proximity of caretakers, instant caretaker responses to a child's crying, and the minimal amount of physical punishment."[12] He is also impressed by how conflicts are resolved: "speedy peaceful resolution, emotional reconciliation between the two sides, and restoration of their previous relationship."[13] He contrasts it with our emphasis on right and wrong, guilt, and punishment for the guilty party, and neglect of the restoration of the relationship itself. Nonetheless, he is not sanguine about certain aspects of hunting-gathering life which include "infanticide, abandoning or killing elderly people, facing periodic risk of starvation, being at heightened risk from environmental dangers and infectious diseases, often seeing one's children die, and living in constant fear of being attacked."[14]

The world for hunting-gathering peoples was sparsely populated by humans and full of friendly and fearsome magical creatures. They lived in extended families and small, fairly egalitarian tribal groups, dependent on each other for food, skills and survival. Time was lived in the present

10. (McWhorter 2008)

11. (Diamond 2012)9

12. (Diamond 2012)208

13. (Diamond 2012)87

14. (Diamond 2012)9

moment, with no abstractions for linear historical time. Certainly, life was brutal and short, but also immediate and intimate, and connected in a way that seems appealing to us. The contemporary poet Mark Strand has suggested how we contemporary humans might feel our way into this spiritual knowing which is still present is some residual way in our own psyche:

> One night when the lawn was a golden green
> And the marbled moonlit trees rose like fresh memorials
> In the scented air, and the whole countryside pulsed
> With the chirr and murmur of insects, I lay in the grass
> Feeling the great distances open above me, and wondered
> What I would become—and where I would find myself –
> And though I barely existed, I felt for an instant
> That the vast star-clustered sky was mine, and I heard
> My name as if for the first time, heard it the way
> One hears the wind or the rain, but faint and far-off
> As though it belonged not to me but to the silence
> From which it had come and to which it would go.[15]

COLLECTIVE KNOWING

What did the transition from hunting-gathering knowing to the collective knowing of agricultural society look like? Come back to a time before recorded history, or if you prefer, before what we call civilization. Most human beings had yet to grow crops for food, animals had not yet been domesticated, we didn't know how to make pottery, and we had yet to even live together in villages. The technical name we have given this time was the Neolithic period, more than ten thousand years ago.

What were the first structures human beings ever built? We have some interesting evidence about that. But when they were first noticed by an American archaeologist in 1964, they seemed so strange they were simply ignored. The best carbon dating places these ruins, located at Gobekli Tepe in southwestern Turkey near the Syrian border, as being built around 11,500 years ago. German archaeologists have been carefully studying the structures since 1994. There is no evidence that people even lived there. The walls of the sites consist of dry unworked stones, like other Neolithic structures built later. Inside the walls are circles of large T-shaped monolithic stones nine feet or so tall, with a pair of similar but larger stones sixteen feel

15. (Strand 2006)39

tall in the center. Animals and abstract designs are carved in relief on the stones. People had to be organized to quarry and move the seven-to-ten-ton stone pillars to the site, a quarter-mile from the quarry.[16]

Nothing even closely this old had been discovered before. To give some perspective, these structures were built 7,000 years before the Great Pyramids in Egypt, 6,000 years before Stonehenge in England, and 6,000 years before human beings learned to write.

Well, what were they, if they were not villages or settlements for people to live in? It turns out they seem to have been temples, built for religious purposes, perhaps as burial sites. Before we human beings even learned to live together in villages, we organized fairly complex societies to construct a series of temples and came, some from significant distances, to worship there. The symbols drawn on them recede so far into our distant past that we don't know what they mean. And since we worshiped there 6,000 years before we learned to write, there is no memory of how we worshiped, or what rituals we used.

Collective knowing later developed with agriculture, resulting in food surpluses that caused dramatic population increase and made possible what we have come to call civilization—first in the form of city-states. Political hierarchies to order the city, money for buying and selling food and other necessities, priests and organized religion, arithmetic and writing, technologies of metal and wheels—all these mental advances made the city-state possible. And in the city-state our primary self-understanding was as a member of it, and the social status we held in it, whether slave or king. Ken Wilber and others call this collective identity the *membership self*.[17] The self is no longer immersed in nature, but defined by the collective to which one belongs. The final guarantor of the membership self is the god of the collective, embodied or represented in the king. Finally, the king himself is god, not even needing any further divine reference. Tiglath-Pileser II in Assyria in 1700 BCE was perhaps the first to no longer join his god's name to his own name.[18]

Names for the god of the collective in Hebrew scripture include the Lord of Hosts, Lord Sabaoth, and Yahweh, the national god of Israel. He embodies the will of the united tribes, and has a covenant or *berith* with Israel, which results in *shalom* when it is obeyed. He is the father of Israel

16. (Curry 2008)54–60
17. (Wilber 1981)113
18. (Wilber 1981)282

who has begotten or created the people. He is warlike, having defeated all other gods (1 Samuel 1:3), except perhaps Chemosh of Moab, who may have been too much for him (Judges 11:24). He is a jealous god, punishing those who dare to disobey him. "I am the Lord, that is my name, my glory I give to no other, nor my praise to idols" (Isaiah 42:8).

The knowing of the collective or membership self is also deeply built into us, influencing or defining how we human beings understand who we are, who we count as allies and enemies, and our deepest values. We tend to define all this by the tribe we belong to. It is difficult to overstate how deeply those assumptions are built into us, how unconsciously and stubbornly we hold to the belief in the essential sacred reality of our tribe as the guarantor of the separate self.

James Fowler and other researchers call this the stage of conventional beliefs and conventional moral reasoning. We accept without question the beliefs and assumptions about the nature of reality held by our tribe, whether the tribe is defined by our nationality, our race, our ethnic background, our gender, our sexual preference, our religion or maybe even our chosen sports team. Not only do we accept their beliefs and assumptions, we go two steps further. We believe that is essentially *who* we are and we believe we are privileged above other human beings *because* that is who we are.[19]

We can feel our way into the enduring sense of the collective knowing of the membership self that still resides at some level of consciousness within us. William Shakespeare gives it classical voice in the panegyric to England in *Richard II*, read by Sir Laurence Olivier, when narrating a film documentary of the coronation of Queen Elizabeth II in 1957. As England rose to a great world power in Shakespeare's time under the first Queen Elizabeth, this reading at the coronation of the second Elizabeth perhaps unwittingly suggests her decline to just another nation among nations.

> This royal throne of kings, this sceptred isle,
> This earth of majesty, this seat of Mars,
> This other Eden, demi-paradise,
> This fortress built by Nature for herself
> Against infection and the hand of war,
> This happy breed of men, this little world,
> This precious stone set in the silver sea,
> Which serves it in the office of a wall

---

19. (Fowler 1981)78–79

Or as a moat defensive to a house,
Against the envy of less happier lands—
This blessed plot, this earth, this realm, this England.[20]

THE AXIAL AGE

Somewhere around 2000 to 1000 BCE, all over the planet, a new literature of alienation, suffering, despair, and lament came into being. Karen Armstrong calls it "the experiences of utter impotence in a cruel world."[21] The surety of collective knowing crumbled, and gave way to a sense of the self as an individual for whom the only thing certain is death. Each individual now must take responsibility for her or his own separate existence. We have been living with that realization and its denial ever since.

Psychiatrist Irvin D. Yalom sums up a contemporary statement of this realization in his book *Love's Executioner and Other Tales of Psychotherapy*. The title is his understanding that the work of the therapist is to disabuse patients of their illusions, attachments, or loves which keep them clinging to their unhappiness. They need to take responsibility for their life by facing up to the four truths of the human condition. Those four truths are, according to him: We are essentially alone; we and everyone else we know will die; there is no self-evident meaning in all of this; and yet we are condemned to the destiny of designing our own lives.[22]

The remarkable response of the human race to this realization was the Axial Age, so named by the philosopher Karl Jaspers, because it marked the axis around which the development of humanity turned. In a tiny slice of human history from around 800 BCE to the time of Christ, in China, India, Iran and the eastern Mediterranean, all the world's major religions and western philosophy suddenly came into being. During that time the great Hebrew prophets taught, Lao Tzu and Confucius lived; Gautama Buddha founded Buddhism; the Bhagavad Gita was written and classical Hinduism developed; Zoroaster, Socrates and Plato lived; and finally Jesus Christ was born.[23]

---

20. (Shakespeare 1997)855

21. (K. Armstrong 2001)11

22. (Yalom 1989)xi—xxiii

23. (Armstrong 2007)xvi

Islam was a later restatement of earlier truths. Jews and Christians both had their own prophets, but the Arabs had been left without one. The Qur'an had been revealed to remedy that lack. As the Qur'an instructs Muslims to say, "We believe in Allah and that which is revealed unto us and that which was revealed unto Abraham, and Ishmael, and Isaac, and Jacob, and the tribes, and that which Moses and Jesus received, and that which the Prophets received from their Lord. We make no distinction between any of them, and unto Him we have surrendered" (Qur'an, surah 2.136).[24]

Spiritual knowing reached its highest development in the Axial Age. The insights realized more than two thousand years ago have not been surpassed, but they have been lost time and again in world religions and the lives of individual worshippers —and been rediscovered and reclaimed time and again by prophets, mystics, teachers, ordinary people, and spiritual communities living them.

The insights are so radical that they break the bounds of language and cannot ultimately be put into words. William James called the highest spiritual insights ineffable and noetic—ineffable because they transcend language, and noetic because they are in fact a knowing, the most profound knowing of which humans are capable. Two historic developments prepared the way for them: the decline in violence and the transformation of sacrifice.

DECLINING VIOLENCE

It is now generally recognized that violence has dramatically declined over the course of human history. Steven Pinker summarized huge amounts of statistical analysis and anecdotal reports in *The Better Angels of Our Nature* to make the case. The word "decline" seems counterintuitive given World Wars I and II in the last century and Korea, Vietnam, Iraq and Afghanistan more recently. However, World Wars I and II rank only sixteenth and ninth, respectively, among the worst massacres in history as a proportion of world population at the time. The appalling honor of first place goes to the An Lushan revolt in the eighth century against the Tang dynasty in China; thirty-six million people were slaughtered, compared with forty million in World War II. Adjusted as a portion of world population in the twentieth century, the Chinese rebellion cost 429 million lives. Our country's killing of Native Americans is seventh—twenty million lives, or the equivalent of

24. (Qur'an Surah 2.136)

ninety-two million in today's world.[25] For two-thirds of the previous century, a new thing happened in world history: Nations stopped going to war with each other. Historians have called this the "Long Peace." And, "since the end of the Cold War in 1989, organized conflicts of all kinds—civil wars, genocides, repression by autocratic governments and terrorist attacks—have declined throughout the world."[26]

The decline in violence goes back in history. During the seventeenth and eighteenth centuries, movements in the Enlightenment fought, often successfully, to abolish "despotism, slavery, dueling, judicial torture, superstitious killing, sadistic punishment and cruelty to animals."[27] And before that, the rise of the nation-state organized and monopolized violence in the service of the state and so decreased homicide rates ten to fifty times in Europe. Generally, every major development toward larger, more effective government reduced violence from the era before it. An archeological study of nine hundred pre-Columbian skeletons in the Western hemisphere showed that 13.4 percent of hunter-gatherers suffered violent trauma, compared to only 2.7 percent of city dwellers.[28] Finally, in our present day there are movements against violence to "ethnic minorities, women, children, homosexuals, and animals" and for "civil rights, women's rights, children's rights, gay rights and animal rights."[29]

Peoples around the ancient world from China to the Middle East began morphing into warring empires more than three thousand years ago. The early Aryans migrated from central Asia into northern India about 1,500 years before Christ. They were farmers who had not yet domesticated horses and lived close to their cattle. But in the next five hundred years they migrated east to the Ganges River, using their newly trained horses as transport and as platforms for their weapons, conquering and subjugating the native peoples along the way and stealing their cattle. Karen Armstrong writes that "They loved their war chariots and powerful bronze swords; they were cowboys, who earned their living by stealing their neighbors' livestock. Because their lives depended on cattle rustling, it was more than a sport; it was also a sacred activity with rituals that gave it an infusion of divine power." They had become hard-living, hard- drinking people who

25. (Pinker 2011)195
26. (Pinker 2011)xxiv
27. (Pinker 2011)xxiv
28. (Pinker 2011)51
29. (Pinker 2011)xxv

loved music, gambling, and wine, expressed in the earliest hymns of the *Rig Veda*.[30] Because they were nomads, they had to burn up the excess beasts they captured in sacrificial violence which included lavish sacrificial banquets, rowdy carnivals, casual sex with slave girls, chariot races, shooting matches, and mock battles which sometimes morphed into serious fighting.[31]

Their heroes were trekking warriors and chariot fighters. Honor, enforced by shame, was gained by killing their enemies. Warriors gained status, renown and virtue, risking injury and death in violent combat to protect their families and tribes, and destroying other persons and groups.

In the tenth century BCE the Aryans migrated further eastward and began to settle. Their fire god Agni had been the *alter ego* of the warrior, carried to new settlements to control and domesticate the population.[32] But by the ninth century the Aryans were settled, and a consensus developed that raiding had to stop. Over time it became a fearful act to kill any being, not to be undertaken lightly. The killer god Indra was given up and complicated sacrifices were developed that would not require harm or injury to the participants. The liturgist suffocated the animal painlessly and told it, "You do not die, nor do you come to harm, to the gods you go, along good paths."[33] So that there would be no possibility of conflict between humans, the sacrifice was done by a single priest and his wife.

Aryans came to understand that the core of their being or self was Atman, who was identical with Brahman—the transcendental reality of the universe who was beyond both existence and nonexistence, death and immortality, and beyond words to describe. Brahman necessitated a revolution in ethics. The ethics of gaining honor through violence was supplanted by the central idea of *ahimsa* —meaning to do no harm, to avoid all *himsa,* or violence. Living beings were not to be injured or killed. To do so would create negative karmic consequences for future life.

In shining moments of the Axial Age, the mental representations and justifications for violence were transcended. In the ensuing course of history the state increasingly monopolized violence for its own benefit—order within and success against enemies without. But of course, violence did not

30. (Armstrong 2007)16–17

31. (Armstrong 2007)20–21

32. (Armstrong 2007)24

33. (Armstrong 2007)92

end. Violence is "largely a male pastime,"[34] especially for young men, and particularly for young men sent into battle by old men. The capabilities of mental representations, supported by the shame-based, emotionally laden virtue of honor, created binary relationships of allies and enemies.[35]

Honor supports, justifies, and excuses violence throughout history and to the present day. As a young Marine Corps officer, I pledged my honor to defend my country against enemies foreign and domestic, intentionally placing myself in harm's way to do so. Decades later as a retired Marine, I watched the Friday night sunset parade at the original Marine Corps barracks at Eighth and I streets in Washington DC. The athletic, precise close-order drill and rifle exchanges ended in the elegiac mournful celebration of taps from atop the barracks roof as the sun went down and darkness settled. I was moved.

Shakespeare, in *Henry IV,* demolishes honor in the words of Falstaff from the viewpoint of the common man or soldier who suffers on behalf of the generals and kings who order and glorify it.

> Prince Henry: Why, thou owest God a death.
>
> Falstaff: 'Tis not due yet, I would be loath to pay him before his day. What need I be so forward with him that calls not on me? Well, 'tis no matter, honor pricks me on. Yea, but how if honor prick me off when I come on? how then? Can honor set to a leg? No. Or an arm? No. Or take away the grief of a wound? Honor hath no skill in surgery, then? No. What is honor? A word. What is in that word honor? What is that honor? Air. A trim reckoning! Who hath it? He that died a' Wednesday. Doth he feel it? No. Doth he hear it? No. 'Tis insensible, then? Yea, to the dead. But will ['t] not live with the living? No. Why? Detraction will not suffer it. Therefore I'll none of it, honor is a mere scutcheon. And so ends my catechism.[36]

Over the long course of human history, violence declines as awareness expands and love becomes more inclusive. In the highest insights of the Axial Age, narrow tribal distinctions of allies and enemies give way to increasing awareness of the sacredness of all life. *Ahimsa* or nonviolence replaces enmity and revenge. Violence has not completely ended, of course, nor has the virtue of honor, deeply rooted in shame, which supports it.

34. (Pinker 2011)xxvi

35. (Armstrong 2007)5–6

36. (Shakespeare 1997)918–919

TRANSFORMING SACRIFICE

In the run up to the Axial Age, the decline in violence is interwoven with the transformation of sacrifice. Sacrifice, of animals and sometimes of humans, was a fundamental religious ritual for hunting-gathering and later for agricultural peoples. Since the time of single-celled organisms, evolution has depended on the energy concentrated by predator-prey relationships. They originated from the emergence of cells called eukaryotes, which are in our bodies and in all multi-cellular organisms. Eukaryotic cells came into being 1.6 to two billion years ago, and the evolution of life beyond the simpler prokaryotic one-celled creatures depended on this great stride forward. Eukaryote cells consolidated energy by invading, eating or merging in symbiosis with other cells, often simpler prokaryotic one-celled organisms.[37] The invention of these predator prey relationships made possible the evolution of all life into more complex forms by this combining of life energy.

What happens with cells happens with us humans beings also. A fundamental fact of being human is that we are predators who survive by killing and eating other life forms. We don't get away from this fact by being vegetarian; every meal depends on killing and eating living beings—plants or animals. We humans evolved from vulnerable, naked, bipedal primates to predators at the very top of the food chain, enabled by technology from spears to strip-mining. And we are capable, with ever-increasing power, of exploiting the energy of all other life forms and even the created order itself for our own purposes. Now we live in such an artificial environment that we seldom are even aware of this basic fact of our existence. I happen to have grown up on a farm, so the reality of raising, killing, and eating plants and animals was perhaps a more direct experience for me.

In contrast, hunter-gatherers lived in communion with the wild animals on which their lives depended. Shamans in trance would seek the advice of animal spirits to tell them where the best hunting grounds were, with animals willing to give their lives to sustain the tribe. Rituals of animal sacrifice recognized, honored, and gave thanks to the animals that were hunted, and on which their lives depended. Shedding their blood renewed the energy that kept the world in being.[38]

37. (Swimme 1992)101–105
38. (Armstrong 2007)5–6

Some vestiges of those rituals continue even into the present day. I once knew an army sergeant who was discharged in Germany after the Second World War. He had become friends with some Germans, and went hunting with them in one of their forest preserves. When they had killed their deer, they put a sprig of juniper in its mouth and sat down around it silently in a ritual they called the "last bite" for a few moments to express their gratitude for its willingness to give its life for them.

In agricultural economies, rituals were needed to renew the fertility of the land each year, so that crops could grow. It may be that people noticed that the menstrual blood flow of a mature woman continued, except when she was pregnant. It must be, then, that the Great Mother of goddess religions needs blood to bring forth new life, to cause the crops to grow again. In the early sacrificial rites the animal or human symbolic consort of the Great Mother is sacrificed. Then the Great Mother follows the dead god/consort into the underworld, and effects his resurrection so that a new cycle of life, fertility, and new moon can begin.[39]

The ancients understood what we grasp only with difficulty: We don't get a free pass for our violence against other life forms; we need to take responsibility for it. Specifically, we need to take action, usually a ritual action, to seek forgiveness and restitution for our violence and its consequences.

The twenty-second chapter of Genesis records the struggles of Hebrew religion to move beyond requiring a human child to be sacrificed. The story is presented as a test of Abraham's faith, or perhaps of God's honor. After preventing him from sacrificing his son Isaac, God says, "now I know that you fear God, since you have not withheld your son, your only son, from me" (Gen. 22:12). And so a ram is sacrificed instead.

The later strands of Hebrew religion refined animal sacrifice. It was not considered a killing of the animal, but a transformation into a spiritual substance. Only domestic animals raised for food could be sacrificed and eaten; they were "clean." "Unclean" or wild animals were not to be killed and eaten at all, so they were not sacrificed.[40] The sacrificed animal was burnt, part was eaten by the priests, and the rest shared with the people.

In New Testament times in the cities Paul visited and evangelized, pagan temples were sort of restaurants in which people could come and eat sacrificed animals. Paul needs to tell his fellow Christians that it is alright to eat that food. But, because some new Christians might be insecure in their

39. (Wilber 1981)126
40. (Armstrong 2007)215

faith and confuse eating the meat with worshiping the idols, he would not do so himself (1 Corinthians 8:4–13).

All across the ancient world during the centuries of the Axial period people began to internalize these ancient rituals. They began to understand them as symbolic invitations to discover the inner worlds of Spirit and their own depth experience. The sacrifice no longer was a literal animal, but the ego that stands in the way of liberation. In India the fire ritual became an invitation to discover one's own inner fire in the Atman, the essential and eternal core of the person.[41]

For the new sect of Christianity, the life, death and resurrection of Jesus Christ realized this transformation. Christ is the eternal definitive symbol of God's self-giving love for humans. Animal sacrifice was no longer needed or relevant. The passage from Hebrews in the New Testament explains: "Therefore, my friends, since we have confidence to enter the sanctuary by the blood of Jesus, by the new and living way that he opened for us through the curtain (that is, through his flesh) and since we have a great priest over the house of God, let us approach with a true heart in full assurance of faith, with our hearts sprinkled clean from an evil conscience and our bodies washed with pure water" (Hebrews 10:19–21).

Paul concludes in Romans 12:1–2: "I appeal to you therefore, brothers and sisters, by the mercies of God, to present your bodies as a living sacrifice [thank offering], holy and acceptable to God, which is your spiritual worship. Do not be conformed to this world, but be transformed by the renewing of your minds, so that you may discern what is the will of God—what is good and acceptable and perfect."

SUMMARY

We have briefly reviewed the history of knowing from hunting-gathering peoples, through the development of agriculture and the emergence of city-states, to the great crises and achievements of the Axial Age and the later divergence between scientific knowing and spiritual knowing. All of the aspects of spiritual knowing still reside at some level in the human psyche.

Declining violence expands awareness to all beings as capable of I-Thou relationships of love. Sacrifice transcends and lets go of the narrow blinders of ego that stand in the way of unlimited awareness and unconditional love.

41. (Armstrong 2007)98

I-Thou relationships can now fulfill their true promise. I-Thou includes my whole being, in love in the whole of reality. And the whole of reality can now be present in any singular I-Thou instance of it —person, tree, divinity. That happens when awareness expands to include all that is, and love is unconditional.

In Michael Polanyi's triad of knowing, the focus of awareness is now the whole of reality present in every singular instance of it, and love is equally omnipresent. Personal knowledge now truly has universal intent, because subsidiaries are no longer limited to partial awareness and unlimited love.

In the next chapter we will examine the great and enduring spiritual insights of the Axial Age—unlimited awareness and unconditional love—in preparation for exploring their interaction with modern science.

CHAPTER THREE

AXIAL AGE INSIGHTS

Emptiness, according to the Victorious Ones (The Buddhas),
is the relinquishing of views.
They have said that the one who holds the view of emptiness is incurable.

—NAGARJUNA[1]

What do unlimited awareness and unconditional love look like? Here is a brief description of their emergence and full articulation in Axial Age traditions.

UNLIMITED AWARENESS

Our awareness expands with the increasing reach of our mental representations of self, others, and ultimate context. Animists evidently had names for the bends in a river, but no name for the river itself. There was a sky god in many traditional religions, although distant and removed from human concerns. Of more immediate interest were gods of rain, wind and other natural phenomena, gods of sacred place, gods of war, and gods of human interaction.[2]

The Hebrew Scriptures illustrate advances in awareness and mental representation. El Shaddai was the mountain god—both mountain and god

1. (Siderits 2013) 145
2. (Armstrong 2007)xx

in human interaction. As Israel coalesced into a nation out of the tribes in Canaan, Yahweh became the national god of Israel, mighty in war, although perhaps not always, as noticed earlier. But the name Yahweh also illustrates the jump to universal mental representations and unlimited awareness.

Moses, herding his father-in-law's sheep, comes to Horeb, a sacred mountain where the Midianites worshiped. Moses has a vision. He sees a bush on fire, but not burning up. He hears a voice speaking to him from the flame, calling him into ministry, to rescue the Israelites from their bondage. He is overwhelmed. But he is also remarkably self-possessed, and wants to know the credentials of the mysterious presence that wants to send him on mission. What is your name, he asks, when I come to the Hebrews? Who shall I say has called me to this daunting task?

The response is *"ehyeh asher ehyeh."* *Ehyeh*, or Yahweh in the Hebrew, can be translated as I AM,[3] or "the one who chooses to be," "I am who I am," or "I will be what I will be." Mystery—being itself, beyond words, beyond definition, the whole of ultimate reality itself—calls poor Moses to a very specific if seemingly impossible mission. Then, ultimate reality itself also cites personal and specific relationships with Moses' ancestors among the Hebrews. Ultimate reality, mystery, being itself, touches down in the concrete reality of the Hebrew people. Ultimate reality spoke to and guided their patriarchs in very specific ways, and now calls Moses to do this one thing.

Much of the history of Hebrew religion involves the struggle between these two poles of awareness and representation: god of the tribe versus being beyond limitation and definition. When Solomon marries his many wives, he also incorporates their gods and goddesses into his household. The tribes in Canaan had any number of gods. But the Deuteronomists insisted that only fidelity to the one God would save them. The fundamental affirmation of Judaism proclaims: *Sh'ma Yisrael, Adonai eleheynu, Adonai echod*—"Hear o Israel, the Lord our God, the Lord is One" (Deut. 6:4).

Monotheism, the belief that there is only one god over all creation and that this one God can be known, is the hallmark and great achievement of mental representations in the Abrahamic religions: Judaism, Christianity, and Islam. Eastern religions articulated the advance in awareness and representation in somewhat different ways. Hinduism has a more relaxed view of the layers of mental representation of the divine. The Hindus' claim that there are 330 million gods is not a body count of separate divinities,

---

3. (The New Oxford Annotated Bible, 3rd edition [NRSV] 2001)87

but "a gesture in the direction of infinity."[4] In contemporary American culture, a granite image of a god is carefully crafted and laboriously installed with blocks, tackle, and ramps into a temple, then elaborate rituals open the divine breath and eyes of the deity present in the carved image. So "Lord Rama resides in Chicago, Vishnu in Pittsburgh, Rabadden Meeakshi in Houston, and the Goddess Lakshmi in Boston."[5]

Precise and rigorous descriptions of unlimited awareness and mental representation are given in the sutras or texts of Mahayana Buddhism. Awareness is no longer limited even by language. It encompasses all reality at once. How do you say this? Buddhism calls it emptiness—empty of all linguistic separations, distinctions, and divisions. It is awareness of everything at once. The description of unlimited awareness or emptiness in Buddhism is a *tour de force* of negating all those separations and distractions that would limit it in any way.

The word for emptiness, *Sunya,* means hollow, void, zero. It is the absence of any distinctions that separate one entity from another and so limit our perception of ultimate reality. Ultimate reality is non-dual, because even the term "one" implies a "not one." Reality is simply non-dual—"not two." Emptiness is not nothing; it's everything at once. Radical awareness or emptiness dissolves all limiting analytical categories.[6] It even negates a basic rule of western logic in Aristotle's principle of contradiction: something cannot be A and non-A at the same time—a chair and not a chair at once.[7] Actually quantum mechanics does something similar, as we will see later.

Just as space ultimately cannot be cut up and named into separate pieces, the same is true for time. Time cannot be stopped and fixed so that events can be made permanent either. The Buddhist term is *anicca*—impermanence. Everything shifts, changes, arises, and passes away in every nanosecond. Space and time are, in the final analysis, artifacts of limited

---

4. (Eck 2001)82

5. (Eck 2001)67

6. (Pine 2004)69 The three characteristics of the non-dual contingent nature of reality—sunyata (emptiness), anicca (impermanence), and anatta (no self)—do not stand alone but are interwoven and interdependent descriptions of ultimate reality beyond words. Red Pine's (Bill Porter's) commentaries on the *Heart Sutra* and the *Diamond Sutra* and the Dali Lama's (Tenzin Gyatso's) *Essence of the Heart Sutra* are accessible guides to understanding them. The specific citations simply indicate various starting points in those texts.

7. (Pine 2004)85

human experience, not final descriptions of reality.[8] On that point, thinkers from Immanuel Kant to Albert Einstein agree in different ways.

In Mahayana Buddhism the greatest delusion is the belief that something exists. Nothing exists by itself, but only in relation to everything else. And the second greatest delusion, as you might imagine, is that nothing exists.[9]

The Buddhist *Heart Sutra* is the most popular text in Mahayana Buddhism, chanted in Buddhist services. It was developed in the seventh century by an ethnic Chinese monk named Hsuan-tsang.[10] It radically dissolves, transcends, and negates any and every distinction that would limit awareness, including the essential teachings of Buddhism themselves. Here are comments on parts of it:

> Form is emptiness, emptiness is form,
> Emptiness is not separate from form,
> Form is not separate from emptiness;
> Whatever is form is emptiness,
> Whatever is emptiness is form . . . .

Form, sensation, perception, memory, and consciousness are the five skandhas or marks of our sensory experience of the world. They are defined as follows: Form, rupa, is the outward appearance of things. Sensation or name, nama, is our recognition of that appearance. Perception, sanjana, is the conceptual combinations or the framework that allows us to know or evaluate the form. Memory, sanskara, is the repository of all that we have previously intended in word, deeds and thoughts that are templates for the evaluation. Finally consciousness, vijnana, is the resulting discrimination or knowledge by which we separate subject from object and one object from another. All are transcended in unlimited radical awareness or emptiness.

> All dharmas are defined by emptiness
> Not birth or destruction, purity or defilement,
> Completeness or deficiency . . . .
> In emptiness there is no form,
> No sensation, no perception, no memory and no consciousness.
> No eye, no ear, no nose, no tongue, no body and no mind;
> No shape, no sound, no smell, no taste, no feeling and no thought;
> No element of perception, from eye to conceptual consciousness;

8. (Gyatso 2005)91–92

9. (Pine 2004)68–69

10. (Pine 2004)17–18

Dharma is a very large term meaning everything from the Buddha's teaching to the basic structure of reality. Dharmas are empty of self-existence, i.e., they do not exist by themselves, but only by virtue of and in relation to everything else. The distinctions we use to separate birth and destruction, purity and defilement, completeness and deficiency are then without ultimate meaning because there is no final separation. As implied above, the same holds for our sensory experience and the organs responsible for perception including body and mind, feelings and thoughts.[11] The Sutra continues:

> No suffering, no source, no relief, no path

Finally the four noble truths which are the essence of Buddha's teaching: suffering, source of suffering, relief from suffering, and path—also dissolve in liberating awareness or emptiness.

> No knowledge, no attainment and no non-attainment . . .
> Live without walls of the mind.
> Without walls of the mind and thus without fears . . .
> See through delusions and finally nirvana.

Walls of the mind are all the limitations negated above that we place on our awareness. Without those walls of the mind we can live without fear, liberated even from the last delusion of nirvana (defined as permanent, self-existent, pure enlightenment).

If this is all true, the perception of an existent self or separate self is also a needless limitation on our awareness. The self is simply a conglomerate of mental capabilities with no other meaning. What the psychologist Gordon Allport called the "proprium," the various meanings of I-ness, has no content, and is not the perception of any entity.[12]

The *Diamond Sutra* makes this point in the strongest possible way. The purpose of the sutra is to lead from the Hinayana Buddhist path of morality and meditation to the Mahayana Buddhist ideal of the Bodhisattva,

11. (Siderits 2013)13, 15 Nagarjuna, the expositor of the Mahayana Buddhist tradition, lists the "famous eight negations": "neither sensation nor origination, neither annihilation nor the eternal, neither singularity nor plurality, neither the coming nor the going [of any dharma, for the purpose of nirvana characterized by] the auspicious sensation of hypostatization. . . . By hypostatization is meant the process of reification or 'thingifying': taking what is actually just a useful form of speech to refer to some real entity." Nagarjuna proceeds to refute any argument to the contrary in order to facilitate liberation.

12. (Allport 1955)41–54

the enlightened being realizing unlimited wisdom and compassion. Here is an excerpt from chapter three:

> The Buddha said to him, "Subhuti, those who would now set forth on the bodhisattva path should thus give birth to this thought: 'However many beings there are in whatever realms of being might exist . . . in whatever conceivable realm of being one might conceive of being, in the realm of complete nirvana I shall liberate them all. And though I then liberate countless beings, not a single being is liberated.'
>
> "And why not? Subhuti, no one can be called a bodhisattva who creates the perception of a self or who creates the perception of a being, a life, or a soul."[13]

There are no such entities as separate beings—myself, or any other being in space or time. All delusions of separate beings, including myself, limit and obscure radical awareness of non-dual ultimate reality. The list of beings that are not a self or a being is meant to be so inclusive that the process of liberation is not even limited by time or space or perceptions of the mind. Only the Bodhisattva's one thought, the liberation of all beings, is so completely altruistic that all thoughts are put to flight.

Radical awareness or emptiness does not annihilate ordinary sensory experience and the everyday need to pay attention to it. But emptiness is the true awareness of ultimate reality within which sensory experience arises and passes away in every nanosecond.

UNCONDITIONAL LOVE

The second great spiritual knowing insight in the Axial Age is unconditional love, or compassion without any boundaries or limitations. In the decline in violence and the transformation of sacrifice, one can see the changing and erasing of those boundaries. The Aryans gave up conquering and killing their neighbors and the virtue of honor that supported it. Now they were committed to *ahimsa*—non-violence toward every living being. It was a giant step toward unconditional love. Equally important is the transformation of sacrifice. No longer is it necessary to kill another living being to atone for the violence of the separate self. The illusion of the separate self is itself the problem. Self-sacrificing that illusion of the self

13. (Pine 2002)71–83 The following remarks are summaries of Red Pine's commentary on Chapter Three of the *Diamond Sutra*

erases the boundary between self and others. What is left is simply love, relationship itself.[14]

Here is a question: if there is one fundamental insight common to all the great religious traditions, what would it be? For Karen Armstrong the essence of religion is not belief, but compassion. And the great expression of compassion and the center of all great religious traditions is the Golden Rule in its various forms.

Perhaps Confucius (551–479 BCE) articulated it first. Confucius did not speak about God, because he considered that beyond the capacity of language to do. But he often said, "My Way has one thread that runs right through it." He called it the Golden Rule, which his followers should practice "all day and every day." This is it: "Never do to others what you would not like them to do to you."[15]

Hillel (80 BCE-30 BCE), the Jewish rabbi and near-contemporary of Jesus, was approached by a pagan one day who promised to convert to Judaism if Hillel could teach him the entire Torah while standing on one leg. Hillel evidently stood on one leg and said, "What is hateful to yourself, do not do to your fellow man. That is the whole of the Torah and the remainder is but commentary. Go learn it."[16]

The radical advance of the Golden Rule, against the conventional religion of the time, is illustrated in the contrast in Luke's gospel between the teaching of John the Baptist and the early Christian community's understanding of the teaching of Jesus: John teaches a conventional code of honor in living ones' social role. Jesus invites us to the radical Golden Rule culminating in the image of God—unconditional, universal love. It is parallel to *ahimsa* as the ethics derived from Atman and Brahman.

For John, soldiers are not to stop being soldiers and using violence to uphold Roman rule, but simply to stop using violence to exploit civilians for private gain. Tax collectors are not asked to stop taking money from citizens to enrich the Roman government, but only to stop skimming the proceeds off the top for themselves. There is also the exhortation to practice charity to those less fortunate (Luke 3:7–14).

Jesus has something more radical in mind, in the Axial Age insight of unconditional love. He puts before us a transcendent invitation to identify with ultimate reality going far beyond the mutual social obligations John

14. (Armstrong 2007)92
15. (Armstrong 2009)24–25
16. (Armstrong 2009)79

recommends: "You have heard that it was said, 'You shall love your neighbor and hate your enemy.' But I say to you, Love your enemies and pray for those who persecute you, so that you may be children of your Father in heaven; who makes the sun rise on the evil and on the good, and sends rain on the righteous and on the unrighteous" (Matthew 5:43–45).

The highest understanding of compassion goes far beyond even a gracious impartial law, bestowing blessing equally on all of the creation. It goes beyond that to a grand reversal of the predatory nature of the human project. Ultimate reality may be called self-giving, unconditional love. However we name it, the fundamental nature of reality essentially loves, brings into being, reaches out in self-giving infinite compassion. No words are adequate, of course, because like emptiness, this insight is ineffable and noetic—beyond language—the highest spiritual knowing of which humans are capable. We are called to live that love.

How we treat each other is a function of who we are—our identity and participation in ultimate reality as we are able to grasp it. We are to love our enemies and pray for those who persecute us, because that is who God is and who we really are, created in the image of God. In Buddhist piety, given the countless lives in which we are incarnated, we are to treat every living being as our mother, as perhaps they once were, down to cockroaches or whatever we regard as the least likely candidate. Marcus Borg has created a short list of parallelisms between the sayings of Buddha and the sayings of Jesus illustrating unconditional love:[17]

> Hatreds do not ever cease in this world by hating, but by love; this is an eternal truth . . .
> Overcome anger by love, overcome evil by good.
> Overcome the miser by giving, overcome the liar by truth.
>
> —*Buddha*

> Love your enemies, do good to those who hate you, bless those who curse you,
>   Pray for those who abuse you. From anyone who takes away your coat
>   Do not withhold even your shirt. Give to everyone who begs from you.
>
> —*Jesus*

17. (Borg 1999)18–19, 24–25

Just as a mother would protect her only child at the risk of her
own life,
> Even so, cultivate a boundless heart toward all beings.
> Let your thoughts of boundless love pervade the whole world.

—*Buddha*

This is my commandment, that you love one another as I have
loved you.
> No one has greater love than this, to lay down one's life for one's
friends.

—*Jesus*

The Johannine tradition continues the insight:

> Beloved, let us love one another, because love is from God; every-
> one who loves is born of God and knows God. Whoever does not
> love does not know God, for God is love. . . .
> Beloved, since God loved us so much we also ought to love one
> another.
> No one has ever seen God; if we love one another, God lives
> in us, and love is perfected in us. . . . God is love, and those who
> abide in love abide in God and God abides in them (1 John 4:7–8,
> 11–12, 16).

STAGES OF FAITH

Unlimited awareness and unconditional love are not separate and unrelated insights. They are more like two sides of a coin, each making the other
possible. Unlimited awareness opens us to unconditional love beyond all
boundaries. Unconditional love opens up awareness beyond all limitations.
Atisha, a thirteenth century Tibetan teacher, said it this way: "The goal of
this teaching is emptiness, the essence of which is compassion."

The great insights are not always known or available to persons and
communities. They have in fact often been scarce, unknown, rejected, or
denied through the history of religious communities and in individual
lives. There has been considerable research in recent times in how people
can grow and realize them. James Fowler carried out extensive interviews, using Jean Piaget's stages of cognitive development in children and

Lawrence Kohlberg's stages of moral development to categorize stages of faith development.[18]

James Fowler found that persons were unable to grasp or understand more than one stage above the one they were in. Further, they were unable to move to a higher stage until their life experience created such dissonance in their present stage that they were forced to move to the next to resolve the difficulty. Ken Wilber, whose stages are also described, mitigates their rigidity by differentiating between states and stages of spiritual development. States are the observation or experiences of spiritual knowing, the first of the two legs of individual discovery described in Chapter One. A person in any stage may be able to experience the most profound state or depth of spiritual experience. But when they come to understand the experience, they must depend on the stage or structure they are in for its insight or explanation—the second leg of individual discovery.[19] How does one move to a higher stage or insight? Wilber and others describe a whole repertoire of spiritual practices for doing so.[20] For Richard Rohr, a Franciscan monk, prayer and suffering open the way to higher stages.[21]

For Fowler, the *undifferentiated faith* of infancy is built on basic trust and relational mutuality. Transition to stage one faith comes with the emergence of thought and language, opening up the use of symbols in speech and ritual play.

Stage one, *intuitive-projective faith*, happens at ages three to seven, and is characterized by fantasy and fluid thought patterns. It is egocentric and unrestrained by logical thoughts. Perception, novelty, and imagination are dominant, along with the first self-awareness. Transition to stage-two faith comes with concrete operational thinking about how things actually are in sensory experience.

Stage two, *mythic-literal faith*, is the faith of the school child, who must sort out what is real from what is make-believe. Symbols are understood literally. Main concerns are reciprocal fairness and immanent justice with rules and works righteousness. This stage is trapped in narrative. Limitations of this stage are either perfectionism or an abiding sense of badness.

---

18. (Fowler 1981)117–211 Following are brief summaries of the stages of faith according to Fowler's research.

19. (Wilber, Integral Psychology 2000)12–13

20. (Wilber 2008)

21. (Rohr 2003)115

Transition to stage three comes with formal operational thought and reflection on meanings.

Stage three, *synthetic-conventional faith*, is the faith of the adolescent who gathers and falls in love with a personal myth of the self, and who moves beyond the family context to larger authorities of school, church, and society. It is a conformist faith that mirrors conventional beliefs. It understands the environment in interpersonal terms, and becomes the final stage for many or most people. Tacit beliefs and ideology hold that because others are different, they are wrong or inferior. Deficiency of faith at this stage is a conformism that leaves no room for autonomy, or interpersonal betrayals that lead to nihilistic despair. Transition to stage four comes from contradictions between values of different authorities.

Stage four, *individual-reflective faith*, comes with adult autonomy, if it comes, usually in one's thirties and forties. It is counter-dependent opposition to authority, with keen awareness of social systems and institutions. Demythologizing prevails, with personal responsibility for beliefs and commitments; focusing on what is relative versus what is absolute; the individual versus the group; self-fulfillment versus service to others. Danger at this stage is overconfidence in the intellect, and insistence on one's own worldview as the only valid one. Transition to stage five comes with the awareness of disturbing inner voices.

Stage five, *conjunctive faith*, if at all, comes when life is more than half over. It is dialogical knowing, resulting from coming to terms with the unconscious, and the deeper self. It is multidimensional, relative, and organically interdependent, in which symbolic power is reunited with conceptual meanings. It, as Fowler puts it, "knows the sacrament of defeat and the reality of irrevocable commitments and acts." It has an ironic imagination and a paradoxical understanding of truth. Danger at this stage is paralyzing passivity with complacency or cynical withdrawal. Transition to stage six is the results of lives and acts divided between an untransformed world and a transforming vision and loyalties.

Stage six, *universalizing faith*, is exceedingly rare. It is the felt sense that the ultimate environment is inclusive of all being. It is redemptive subversiveness, and an ideal limit of faith. One example would be a person such as Martin Luther King, Jr.

Carol Gilligan, in *A Different Voice*, critiqued maps of spiritual development like Fowler's as being too dominated by male perspective. The male approach is that individuals have certain basic rights and that you have to respect the rights of others—what she called a "justice orientation." Women hold that people have responsibilities toward others and the imperative is to care for others—"a responsibility orientation." There are three stages in a responsibility orientation: from selfish to social or conventional morality to post-conventional or principled morality.[22]

Ken Wilber adds a description of higher stages of Axial Age insights "not imagined, felt." His *vision-logic* stage integrates reason and symbol. His metaphor for it is the Centaur, a mythical beast with a human head and a horse's body, thus integrating human reason with instinctual and unconscious energies in imaginative images and symbols.[23] Next higher is the *psychic* stage of the soul. It is the stage of nature mysticism, the path of yoga, of refined shamanism, and of esoteric spiritual disciplines with imaginative symbols and energies. Above that is the *subtle* stage, also involving the soul. It is the realm of saints, who live in the ultimate universe inclusive of all being. It is the realization of the pure formless witness that has never been absent. Wilber introduces it in a guided reflection:

> So tell me: Who are you? You are not your thoughts, for you are aware of them. You are not your feelings, for you are aware of them. You are not any objects that you can see, for you are aware of them too. Something in you is aware of all these things. So tell me: What is it in you that is conscious of everything? What is it in you that is always aware? Always fully present? Something in you right now is effortlessly noticing everything that arises. What is that? That vast infinite witnessing awareness, don't you recognize it? What is that Witness? You are that Witness, aren't you? You are the pure Seer, pure awareness, the pure Spirit that impartially witnesses everything that arises, moment to moment. Your awareness is spacious, wide open, empty and clear, and yet it registers everything that arises. That very Witness is Spirit within. . . .[24]

Finally comes the *causal* stage of Spirit, the highest realm of the sage. Wilber again:

> And then the strangest thing happens. Resting in the pure Self, abiding as the timeless Witness, noticing that the clouds float by in the vast expanse of Emptiness that is my own ever-present awareness, the Witness itself suddenly cannot be found . . . The

22. (Gilligan 1982) 19
23. (Wilber 1981) 9
24. (Wilber 2004) 4

Seer vanishes into everything seen, which sees itself eternally. I no longer witness the clouds, I am the clouds: I do not hear the rain, I am the rain: I can no longer touch the earth, for I am the earth . . . Precisely because I am not this, not that, I am fully this, fully that. Beyond nature, I am nature; beyond God, I am God: beyond the Kosmos altogether, I am the Kosmos in its every gesture.[25]

Underlying this highest stage, and indeed all stages, whether recognized or not, is the non-dual nature of reality which is the true nature of being. Wilber recognizes confusion in realizing these insights. He calls it the pre-trans fallacy. The fluid thought patterns of infancy and early childhood—pre-rational or pre-personal—can be confused with the highest insights only realized by going through all the stages of personal spiritual development, trans-rational or trans-personal. Both stages are fluid, open, not caught in fixed linguistic boundaries. But they are at the opposite ends of the spectrums of spiritual relational knowing, not equivalent.[26]

The great Axial Age insights of unlimited awareness and unconditional love are accessible to all persons, albeit according to their own varying growth in stages of spiritual knowing. These stages range from the undifferentiated faith of infancy to the highest causal stage of spirit. Ken Wilber notes the *pre-trans fallacy* which confuses the pre-personal fluid thought patterns of infancy and early childhood with the trans-personal highest insights of personal spiritual development, beyond language, at the opposite end of the spectrum.

SUMMARY

Unlimited awareness, called emptiness in the Buddhist tradition, transcends all divisions and separations, even the illusion of separate beings themselves. The evolution of the Golden Rule culminating in unconditional love also transcends all barriers and limitations. For Jesus, unconditional love is the image of ultimate reality. Unlimited awareness and unconditional love are inseparable dimensions of ultimate spiritual knowing. Persons are able to grasp them according to their own capabilities. This description of these unsurpassed spiritual insights now enables us to explore how they interact with scientific knowing in scientific and technological advances.

25. (Wilber 2004)5
26. (Wilber, Integral Psychology 2000)244, n.17

CHAPTER FOUR

EVOLUTION OF SCIENTIFIC KNOWING

Now my charms are all o'erthrown,
And what strength I have's mine own,
. . . In this bare island by your spell,
But release me from my bands
With the help of your good hands.
Gentle breath of yours my sails
Must fill, or else my project fails,
Which was to please. Now I want
Spirits to enforce, art to enchant,
And my ending is despair,
Unless I be reliev'd by prayer,
Which pierces so, that it assaults
Mercy itself, and frees all faults.

—William Shakespeare, *The Tempest*[1]

A BRIEF HISTORY OF SCIENTIFIC KNOWING

The origins of scientific knowing also go far back in the human experience. But in contrast to spiritual knowing, scientific knowing flowered much later, in the Renaissance and Enlightenment. And they did not peak then, but continue to advance, faster and faster, into an unlimited future.

One example of the original unity of religion and practical knowledge is the golden proportion. It supposedly mimics the proportions of the human body and is the basis of Egyptian architecture, later imported to

1. (Shakespeare 1997) 1685–1686

Greece. It can be drawn geometrically and stated numerically as 1.616 (...). Much later, in the thirteenth century, the Italian mathematician Fibonacci defined it arithmetically as a sequence of numbers such that each number is the sum of the two previous numbers. You can see it when you look at the expanding whorls of a nautilus shell. When you show people geometric examples of the golden proportion, they will most often prefer it to geometric examples of other proportions. When stated as a ratio, a:b=b: a+b, it was considered a spiritual definition of perfect meditation, or relationship between God and humans. There are only two entities in it—a and b, or God and humans.[2]

And then there were the Pythagoreans. Named after the Greek philosopher Pythagoras (ca. 570–490 BCE) who influenced Plato and Aristotle, they believed and tried unsuccessfully to prove that the universe could be understood in terms of whole numbers. Aristotle wrote "The Pythagoreans say that things exist by 'imitation' of numbers, and Plato, by 'participation' but these are the same, and Plato only changed the name." Their *tetraktys* presented harmonic laws. It was a pyramid of pebbles—one on the top row, two on the second row, three on the third, and four on the bottom row. The second row was twice the first row. When you cut a vibrating string in half, the sound it produced was an octave higher. The ratio of the second row to the third row 2:3 produced the musical interview of the fifth, when you cut the string by the same ratio. Here were the unified, cosmic, numeral laws of music. Pythagoreans swore their oath "on he who gave our soul the *tetraktys*."[3] A point was associated with 1, a line with 2, a plane with 3, and a solid with 4. Their sum, 10, was sacred and omnipotent. Heavenly bodies as they move give forth musical sounds, the "music of the spheres," as Plato wrote. Because we are used to it from childhood, we cannot hear it. But music *is* number and the cosmos *is* music.

The symbolic capabilities of the human species could in time be stripped of all their messy connotations and reduced to pure monochrome number. At once cosmic and empirical, number could explain the universe. Although it would take a couple of millennia, the advance of number in mathematics could even shed associations with divinity. Like Tiglath-Pileser II who no longer needed to add a god's name to his own, number could now rule the world, unaided, by itself.[4]

2. (Lawlor c. 1982, pbk. ed. 1989)44–64
3. (Latura 2012–13)64–65
4. (Wilber 1981)282–3

When first discovered, advances in scientific knowing often were held to be true for a long time. Euclid's geometric axioms and proofs were so regarded for over two thousand years. His first axiom, for example, stated that between any two points, a straight line can be drawn. Then, in the nineteenth century, mathematicians realized that was only true for two points on a plane. On the surface of a sphere, no straight line can be drawn between two points.[5]

Natural philosophy or theology—the study of the "Book of Nature," what we call science— and the study of the "Book of God," or theology, were not sharply distinguished. Scientists were often priests (in fact, some still are).

The legacy of the Axial Age was complicated around the Mediterranean. When Christianity spread beyond Palestine, Hebrew ways of knowing met Greek ones, Jerusalem met Athens. What was known as faith and reason became key features of Christian theology. What could be known by reason in the world, and what would only be known though faith in Christ?

Saint Augustine created the most important synthesis in his doctrine of the two books: the *book of Scripture* and the *book of nature*. Depending on a tradition of earlier writers including Clement of Alexandria, Augustine made four points. First is the unity of truth. There cannot be one truth for theology and another for the natural world. They must be resolved by reason. In the second place, because of the unity of truth, the book of Scripture and the book of nature are both ways in which God reveals himself, so they cannot contradict each other. Third, both books must be carefully interpreted. The Bible has literal, allegorical, analogical, and moral meanings. Contradictory to modern-day biblical literalists, in his "literal interpretation of Genesis" there is no six-day or six-epoch creation. For Augustine, biblical passages are accommodated to their contemporary hearers. God is the final source of sacred scriptures, but their human writers partially obscured that. His central principle of accommodation means that biblical interpretation is difficult, may be only provisional, and requires the careful use of reason. Finally, faith knowing is primary, and scientific knowing is an important handmaiden or "ancilla" that assists it.[6] Augustine's insights were normative in succeeding centuries as theologians continued to depend on Greek philosophical concepts in understanding faith and reason.

5. (Burger 2005)289–298
6. (Principe 2006)34–36

The Bible begins with the great statement: "In the beginning when God created the heavens and the earth, the earth was a formless void, and darkness covered the face of the deep" (Genesis 1:1–2a). Theologians in the early centuries tried to make sense of all this. How does God create, and how can we recognize God's continuing creative activity around us? They depended on Greek cultural ideas and categories of their time. God was the cause of it all. The creation was and is the effect or the result of what God caused.

But the theologians also recognized that the world sort of continued on its own, was even predictable in the way it operated. When you dropped a stone, it fell to the ground, not just sometimes, but all the time. Fire burned wood, unless it was too wet, consistently. So was God around all the time, making sure that stones dropped and fire burned? That seemed a little excessive, not quite right. The world had a reality of its own, went on by itself. So maybe God didn't need to directly cause every single effect in the world all the time. Maybe God just needed to set things up so they would work predictably, consistently. There was a kind of secondary causation in the world. God was the primary cause, but things in the world could continue to cause things on their own, in secondary causation, without God having to prop them up all the time.[7]

But as science and technology continued to develop, some people began to wonder if one needed God at all. Maybe the laws of cause and effect just worked on their own. There was no need for some external cause like God to push things along. Early scientists like Sir Isaac Newton wrote as much theology as they did physics, trying to make it all hang together, but the effort seemed less and less necessary as time went on.

Augustine's insights on the relation between spiritual and scientific knowing continued to be normative, even many centuries later, e.g., in the Galileo affair. Galileo, following Copernicus, adopted the revolutionary idea that the earth revolved around the sun, instead of being the still center of the universe. That seemed to contradict the biblical story of Joshua stopping the sun to lengthen the day. Cardinal Roberto Bellarmino, a friend and a leader of the Council of Trent, verbally warned Galileo that he could hold the rotation of the earth as provisionally true, but not as literally true, and Galileo agreed. But Bellarmino agreed that if Galileo could prove it to be true, then Scripture would have to be reinterpreted to agree with it. However, Galileo's attempted proofs, such as the phases of Venus, or the

7. (Principe 2006)55–56

earth's movements causing the tides, were either wrong or inconclusive. So the unity of truth was preserved for the moment.[8]

Buddhism has a similar perspective. At a conference in 2007, the Dalai Lama was asked what he would do if current brain research on meditation showed that Buddhist teachings were inaccurate. He replied that Buddhist practice and teachings would have to be revised in accordance with scientific findings.[9]

Through the seventeenth into the nineteenth centuries, scientific discoveries were often thought to be the best way to establish religious beliefs. Scientists were often deeply religious, exploring theology along with physical matter. Sir Isaac Newton's (1642–1727) *Principia Mathematica* is both a fundamental text of classical physics and a discussion of the "attributes and activities of God."[10]

The seventeenth century was also the time of scientific revolution, establishing the foundation of modern scientific knowing. Galileo was a key proponent of the essential need for indirect measurements, on which science has depended ever since. Our unaided senses have severe limitations when it comes to discovering what is really out there in the world. We just can't see closely or far or clearly enough. But now using telescopes and microscopes to augment our vision, scientific knowing was on its way to its subsequent great advances.[11] Galileo also advocated experiments, both in thought and in empirical observation, to test his ideas. He called them *cimenti*—"trial by ordeal."[12] Now the panoply of resources for scientific knowing was in place: number, advanced since the Pythagoreans; indirect observation; and experiment.

Sometimes a new discovery will drive the need for a new mathematics. Both Newton and Leibniz independently created calculus in the same period. Newton invented calculus in order to apply his physical laws.[13] Sometimes new mathematics will spur scientific discoveries. For example, the development of knot theory facilitated the discovery of the double helix of DNA.[14]

8. (Principe 2006)65–68

9. (Siegel 2007)102

10. (Principe 2006)98

11. (Randall 2011)26

12. (Deutsch 2011)14

13. (Starbird 2006)7–8

14. (Burger 2005)374–376

New scientific discoveries are often held with great confidence. La-Place, for example, boasted to Napoleon that he could predict the exact occurrence of any event two hundred years into the future using Newton's laws, if he just knew the exact position of all the particles now.[15]

Every scientific or mathematical discovery involves a more powerful abstraction that simplifies reality in order to understand and control some aspects of it. Sooner or later what has been left out intrudes in some rude way. In the early twentieth century the "Vienna Circle" of mathematicians, following the doctrine of logical positivism, insisted that mathematics, just like logic, was devoid of any descriptive content. They had grown tired of having their discoveries come up against inconvenient physical realities. They determined to create mathematical systems that were perfectly consistent within themselves, apart from any reference to physical reality.[16]

Almost immediately the mathematician Kurt Goedel, an outlier in the circle, created the Incompleteness Theorem. It proved both mathematically and logically that every rigorous formal system had within it a statement that is undecidable. It cannot be proven true or false within the system itself. It may be, in his words, "Completely (materially) true but unprovable in the formal system of classical mathematics."[17] There is a corollary. Since that is the case, no system can be proven to be consistent within itself. He established the theorem and corollary both in mathematical form and in words.[18]

The basis of his proof is in the epistle of Titus in the New Testament, which agrees with Greek racist attitudes toward Cretans. Titus 1:12–13 reads, "It was one of them, their very own prophet, who said, 'Cretans are always liars.' . . . That testimony is true." The same idea can be written "a Cretan once said, 'all Cretans are liars.'" The statement is an example of the self-referential paradox, or the liar's paradox. In its simplest form, it goes "This very statement is false." Now, if that statement is false, it is true, and if it is true, it is false. Not a happy situation. Any time I use a member of a set or group to prove the truth of the whole set, it doesn't work.

Scientific and mathematical advances, along with their inevitable technological applications do not end, even when scientists or mathematicians think they do. At the close of the nineteenth century prominent physicists

15. (Holt 2012)6
16. (Goldstein 2005)86
17. (Goldstein 2005)156
18. (Goldstein 2005)154–156

warned their graduate students not to go into the field, because all the essential discoveries had been made and there was nothing left to do but to tidy up some loose ends.[19] Of course, the grand discoveries of quantum mechanics, special relativity, and general relativity came shortly thereafter.

Science doesn't always proceed by filling in the gaps, putting chinks in the slight openings of its present knowledge to create even greater certainty. Sometimes the cumulative weight of difficulties will sink a whole way of viewing things, leading to a paradigm shift in theory. A gap turns out to be a gaping insufficiency in understanding how things worked, and an invitation to dive into the possibility of a new way of seeing things.

Science doesn't move from certainty to certainty either. When a new area of discovery opens, it is often muddy, confused, or uncertain. Only over a great deal of time and effort is a new simplification discovered that does make sense.

Newton's laws, powerful and universal as they are, quickly reached their limit in accounting for complex real-world situations. For example, Newton beautifully derived the planetary laws of motion by assuming that only the sun exerts gravitational pull on a planet. Now it might occur to us that there are other planets around also, and we would be right. The so-called two-body problem worked only because it simply ignored their existence and effects because they were so small. When you try to derive the motion with three bodies involved—say the sun, earth, and moon—the resulting three-body problem was so complex that it remained unsolved for two hundred years. The calculus Newton invented to apply his laws assumes that any point on a curve in a graph can be treated as if it were a straight line. Well, we say, but it isn't. Of course we're right, it isn't. But the simplification worked for centuries and still does, for most purposes.[20]

Calculus loves straight lines, gentle even curves, and smoothness that it can work with mathematically. But if you go out into the woods and look around, you don't see much smoothness; you see ragged edges, sharp differences, and roughness. So if you want to explore some of that roughness, like weather patterns over time, or even bodily rhythms like brain waves or heartbeats, perhaps you had best give up the illusion of certainty that assumes smoothness, and try to understand the greater complexity of roughness. One of the problems in even estimating environmental damage is the reliance on linear mathematical models of change when the reality seems

19. (Wheeler 1998)90
20. (Starbird 2006)15–16

chaotic, in fish and other creatures. "Scientists discovered total population numbers could remain stable for thousands of generations, then without warning suddenly boom or crash, without notable changes in the environment as the trigger."[21]

We will look later at chaos theory, fractals, and complexity theory which add a little more complexity into the equations, and let go of certainty regarding smoothness. At first complexity theory, chaos, and fractals were messy, confused, and uncertain; in some ways, they still are. In fact, those fields weren't even possible until computers made rapid calculations and iterations possible that previously would have taken lifetimes to do before their invention.

But the results again were astounding. To take one example, it turns out that brain waves are not smooth; they are chaotic in shape and rhythm. (We will explain later what "chaotic" means mathematically.) In fact, when they are smooth and regular, what you have is called an epileptic seizure.[22]

Medical research illustrates the uneven and lurching progress of science and technology, influenced by the imperatives of market capitalism. Greek mathematician and physician Athina Tatsioni has carried out and published extensive secondary analyses of biomedical research in peer reviewed journals. He charges that "as much as 90 percent of the published medical information that doctors rely on is flawed." He developed a sophisticated mathematical model to predict rates of error resulting from "manipulating data analyses [and] chasing career-advancing findings rather than good science." He studied the forty-nine most cited and most highly regarded research findings over the past thirteen years. Forty-five of the studies claimed significant advances. Thirty-four of them were retested. Dr. Tatsioni reported, "14, or 41 percent of the claimed advances, have been convincingly shown to be wrong or significantly exaggerated."[23]

Medical practice is based on the state of the art of medical knowledge and practice at any given time. It is the best we know. As supposedly some professors tell their students at the beginning of medical school, "Half of what we will teach you is wrong. We just don't know which half."

21. (Rasmussen 1996)156

22. (Strogatz 2008)95

23. (Freedman 2010)78–81

SCALE OF SCIENTIFIC KNOWING

The amazing growth of scientific knowing in history and to our present day is shown in its range of size or scale.[24] Scale refers to what scientists know at different sizes. Human beings are sort of in the middle of the scale, between the smallest we know and the largest we know. Human scale would include the tallest building we have made, Burg Khalifa in Dubai, at 828 meters (2,717 feet); the world's tallest mountain, Mount Everest, at 8.8 kilometers; and the deepest place in the ocean, the Mariana Trench at 11 kilometers. Lisa Randall calls that the human scale, since it is the size humans know about on earth. The movement of gravity and physical bodies on this human scale was worked out by Sir Isaac Newton some centuries ago, and scientists who want to know about the movement of physical bodies in the human scale still use this.

The next larger physical scale above the human scale can be called the sub-galactic scale. It goes from the size of the earth (twelve million meters), to the size of the solar system—ten trillion meters. On this scale, Newton's laws work fairly well, but not entirely. Einstein's theory of general relativity was needed to explain the perihelion of Mercury, which is "observed change in its orbit around the sun over time." Newton's laws work when densities are low and speeds slow enough; but now Einstein's more comprehensive theory of general relativity, which includes Newton's laws, is needed.

Even bigger is the cosmological scale. The black hole at the center of our own Milky Way galaxy is about ten trillion (10^{13}) meters in radius. The mass in a black hole is about four million times the mass of the sun. Gravity is so intense in a black hole that even light is sucked into it—nothing escapes. Newton's elegantly simple understanding of gravity is totally inadequate; the space-time continuum of Einstein's general relativity is needed.

Space/size and time are now intertwined. Scientists can now reason back to the beginning of the known universe and determine that the big bang which started the whole thing happened 13.75 billion years ago. The physical size of the whole universe at the time of the Cosmological Microwave Background, around 380,000 years after the beginning, was 10^{24} meters across. The universe continued to expand in size. The entire visible universe is now 10^{27}—100 billion light-years—across. That is peculiar, since that is bigger than we can observe in light-years from the beginning of the

---

24. (Randall 2011)The following discussion of scale summarizes pp. 70–87.

universe 13.75 billion years ago. That means we can observe parts of the universe that are so far apart they cannot see each other.[25]

The equations of general relativity explain that when scientists say the universe is expanding, they mean that the *very fabric of space itself is expanding*. It has been expanding ever since the big bang, but not at a steady constant pace. Very, very early, infinitesimally early, maybe as early as 10^{-39} seconds after the beginning, the cosmological inflation occurred. I can write these figures down. I cannot possibly understand them. When the age of the universe had multiplied by sixty times, the size of the universe had increased more than a trillion-trillion-trillion times. A scientist named Alan Guth worked this out in 1930 using field theory, combining Einstein's special relativity and quantum mechanics.[26] Since the end of the cosmological inflation, the universe expanded at a steady pace. In the 1990s two independent research teams discovered that the universe—space itself—is again expanding faster and faster, similar to what happened in the cosmological inflation but at a much slower rate.

What would possibly be causing all this expansion? The leading candidate is something called dark energy. It is exceedingly mysterious. The amount of dark energy is remarkably small and spread throughout the universe. But its density does not change, no matter how much the universe grows. It doesn't dissipate. When the universe was very small and young, energy in the form of radiation was dominant; later, energy transformed into matter was dominant (Einstein's e=mc2). And now, dark energy is taking over. Early in his career, Einstein invented a figure he called the cosmological constant to make his equations come out right. He later discarded it and called it the biggest mistake of his career, but now it seems to be the best measurement we have of the negative pressure that dark energy exerts upon the universe, causing it to expand faster and faster while gravity alone would seem to cause it to collapse.[27]

Where does this all end? We don't know, of course. Maybe it doesn't. Probably it doesn't. Probably, the universe is infinite. There may be nothing outside it, and it keeps expanding, infinitely. Some scientists speculate that there are actually many disconnected independent universes—a multiverse.[28]

25. (Randall 2011)350
26. (Randall 2011)362
27. (Randall 2011)373
28. (Randall 2011)351

But we have gone as large as we can in size. Now, will proceed to go smaller than human scale.

Moving smaller down the human scale, red blood cells are 10^{-3} meters, or seven micrometers long—one hundred times thinner than a credit card. William Harvey discovered the connections of arteries and veins. Later, Marcello Malpighi with better technology discovered the capillaries that connected them circulating the blood cells through the body. Harvey had discovered a system in which the connections among the elements, rather than just the elements themselves, determine what happens. Further down the human scale is DNA—two nanometers or a tenth of a micron, or ten million times smaller than a meter. Understanding how DNA works is increasingly difficult in the emergent behavior of the interconnections in the system. In chemistry and molecular physics "functional biological systems are complex and intricate and often have difficult-to-anticipate consequences."[29]

Even smaller is the atomic scale, 100 picometers, 10,000 million times smaller than a meter. Size is variable here and harder to determine. Electrons keep moving around a nucleus. In the electro-magnetic field the light we see by is between 380 and 750 nanometers in length but the size of an atom is only a tenth of a nanometer. In other words, we can't see an atom. And scientists find that the laws of physics operating here are very, very different than at larger scales.

The atom is mostly empty space. The nucleus at its center is around ten thousand times smaller in radius than the electron cloud around it. The volume of a nucleus is a mere trillionth of the volume of an atom. Quantum mechanics rules here, and Newtonian physics break down. Werner Heisenberg developed the uncertainty principle in 1926: all we can know is the probability of the position in space of a subatomic particle. We cannot know both the location and the momentum of a particle at the same time. All we can know are probabilities, but they are still precise equations.

Niels Bohr in 1912 discovered that electron orbits depend on fixed quantities of energy and that electrons can only jump between those quantities. We have left Newton behind, even though his laws work perfectly well at larger scales described above.

Still further down we can go inside the nucleus of an atom. While the electron seems to be a fundamental elementary particle, inside the nucleus are protons and neutrons which are not fundamental. Because inside them

29. (Randall 2011)76

are quarks—two up quarks and one down—that the strong nuclear force binds together to form protons and neutrons.[30] The quarks are free to move around inside the proton or neutron, but you can't isolate or pry them loose. Hence they are called "gluons," because they are so sticky.

The standard model that identifies all these particles has been experimentally confirmed as very accurate.[31] It takes incredibly large amounts of energy to probe these tiny subatomic distances. The Large Hadron Collider on the border of France and Switzerland has involved millions of dollars, a number of countries, and years of work to create the energy to take the search even further. Hadrons, subatomic particles bound by the strong nuclear force such as protons, collide together at enormous velocities in the hopes that in the collision they will decay into yet more exotic particles. Every time a quark is formed, an anti-quark with an equal and opposite charge must also be formed. And "inside a proton is a sea of virtual particles that is, quark/antiquark pairs and gluons."[32] Enormously high energy collisions in the Large Hadron Collider, we hope, will eventually tell us even more about what's there.

And even further down we come to impasse, mystery, what we don't know. Einstein determined that the mass of a particle tells how much energy a particle has at rest. (There are also particles that have no mass, like photons and they are never at rest.) "Experimenters have measured these masses, but the simplest physics rules simply don't allow them."[33] Particle physicists think something very big happened that "changed the very nature of the universe" very early in its history. Before that, particles had no mass and flew around. After that, they had mass and slowed down. That something is called the Higgs boson or Higgs field, after one of the first scientists to think of it. The Large Hadron Collider, very recently, has found evidence of it. But for now, "Calculations based on quantum mechanics and special relativity tell us that without a richer theory, masses should be much greater—in fact 10 quadrillion, or 10^{16} times as big."[34] It's called the hierarchy problem, and it doesn't make any sense. But there it is—infinity at the largest scale, and mystery at the smallest scale.

30. (Tippett 2010)259–260 Murray Gell-Mann had read James Joyce's *Finnegan's Wake*'s line, "Three quarks for Muster Mark!"
31. (Randall 2011)273
32. (Randall 2011)85
33. (Randall 2011)116
34. (Randall 2011)118

This brief history of scientific knowing focused on physical sciences. Richard Feynman taught that the most succinct and comprehensive statement of scientific knowledge is this: "All things are made of atoms—little particles that move around in perpetual motion, attracting each other when they are a little distance apart, but repelling upon being squeezed into one another."[35] All other sciences are dependent on and derivative of the basic laws of physics. It is true that other disciplines have to translate their questions into the language of physics in order for it to be helpful. And it is true that physical knowledge is far from complete, as noted earlier. Perhaps the laws of physics change over time, although at present we don't think they do. Turbulent fluids, the hierarchy problem and other issues remain. But for now, the clearest and best way to understand scientific knowing is by means of physical sciences.

UNINTENDED CONSEQUENCES

There are at least three huge developments, and unintended consequences, from the continued advance of science and technology into the future which threaten to wreck the whole enterprise.

The first is the explosion of population. In hunting-gathering times there were perhaps four million human beings on the planet. Now with populations aging in parts of the world from China to Europe, scientists are hoping population growth will top out at about 10 billion human beings around 2030.[36] Even with technological advances, that explosion strains every aspect of the ability of the earth to sustain the life and welfare of living beings.

The second consequence of scientific and technological advance is moving from dependence on natural energy from the sun (through photosynthesis into food, wood, and wind) to essential dependence on stored energy in fossil fuels and other nonrenewable resources. "Every day the world wide economy burns an amount of energy the planet required 10,000 days to create. Or, to put it another way, 27 years' worth of stored solar energy is burned and released by utilities, cars, factories and farms every 24 hours."[37] Even with the increasing availability of renewable energy, there are various estimates of how many planets of our size and resources it would take to

35. (Feynman 2011)4

36. (Rasmussen 1996)3

37. (Rasmussen 1996)59

sustain this depletion of our energy and resource capital as the rest of the world strains to catch up with the profligacy of the United States.

The third consequence of scientific and technological advance is the irresistible appeal of a relatively new ideology or belief system spreading across the planet. It is called market capitalism, and it co-opts scientific and technological advances to its seldom challenged or even questioned ultimate goals of permanent economic growth, development, and consumption. It has brought enormous and continuing gains in economic development and standards of living around the globe. Entrepreneurship especially thrives on its open-ended promise of individual gain. It often is associated with the spread of democracy and it exists in diverse (even bewildering) variations, from "socialism with Chinese characteristics" to American libertarian enthusiasms. Few can resist its confident assurance that things will keep getting better and better forever, materially speaking, whether they be individuals or even authoritarian regimes like China.

Like water to the Wicked Witch of the West, what is toxic to market capitalism is community—the community of the planet itself, the community of all living beings together, and the community of humans among themselves and with their natural environment. The popular irrational and excessive ideology of market capitalism is that individual units—corporations and persons—each getting everything they can for themselves without any other consideration, will make things better for everyone. In spite of ameliorative efforts by outliers such as entrepreneurs, venture capitalists, religious communities, foundations, non-governmental organizations, and even some governments, the belief often prevails.

One can certainly criticize aspects of hunting-gathering peoples. They sometimes practiced slash-and-burn agriculture; they might soil a bit of land and then move on; and their understanding of the communion of living beings in and with nature was unconscious, naïve, magical, and at times violent. But they did live communion in nature in an age as lost to us as participation in origin-myth initiation rites.

It is hardly possible to overstate the damage done by scientific and technological advance, often in the service of market capitalism, to our earth-human community. At the beginning of the twentieth century it was not yet true that "every natural system on the planet [was] disintegrating . . . soil erosion was not exceeding soil formation. . . . Species extinction was not exceeding species evolution. Carbon emissions were not exceeding carbon fixation. Fish catches were not exceeding fish reproduction.

Forest destruction was not exceeding forest regeneration. Fresh water use was not exceeding aquifer replenishment. Half the world's coastlines, the most densely populated human areas were not imperiled." By the end of the century all of that was reversed and human power over and against the rest of creation changed "fundamentally and dramatically."[38]

A few decades ago astronauts brought back the first picture of earth taken from space. It was astonishingly beautiful: shimmering vibrant blues and greens and whites framed against a limitless void. Even when the orbiting space craft showed the moon up close, it was pretty much what we expected it would be: a large rock, colorless, inert, dead. But this earth, this green and pleasant orb set in the dark sky, this earth is alive! It became a new art form. We hung the image on our walls. We enshrined it in the marketing materials of advocacy groups and for-profit corporations.

Trees demonstrate the resulting damage human beings are doing to the planet from all three consequences: population growth; depletion of stored energy, and the excesses of market capitalism. Trees anchor the ecosystem. They hold the soil, nourish, protect and maintain its fertility, richness, and diversity. They complete the water cycle, moderating the falling of rain to prevent drought, floods, and mud slides. In and under their canopy they shelter innumerable living beings, from microbes vitalizing the soil to mountain lions atop the food chain, keeping the soil soft and hospitable to growing things. They capture and transform enormous amounts of solar energy in photosynthesis.

Jared Diamond has demonstrated what happens when humans mess with this arrangement. There are case studies from the Easter Islanders to the temples and wats in Southeast Asia, to the Anasazi in the Four Corners region of the American southwest where Utah, Colorado, Arizona, and New Mexico meet. Whenever humans in their relentless ambition kept harvesting trees to fire kilns for clay images of the divine, roll huge stone statues into place with logs, use wooden beams for temples aligned with solstice and equinox, whatever, the results were always the same. When all the trees had been cut down, the ecosystem collapsed; the civilizations vanished; the people perished.[39]

Say you produce a little film from Neolithic times (10,000–8,000 BCE) to the present, in which each millennium takes up one minute. Alan Durning did this, and Larry Rasmussen tells what you would see in the film: "For

38. (Rasmussen 1996)4
39. (Diamond 2005)77–309

seven minutes, the marbled blue planet looks like a still photograph. Forests cover one third of the land. The agricultural revolution makes changes, but on a small enough scale they are hardly visible. Then at about seven and one-half minutes the islands and lands of the Aegean Sea begin losing their forests. At nine minutes, that is, one thousand years ago, scattered parts of Europe, Central America, China and India show threadbare sections of the forest mantles. Six seconds from the film's end, a century ago, eastern North America shows the same. Still, forests cover 32 percent of the earth's lands.

"Suddenly in the last three seconds—since 1950—an explosion occurs. Forests vanish in Japan, the Philippines, mainland Southeast Asia, Central America, the horn of Africa, eastern South America, western North America, the Indian subcontinent, West and Sub-Saharan Africa, the Amazon basin, Papua New Guinea, Malaysian Borneo. In only 45 years, forests fall to 26 from 32 percent of earth's land cover. And only 12 percent of this is intact forest ecosystems."[40]

INFINITE REACH

The Axial Age insights of spiritual knowing have never been surpassed while scientific knowing continues to advance into an unlimited future. However, both scientific and spiritual knowing share a common aim. David Deutsch calls it "infinite reach." Both scientific and spiritual knowing are infinitely open-ended quests. In its popular meaning, infinity simply means something goes on forever. It never stops, never ends, has no final constraints or limits. Its symbol is a figure-eight drawn on its side. Infinity may be mysterious, appealing or even, in some contexts, disturbing.

Infinity also has a specific mathematical definition. Georg Cantor developed it in the 1870s. Infinity is a one-to-one correspondence between the whole and a part of the whole. You can demonstrate it by pairing up members of one group with members of a part of the group one-to-one. It is called cardinality.

You can do cardinality with natural numbers. Have one group or set of natural numbers beginning with 1 and go on 2, 3, 4, and on infinitely. Then, put part of them in another group or set beginning with 2 and go on 3, 4, and on infinitely. When you try to pair them up it looks like a number in the whole group has no partner, no buddy, is not part of a pair in the partial group. So there is no cardinality. But Cantor developed the

40. (Rasmussen 1996)217–218

"diagonal method," pairing 1 in the first set with 2 in the second set, and so on infinitely. There is cardinality after all, one-to-one correspondence between pairs of numbers, in the two groups—between the two infinities—the whole beginning at one and the part beginning at 2. They are both infinite.[41]

Cantor went even further: Take real numbers—i.e., natural numbers plus decimals, zero, and negative numbers—and pair them up with natural numbers using the same diagonal method. Do they also demonstrate cardinality, one-to-one correspondence? No. Cantor demonstrated that you can create a real decimal number that is not part of any pair with a natural number. Therefore, there are more real numbers than natural numbers. The astonishing conclusion: There is no infinity without another larger infinity. There are infinitely different sizes of infinity and infinite numbers of infinities.[42] For daring to make these suggestions at that point in history, Cantor was personally attacked, and spent much of his later life in an insane asylum. And yet, he was proven correct.

The scientific idea of fallibilism, as David Deutsch noted earlier, implies that scientific knowing will advance infinitely. There will be no end to new and improved good explanations. We can create and shape reality more and more, infinitely. Perhaps when the sun finally cools, or the earth becomes too polluted to support life, we will not even need this planet. We can create our own. Already, 22,000 miles above the planet, "geo-synchronous communication satellites, unaffected by atmospheric drag, will remain in our orbit until the sun consumes the earth."[43] Perhaps someday all it means to be human can be encoded in a microchip, or some other device, so we will not even need our bodies. These fantasies are entertained by some. What we do know is that scientific knowing, as practiced now, has no known limits. Explanations will still be decided by finite physical testing of predictions. But of the infinite number of infinities, physics uses only one or two—the infinity of natural numbers, and the infinity of a continuum.[44]

Scientists seem drawn to religious metaphors to express their ambitions for infinite reach. Lisa Randall titled her recent book on particle physics and the Large Hadron Collider *Knocking on Heaven's Door: How Physics and Scientific Thinking Illuminate the Universe and the Modern World*. And

41. (Burger 2005)150, 140

42. (Burger 2005)163,174

43. (Weiner 2012)60

44. (Deutsch 2011)195

Time magazine titled its picture of the Large Hadron Collider and its discovery of the Higgs Particle, "The Cathedral of Science."[45]

Spiritual knowing also has infinite reach, illustrated by the mathematics of calculus. Calculus is indispensable in engineering and technology from engines to electrical circuits, to financial derivatives, from economics to architecture.[46] Precursors of calculus go back as far as Archimedes (287–212 CE), but it was created independently by Sir Isaac Newton (1642–1727) and Gottfried Wilhelm von Leibniz (1646–1716) in the seventeenth century. Newton circulated his ideas in the 1660s, but did not publish them until 1704 and later.[47]

Infinity is central in calculus. Infinity in calculus approaches a limit. The concept of limit, essential to calculus, did not become clear until the mid-1800s. As a quantity becomes closer and closer, infinitely closer, to a fixed value, that fixed value is the limit.[48] There are infinite series of numbers that "come infinitely closer" to a finite number, e.g., 1/2+ 1/4+ 1/8+ 1/16 comes infinitely closer to 1. There are also infinite series that do not, e.g., 1+1/2+1/3+....

Calculus has two fundamental ideas, or ways of analyzing change and motion. Both depend on the limit. The first, the derivative, arrives at the limit by subtracting and dividing. The second, the integral, arrives at the same limit by adding and multiplying. The fundamental theory of calculus is that both solutions are equivalent—giving two alternate and equivalent ways of solving a problem—which is the great usefulness and applicability of calculus.[49]

When you plot the relevant numbers on a graph, they must create a smooth, visually curved line. It is called compatibility. When you magnify the curve, it looks like a straight line. And calculus uses that straight line, called a tangent line. If the line jumps all over the place, or takes sharp turns, you can't use calculus. Much of nature does not conform to that constraint, and so calculus is not applicable.[50]

Calculus can, however, help us help understand the key insights of spiritual knowing developed in the Axial Age: unlimited awareness and

45. (Kluger 2012)32–33
46. (Starbird 2006)123–124
47. (Starbird 2006)23
48. (Starbird 2006)70–71
49. (Starbird 2006)22
50. (Starbird 2006)73

unconditional love. The two insights have infinite reach. Unlimited awareness or emptiness is unlimited. Unconditional love erases all boundaries;
it is unconditional. These two insights are not unrelated; they each depend
on the other. And they both infinitely approach a limit, as in calculus. That
limit has various names in the traditions: liberation, enlightenment, perhaps even salvation. Thomas Merton called it the palace of nowhere—the
infinite limit of spiritual relational knowing.

Spiritual knowing comes infinitely close in two intertwined ways. The
first is unlimited awareness, or emptiness. Like the derivative in calculus,
radical awareness subtracts and divides all the distinctions, separations and
linguistic barriers by which we limit and restrict our awareness until we
finally come infinitely close to emptiness—no restrictions at all, undivided
awareness of everything at once—in time, in space, in dissolving all illusions. Unconditional love, like the integral in calculus, adds and multiplies
the breadth and depth of compassion until it comes close, infinitely close,
to the limit of love without any boundaries, any conditions, any restrictions, any limits at all. The Golden Rule evolves in the Axial Age. Love of
family and friends, and hatred of enemies evolves for Jesus Christ into unconditional love for all. As God provides the sun and rain for all without
partiality, restriction, or limitations, we are to love all without partiality,
restriction, or limitation. In Buddhism, the Bodhisattva's vow for the liberation of all beings, including the illusion of beings, intends unconditional
love without partiality, restriction, or limitations.

Unconditional love and unlimited awareness both infinitely approach
the limit of final liberation. They depend on each other. They journey to
the same infinite no place. This liberation in awareness and love is not a
static inhuman or robotic perfection. We can even say it is the realization
of our full humanity. It is an open-ended journey of infinite reach to who
we really are.

Adam Gopnik, an art critic and cultural commentator, illustrates the
human experience of developing awareness and love.[51] He is at a dinner
party. The hour is getting late; people are worrying about paying the baby
sitter and getting up in a few hours to go to work. But the oblivious host
keeps bringing out new exotic dishes he has just cooked. Adam has exhausted the possibilities of conversation with the guest on his left and then
with the guest on his right. Finally he introduces himself to the guest sitting
opposite and asks him what he does. It turns out that he is an artist who

51. (Gopnik 2011)56–63

teaches drawing. For some reason, Adam finds himself asking, "Would you teach me how to draw?"

The teacher agrees; Adam shows up at his studio with pencils, erasers, and paper. The studio is cluttered with copies of classical statues, and he is given a large plaster cast of an eye to draw. He begins; he draws; when he looks at the paper, what he sees is appalling compared to the statue. He grips the pencil tighter and tries harder; he hasn't felt this bad about himself since grade school. After a few more equally painful sessions, the teacher invites him to his private studio to watch him draw. He goes and watches the teacher look, draw a line, perhaps erase it, look, draw again, patiently, easily, slowly—above all, paying attention, being present, caring, one might even say meditating through drawing. Adam begins to learn to do something like that himself. And the day comes when what he draws resembles what he sees before him. He graduates to live models, and one day the teacher stops by and says something like, "Do you see what looks a little like a rabbit under his ribs?"

So now Adam begins to realize drawing is not just mechanically putting down only what his senses register. As brain-mind research teaches, he also needs the creative input of his mind. He needs to express the full range of his humanity. The remarkable thing is that as he begins to do so, what he draws looks even more like the model, more alive, more interesting, than when he was just trying to copy what he saw. Even putting pencil lines down on paper is a creative act. The pencil shades gradually become shapes, and the shapes begin to take on meaning. They become symbols, become interesting, become art.

The challenge here is for the mind's input to be fresh, created in this moment. His "I" needs to meet the "thou" of what he is drawing, instead of automatic mindless imposition of past stereotypes or judgments. To say it another way: He needs to see with the eyes of the heart. The infinite reach of spiritual knowing in unlimited awareness and unconditional love does not end in a static, inhuman perfection. It makes us more human, truly human, not less human. Human spiritual knowing is an open-ended quest; an infinite reach into liberation, full realization, and infinite limit of our humanity. In the gospel of John, Jesus promises "Very truly, I tell you the one who believes in me will also do the works that I do, and in fact will do greater works than these, because I am going to the Father" (John 14:12). The first letter in the Johannine tradition says, "Beloved, we are God's children now; what we will be has not yet been revealed. What we do know is this; when it is revealed, we will be like him, we will see him as he is" (1 John 3:2). Bodhisattvas and Buddhas are not made from cookie cutters, nor are they interchangeable numbers. Each is a unique manifestation of emerging human liberation. In spiritual knowing we are called to come closer, infinitely closer to infinite spiritual limit, becoming ever more truly human, becoming who we really are, in the process. Good drawing, good meditation, good living, and spiritual knowing are the fresh creative images of the heart interacting with and enlivening what the senses see, hear, touch at this moment.

SUMMARY

Scientific knowing, called natural theology or philosophy, was originally undifferentiated from spiritual knowing. In the seventeenth century the full panoply of resources for scientific knowing was developed as it diverged from spiritual knowing. The advances of scientific knowing are illustrated in its scale.

There are at least three large developments and unintended consequences from the continuing advance of science and technology. They include the rapid expansion of population which strains the earth's ability to sustain the life and welfare of living beings; the depletion of stored energy from fossil fuels and other non-renewable resources; and the appeal of market capitalism, which tends to neglect communal responsibilities. The decimation of trees on the planet illustrates the consequences.

Scientific knowing and spiritual knowing share infinite reach. In scientific knowing it is called fallibilism. The mathematical metaphor of calculus describes infinite reach in spiritual knowing. The infinite limit of unlimited awareness and unconditional love is the full realization of our humanity, who we really are.

CHAPTER FIVE

BRAIN-MIND RESEARCH AND MEDITATION

I do think all religions are the left hemisphere story
that helps us get into the right hemisphere experience.

—JILL BOLTE TAYLOR[1]

We have described differences and similarities in scientific knowing and spiritual knowing. We have briefly traced the historical development of each, culminating in the Axial Age for spiritual knowing, and advancing exponentially into the future for scientific knowing. Now we are prepared to explore their interactions with each other in personal experience. Scientific knowing explains personal experience in brain-mind research and clinical experience. Scientific knowing in inner experience ends in "qualias," the subjective experiences that are finally known only to the person having them.

This chapter begins with a definition of brain and mind, and a brief description of meditation based on brain-mind research and clinical

1. From Taylor's June 25, 2008 radio interview with Terry Gross on NPR's Fresh Air from WHYY. Fuller excerpt: "Religion is the story that different people tell themselves because ultimately, whether you're Christian based or you're Buddhist based or whatever your choice of religion is, there's a story that you tell yourself, that gets you, allows you to quiet your mind, whether it's through mantra or whether it's through prayer, to quiet that left hemisphere language center, in order for you to be able to feel that you are in relationship with something that is greater than you are as a single individual. So I do think that all religions are the left hemisphere story that helps us get into the right hemisphere experience."

experience. Then we describe the layers of the self from brain-mind research and the central role of the medial prefrontal cortex. After that we describe spiritual knowing as mindfulness meditation in the Buddhist tradition of *vipassana*. Mindfulness meditation manifests in awareness of body rhythms, reports of personal experiences, and related descriptions from personal growth modalities. The aim and full development of meditative practice is self-transformation. Finally, we describe how scientific knowing in brain-mind research explains and supports self-transformation in mindfulness meditation in eight levels of integration.

For scientist and clinician Daniel Siegel, who draws on brain research and clinical experience, mind is the "flow of energy and information, while the physical brain consists of neural connectors and their complex patterns for firing."[2] We live out our ultimate vocation in spirit in the midst of the physical creation of gravity, matter, electricity, and neurons in the brain.

Siegel goes on to describe what the experience of meditation is like, based on brain research and clinical experience: "The mind is like the ocean. And deep in the ocean, beneath the surface, it's calm and clear. And no matter what the surface conditions are, whether it's flat or choppy or even a full gale storm, deep in the ocean it's tranquil and serene. As from the depth of the ocean, you can look toward the surface and just notice the activity there, so from the depth of the mind you can look upward toward the brainwaves at the surface of your mind, where all that activity of the mind, thoughts, feelings, sensations and memories exist."[3]

THE SELF IN BRAIN-MIND FUNCTIONING

The self functions at different levels in the brain. If a metaphor is useful, think of them as levels or stories of a house. Like stories in a house, they contain "stories" about who we are. We don't often go into the basement or proto-self. That means we are not, by and large, consciously aware of the rich mix of information there that forms the foundation of who we are.

Above the basement is the first floor or core self. We are consciously aware of the core self. It is our basic experience of who we are. And above the first floor is an open sun room called the autobiographical self. From there we can see in all directions; tell stories about our past as we remember it; anticipate the future; and create stories about what the present means.

2. (Siegel 2007)48
3. (Siegel 2007)285

Begin with our proto-self, to use Antonio Damasio's term—our most basic experience of who we are. It is not exclusively a human attribute; we share it with some animals. Our brain receives and shares a rich and continuous mix of information from our body. There are three fundamental divisions of that information: internal milieu and viscera; vestibular and musculoskeletal; and fine-touch. The internal milieu and viscera division senses changes in the chemical composition of the blood, receives pain signals, and contracts and dilates the smooth muscles including blood vessels. Except for partial control of our breath, it is beyond our conscious control. We can exercise conscious control over the second division, the striated voluntary muscles connected to our bones. That information comes in through neurons at different levels from our spinal cord to our cerebral cortex. It also includes our vestibular system which maps our location in space. Finally, specialized sensors in our skin comprise the fine-touch division when they touch an external object, registering texture, form, weight, temperature.[4] They register external, rather than internal signals.

All of that information is essential to our life. The brain automatically uses it largely below our consciousness to maintain the homeostasis of life functions. Homeostasis means that those functions must be stable within a fairly narrow range if we are to survive.[5]

Next up the ladder of complexity is the core self. Whenever any sense encounters any "object," externally or internally, from an inner state of bliss to a car moving down the street, the proto-self is affected, and the core self comes into being. The essence of the core self are non-verbal neuronic accounts of the proto-self being modified by events. Because that happens all the time, the core self appears to be continuous.

We are conscious of the core self. What does it mean to be conscious? We can usually tell if another person is conscious by noting whether they are awake, alert and at least minimally attentive to their surroundings.[6] We can usually also sense their background emotions; are they edgy, relaxed, preoccupied, really present? And we can tell if they are paying minimal attention to what is going on around them. That is consciousness as noticed externally by another—wakefulness, background emotion, minimal attention.

---

4. (Damasio 1999)149–153
5. (Damasio 1999)39–40
6. (Damasio 1999)55, 88–91

We ourselves know internally that we are conscious because we are experiencing specific emotions, and engaged in specific behaviors for specific purposes. Others may surmise the validity of the subjective experiences we are having, but only we can directly know those "qualia" or subjective experiences.[7]

Interestingly, nearly all of the portions of the brain responsible for core consciousness are located near the midline of the brain, from the cortex to the brain stem, where left and right sides of the structures face each other across the midline.[8]

Emotions developed in the course of evolution to do two things. First, they produce specific reactions to a situation. i.e., to flee, to fight, to freeze. Second, they prepare the organism to carry out the reaction, e.g., to increase blood flow to the muscles to fight or flee. As we all know, they may be induced either from present events or from memory.[9] There is no consciousness without emotion. For example, in what is called an absence seizure, when consciousness is impaired, all emotion is suspended.[10] Emotions are a necessary step on an interconnected ladder of life regulation. The ladder goes from simple automatic responses, to emotions, to images we experience as feelings, to creative conscious responses.

Feelings are a step above emotions in the ladder. When we become conscious of or feel emotion, the brain is creating an image of the emotion.[11] Then, when we *know* that we feel a feeling, the brain is creating three interwoven images: the proto-self; the "object"—in this case, an emotion; and the changes in the organism from the interaction of the two. That can only happen with the emergence of consciousness in the core self.

Emotion is necessary for consciousness, but language is not. Language is a translation from the non-linguistic images we have been discussing. Persons with global aphasia, for example, have no language capabilities, but are fully conscious.[12] They can communicate, are aware, and so on. They simply cannot translate their images into words.

Finally, above the core self is the autobiographical self. The autobiographical self is based on personal memories of past experiences and

7. (Damasio 1999)9
8. (Damasio 1999)106
9. (Damasio 1999)53–54
10. (Damasio 1999)96–100
11. (Damasio 1999)280
12. (Damasio 1999)107–109

INFINITE REACH

anticipated futures.[13] The memories are recorded as permanent neural patterns of core consciousness activated as images. Those records can be modified through later experiences. They describe "who we are," our conscious identity and autobiography.

The autobiographical self requires an extended consciousness beyond the here-and-now experience of core consciousness in the core self. Extended consciousness requires a building up and reactivation of memories, and the ability to hold many images together in awareness. Extended consciousness in the autobiographical self remembers the past, anticipates the future, and holds everything together in a larger context of lived life.[14] When researchers conclude that the self arises at perhaps eighteen months of age, they are probably referring to extended consciousness in the autobiographical self.

Sensory input portions of the brain in the cerebral cortex and other portions of the higher brain hold dispositions—dormant records for how to produce actions and process current images and all memory. Dispositions in themselves are never conscious. There is in fact a vast unconscious underground beneath our conscious images, consisting of not-activated neural patterns and their interrelationships, and records of neural patterns in memory.[15]

THE MEDIAL PREFRONTAL CORTEX

The left hemisphere of our brain deals in words, concepts and stories, or the four L's: language, linearity, logic, and literalism.[16] It organizes things for us, and carries out the executive function; it is in charge of making decisions. Portions on the left side of the cortex of the higher brain, called the anterior cingulate cortex, focus attention and choose what to focus on. That portion of the cortex is related to the big bundle of nerves called the corpus callosum, which connects the left and right hemispheres of the brain.

The executive decision takes effort. For example, when I was trying to write this, I was put on hold on the phone for tech support to figure out how to back up my virus control. I had to listen to some annoying music in

13. (Damasio 1999)174–175
14. (Damasio 1999)106–108
15. (Damasio 1999)222–223, 319
16. (Siegel 2007)45

the background. It was difficult to both write and suffer the muzak at the same time.

When we decide to focus in meditation, brain activity then shifts to include non-verbal imagery and bodily sensations in the right hemisphere, midbrain functions of emotion, and brainstem functions of life support. Now the focus of activity is a portion of the brain called the medial prefrontal cortex (medial meaning in the middle, and prefrontal cortex, meaning the front part of the brain). When we shift to this integrative function of the medial prefrontal cortex, no more effort is needed, it continues without effort. We can just rest, effortlessly.

There are several fascinating things about this part of the brain. The chakra called the Ajna center, or the third eye, is in traditional lore the center of spiritual insight. The medial prefrontal cortex would be reminiscent of this very same location. Over literally thousands of years, meditators and mystics have discovered wisdom about our human physiology and brain functioning that brain researchers are now confirming.

The medial prefrontal cortex rests on top of another part of the cortex called the insula, which connects to the brain-stem structures which regulate life functions—breathing, waking and sleeping, autonomic nervous system—and the midbrain structures like the amygdala which store, access, and regulate emotions.

The medial prefrontal cortex has a remarkable list of integrative functions. They include the following: bodily regulation; attuned communication to others' and one's own mind; emotional balance; response flexibility; empathy; insight or self-knowing awareness linking past, present and future; fear modulation; intuition including input from the visceral neural areas around heart, lungs, and intestines—"gut feelings"; and morality—what is best for the whole.[17] The medial prefrontal cortex is the center of the experience of the integration of the whole being. It is the site of non-verbal self-reflection, pure awareness and meta-awareness, or awareness of awareness itself.

VIPASSANA MEDITATION

There is a wide diversity of methods, experiences, and practices of spiritual knowing. Spiritual insights which explain those experiences cover an equally broad area. Brain-mind research has considered mindful awareness

17. (Siegel 2007)43–44

or mindfulness meditation to be a useful and central method or paradigm of spiritual knowing, and integration as an adequate explanation of the insights it brings. That practice is followed here. Mindful awareness or mindfulness meditation is derived from *vipassana* practice in Buddhism.[18] Here is Buddha's teaching of *vipassana* in the *Diamond Sutra*, spoken as the sutras supposedly were perhaps within a decade of 400 CE, when the Buddha was 65:

> Thus have I heard. . . . One day before noon, the Bhagavan put on his patched robe and picked up his bowl and entered the capital of Shravasti for offerings. After begging for food in the city and eating his meal of rice, he returned from his daily round in the afternoon, put his robe and bowl away, washed his feet, and sat down on the appointed seat. After crossing his legs and adjusting his body, he turned his awareness to what was before him.[19]

The voice that begins all sutras is that of Ananda, Shakyamuni's cousin, who had "perfect" memory. Late in his life, Buddha instructed him to begin all sutras with these words: "Thus have I heard."

Although most sutras begin with a miraculous event, this one begins with the Buddha's everyday activities, emphasizing that the highest teachings are about compassion and wisdom in ongoing daily life. In his final *Testament Sutra*, Buddha said, "Renounce fashion and beauty, put on the faded robe, take up the vessel of humility and support yourselves by begging. And when you do so, should feelings of pride arise, get rid of them at once. . . . For the sake of liberation, humble yourselves and practice begging."

His appointed seat is elsewhere called the Lion's Seat; it is a large stool, and sitting on it signifies that he wishes to address the monks. He sits precisely in a meditation posture. "Turning his awareness to what was before him," meaning that he is practicing mindfulness meditation or *vipassana*. One is mindful, or pays "bare attention" without interpretation, naming, labeling or language, or any intermediary between the mind and what is before us, body, sensations, emotions, thoughts, and dharmas.[20]

I once spent an afternoon in a Rinzai Zen Buddhist community in the Catskills, doing mindfulness meditation. We spent the afternoon just listening, nothing more, just listening to the sounds on that sultry summer afternoon—slight breeze in the trees, bird songs, barely audible insects, the

18. (Siegel 2007)11
19. (Pine 2002)41,47,49
20. (Pine 2002)47–53

occasional rustling of clothes and bodily movements of others in the community, my own breathing and heartbeat. We were not to say to ourselves "O that's a robin" but simply listen to the sounds without naming, judging, analyzing, or thinking about what they were. We were to just pay bare attention to sound, engage in pure awareness.

Erich Berne, the founder of a school of therapy called transactional analysis, tells the story of a little child sitting by a window and hearing a high-pitched sound outside which attracts her attention. Her careful parent instructs her, "That's a robin." So ever after, whenever the child hears a sound like that, she says to herself "robin" and closes off any further curiosity or exploration. And that's why, according to Berne, most of us have never really heard a bird song since we were five years old.

MEDITATION AND THE BODY

Awareness of bodily rhythm is central in meditation. My first introduction to Zen meditation was at the San Francisco Zen center. Our engaging teacher, Tommy, had been a female impersonator in the city before he entered the community. For an hour he discoursed carefully and exhaustively on only two topics: how to sit, and how to breathe. Our entrance into the depth and mysteries of Soto Zen Buddhism was focused solely on the body—how to sit and how to breathe. The intricacies and nuances of the *Heart Sutra* and other Buddhist teachings would come later. But the essential and sufficient entrance to them was the body—how to sit and how to breathe. At the end of his discourse he bowed—*gassho* to us—and said, "Now please forget everything I have said to you." For teaching purposes he had engaged our left brain, but it could not take us very far; it was not a sufficient vehicle to carry us where we wanted and needed to go. For that, we needed to let it go and return simply to the body in *shikantaza*, "just sitting"—the hallmark of Soto Zen Buddhist practice.[21]

Peter Levine is a therapist who works with bodily rhythms, especially with patients recovering from trauma of various sorts. In learning how to treat them, he came to realize that their physical and mental suffering reminded him of animals fighting or fleeing from other predator animals attacking them. Deep in our psyche and in our bodies are the patterns we learned long ago, even as animals to defend against those intent on destroying us. Those patterns reside especially in the dialogue between two parts

21. (Suzuki 1999)72

of our nervous system. Together they are called the autonomic nervous system, because until recently it was thought that they were outside our conscious awareness and beyond our ability to affect their responses.

One of the dialogue partners is called the sympathetic nervous system. Like our animal forbearers, when we are faced with danger, it gears us up for action—to fight, to run away, or to freeze like a rabbit hoping no one will notice. The sympathetic nervous system is necessary for our life. It enables us to act in the world. It alerts us, energizes our muscles, increases blood flow of oxygen and glucose, and gives us the vitality we need and rejoice in.

To do all that, it needs its dialogue partner, the parasympathetic nervous system. That system relaxes, renews, and heals us. The vagus nerve, direct from the brain and bypassing the spinal cord, connects to various organ systems in the body. It enables the parasympathetic nervous system to increase blood flow, to feed nutrients and oxygen to internal organs, and to activate all the restorative patterns we know deep in our bodies and share even with our animal forbearers. When we feel safe, restored, blissful, and quietly happy, that's the parasympathetic nervous system at work. It is the necessary and cherished background for the rest of our life.

We need them both: sympathetic and parasympathetic nervous systems, action and rest, exertion and renewal. They need to be in intimate dialogue and rhythm with each other. When they are, we experience equilibrium, a relaxed readiness, what the mystics called equanimity. Like a deer quietly grazing in a meadow, or a wolf looking calmly from the edge of a forest, we are deeply in touch with life, in tune with the deepest wellsprings of our existence, healing and acting in rhythm and concert.[22]

Meditation often focuses on the bodily rhythm of breath awareness. Our breathing changes moment by moment, as our sympathetic system needs more oxygen for action, and as our parasympathetic system invites our breath to slow down, open, and relax.

Breathing patterns perhaps even have evolutionary advantages for us relatively hairless bipedal apes. In contrast to the great cats, for example, running on two legs untethers our breathing from our stride. We can breathe as we need, regardless of how may steps we take while doing so. And our naked skinny bodies dissipate heat more effectively so we can run longer without overheating. Prey animals certainly can run faster, but we can run longer, farther, steadier. Antelopes dart away as we approach, but

22. (Levine 2008)85–97

then fall exhausted, then dart away again as we keep on running after them until finally chasing them down to kill and eat.[23]

Breath awareness is a fundamental meditative practice in so many traditions. Even the word for breath and the word for spirit are often identical: *pneuma* in Greek, *ruah* in Hebrew, *prana* in Sanskrit, *ha* in Hawaiian. Breathing lives at the intersection of conscious choice and involuntary regulation in the brain. We can choose to hold our breath, but only for so long. Little kids in tantrums can hold their breath until they are blue in the face. But after time their bodies will breathe again, in spite of their stubborn intent. Our first breath is our inauguration to life outside the womb, and our last breath and death rattle is our final exit.

Some of us tend to hold our breath when we are anxious. We hold our breath in at the top of our chest to protect ourselves. Others of us have difficulty letting it all go and exhaling all the way. There is even a personal growth modality called "rebirthing" that diagnoses such difficulties, and induces hyper-ventilation until conscious control is released and our natural way of breathing returns.[24] We all knew our natural breath as little babies. If you want to see it, just watch an infant breathe—a full breath from the depth of the abdomen to the top of the chest and back again—easy, relaxed, without pause or strain.

There are many rhythms accessible in bodily spiritual knowing. In addition to breath awareness it is possible to experience our heart rhythm, dispassionately tracking its slow return to equanimity from the pressures our anxious mind, often our left brain, imposes on it. Then there is the rhythm of the cranial sacral fluid. This clear, sparkling liquid produced six to twelve times a minute in the fourth ventricle of the brain, flowing around the brain and down through the spinal cord, protects, nourishes and heals. For some of us, it is even possible to intuit the isoring—that marvelous still point of the ceaseless rhythm of the body—where capillaries from arterioles meet venules connecting to veins. This is where cells are nourished, waste collected, and balance found and attuned in the centerless center of our body.

Finally, for a few, even the deep, intimate and distant thrum and rhythm of the cells themselves are available, faintly calling us to the deepest

23. (Grippando 2008)
24. (Orr 1977)

wellsprings of spirit life.[25] Erich Schiffmann calls the awareness of these rhythms "moving into stillness," in relation to yoga:

> Stillness is like a perfectly centered top, spinning so fast it appears motionless. . . . Stillness is not the absence or negation of energy, life, or movement. Stillness is dynamic. It is unconflicted movement, life in harmony with itself, skill in action. It can be experienced whenever there is total, uninhibited, unconflicted participation in the moment you are in- when you are wholeheartedly present with whatever you are doing. . . . Stillness is a higher energy state than what we're used to. This is because we are rarely wholehearted, or unconflicted, about anything. . . . Yoga is a way of moving into stillness in order to experience the truth of who you are. It is also a way of learning to be centered in action.[26]

EXPERIENCING MEDITATION

Meditation engages a wide range of human experience. My experience of chronic illness and pain tore away some of my mental resources. In medical jargon, chronic pain does not habituate; that means you don't get used to it. How to survive the next fifteen minutes of stinging and stabbing is just as problematic as the last fifteen minutes, and this year as threatening as the year before. At the worst, I was only able to sleep for about twenty minutes at a time without getting up and applying some pretty much useless palliative support. I would say to myself, "I'm dying." I knew I wasn't, not literally, not then. But pretending to entertain it was a tiny incremental step toward mindfulness, the full experience and integration in spiritual knowing of what was there immediately before me. Later on I would pretend "I'm going crazy"—which was, of course, an improvement. I had insufficient mental energy and no possibility to muster a prayer. I was far from being present enough to do that. But I did have, in the depths, some intimation that spirit was around somewhere, perhaps, even taking care of things. I couldn't do anything about it, certainly couldn't reach out or respond, but that was all right; it wasn't required.

A close friend shared these portions of her story over years of conversation:

25. (Cohen 1993)
26. (Schiffman 1996)3–4

The one thing you knew growing up was that your family didn't work. Not grossly dysfunctional, your stepfather was a psychiatrist, after all. Just lacking the one essential thing—love, true connection and nurture, intimacy. Painstakingly over the years, you built the foundation for a true loving family—education, career in teaching, loving attentive husband. Then the child came—a beautiful, sensitive, aware little boy. He charmed everyone who met him. Your hopes and dreams and patient work were now fully realized in a loving family. Then the little boy slowly and irrevocably died of leukemia at the age of six. Your world is gone. You have to learn with difficulty things you never knew you had to learn. The asphalt road you are driving on may, without warning, melt away. You have to learn simple skills, like eating. Interpersonal transactions could be almost impossible puzzles. You are not suicidal, just patiently waiting out your body's unreasoning insistence on keeping on, because you are already dead in every way that counts. And you never stop crying, at night, alone. But you wade into all that again, again and again. Until after an inordinate amount of time, and mostly unrecognized when it occurs, energy begins to shift, and life becomes—interesting again. Simple things, like a bakery that sells a certain cheese bread, are even delightful.[27]

When I was a little kid, I was terrified, and even sort of teased myself with being in the basement, lights out, totally black, and the door of release atop the stairs closed. The hairs on the back of my neck would literally rise, some unknown monster presence was approaching to do some unknown terrible thing to me and I would stumble up the steps to throw open the door to light and safety.

In some unknown way the fear was connected to fear of heights. Standing on the rim of the Grand Canyon, it seemed without a sufficient guard rail, I was powerfully tempted, almost irresistibly drawn to take those thrilling, deadly, final two or three steps to freedom and oblivion.

Vipassana bestows bare attention on all of those experiences, until energy shifts, insight and blessing come in the darkest places as well as in occasions of joy and wonder. There is an essential dynamic in spiritual knowing which contrasts with scientific knowing. Scientific knowing must precisely and rigorously separate subject and object, I and it. There must be no spillover from the passions and the biases of the scientist into the findings of the scientific query. In contrast, in spiritual knowing, those very passions, intuition, and connotations are the very stuff of spiritual knowing.

27. Used by permission from a confidential source.

Not as they are, but as they will become and be transformed in the quest. Dispassionate unbiased truth is the aim of both endeavors. But in spiritual knowing, it comes not in spite of but in and through transformation in those depths.

PERSONAL GROWTH METHODS

A couple of personal growth methods may help describe the rhythm of mindfulness meditation. The first method is focusing. Eugene Gendlin at the University of Chicago extensively studied examples of successful therapies across different theoretical orientations. Regardless of what they thought they were doing, Gendlin noticed therapists were actively engaged in a similar educational method: teaching a process clients could learn to do themselves. He called it focusing.

Focusing begins with mentally listing whatever concerns are troubling a client. Then the client is asked to set them all aside, trusting they will be addressed later, and to choose one for whatever reason. The client is then asked to simply be aware of the whole of that concern—thoughts, feelings, bodily sensations, images, the "whole ball of wax" as it is sometimes called, including textures, colors, shapes and all that occurs to the client. The client is asked to get a "felt sense" of that wholeness, and the therapist waits patiently until she or he lifts a finger or gives whatever nonverbal sign they have agreed on. Words are avoided here to keep from interrupting the focus. The client is instructed to look at and get a felt sense of that wholeness, but not to "go into it" or "go inside it." This full awareness without identifying is essential. The purpose is not to relive or to be overwhelmed or preoccupied by the feelings, thoughts, and images, but to remain within oneself, looking on dispassionately. It is like the "bare attention" of *vipassana*—no interpretation, no analysis, no getting lost or becoming overwhelmed by the focus, just looking and not going inside it. Then the client is asked to wait, and "allow" an image to come from the felt sense. The passive mode of the verb is also essential here. Again, as in *vipassana*, there is to be no reaction, no interpretation, no deliberate attempt to think up an image; the left brain and ego are not to act and take over. The client waits quietly until the image emerges from the depths by itself. The image is then shared with the therapist.

That's it. There need be no applications of the image to problems, no thinking through of what it may mean for daily life. The process is complete in itself, because a feedback loop has been opened for ongoing dialogue between conscious awareness and psychic depths. Again, as in mindfulness meditation, that dialogue itself occasions increasing awareness and even unbidden resolutions. Insights are discovered, not thought up. The client may feel some resolution, or at least a stopping point, with the first image, or may use it to begin a new round of focusing.

Insight is known in the "body shift," some change in the body itself: breath, posture, laughter, sighs, tears—some shift in bodily energy, tension, and rhythm. When bodily rhythms spontaneously change, that is insight that makes a difference. *Satori,* or liberation in Zen Buddhist practice, is known by "mingled tears and laughter"; it is real change because the body knows and experiences it.

Here are four essential characteristics of mindfulness meditation, described in the process of focusing: full-depth experience and awareness; letting go of reaction or reliving; trusting and waiting for insight instead of thinking or making it up; and resulting changes in being itself, known in the body.[28]

Sedona, the second method, emphasizes a similar rhythm. It begins, along with mindfulness meditation and focusing, with full and complete experience of the feelings and internal states. The second step in the process is expressed by three questions. There is no right or expected answer to them; they are simply asked again and again until the person is satisfied and ready to move on:

> Could you let go of (feeling, internal state)?
> Would you let go of (feeling, internal state)?
> When?

The final step, change in the body itself, is signaled by the lasting experience, "not imagined, felt" of "freedom and imperturbability."[29]

SELF-TRANSFORMATION

In spiritual knowing our identity changes—how we see, what we love, who we really are, what we consider and believe to be our true real self. Earlier we looked at how our identities expand, to include more reality in the stages of spiritual growth. Fowler and Wilber trace that growth from infant,

28. (Gendlin 1982)
29. (Dwoskin 2007)

to tribe, to autonomous reason, to identification with the whole in the highest causal stage in which "I no longer witness the clouds, I am the clouds. . . . Precisely because I am not this, not that, I am really this, fully that . . . I am the Kosmos in its every gesture."[30]

We love, suffer, struggle to transcend our limited, narrow identities into more holistic ones. In the traditions this drama is often called transcending our ego. This evolution in self-identity is a drama, filled with all the protagonists and antagonists, progress and setbacks of any real drama. The Hindu teacher Ramana Maharshi taught the method of self-inquiry. For him it was the only sure way to reach enlightenment. You simply ask yourself, every day, "Who am I?" No matter what answer you discover, you just keep asking the question until all narrow definitions melt into unlimited awareness and unconditional love, revealing your true nature and self.[31]

There is even a mathematical way to understand transcending ego. Kurt Goedel's Incompleteness Theorem, described in Chapter Four, demonstrated that within any formal mathematical system there is an undecidable statement that can neither be proven true nor false within the system itself. His demonstration is based on the "liars paradox"—in its simplest form expressed in the statement: *This very sentence is false.* If it is false, then it is true, and so on. His corollary or second theorem is therefore: even the consistency of the system cannot be proven true or false within the system itself.

The spiritual practice of asking "Who am I?" acts out this mathematical demonstration in the process of self-transformation. If we think we know who we are, if we have tied our self-identity to any mental representation, then we are subject to the corollary of the incompleteness theorem. Since it is this particular conscious "I" who is stating and determining the wholeness of my being, then I am in the position of the liar's paradox. Part of my whole being is attempting to define the whole. It is fallacious mathematically and it doesn't work spiritually in realizing who I truly am. Only in transcending all mental representations of who I am can I realize the truth in unlimited awareness and unconditional love.

Thomas Keating, the founder of centering prayer, combines developmental psychology and traditional monastic disciplines for his description of the drama. In order to survive the stresses and challenges of our early life, we had to develop three strategies. We needed to find ways to be *secure*

30. (Wilber 2004)5
31. (Zaleski 2005)220

and belong in our problematic environment. We needed to find *intimate connections* with others. And we needed to develop strategies to exercise some *control and power* over our existence. These strategies together create the false self which blocks and prevents true intimacy and full spiritual knowing. The practice of meditation itself allows the strategies of the false self to "unload" and melt away, so the true self and true intimacy with God and others can emerge.

Spiritual traditions have many descriptions and prescriptions for transcending the ego or "false self." They are carefully calibrated to thwart the ego's characteristic self-serving and restricting demands, opening the way to self-transformation. They have surprising similarities. For example, the vows of mendicant orders, which became normative for all monasteries in the Roman Catholic Church in 1917, create a community for transcending ego in three ways. The first vow is poverty. The hierarchical community takes full responsibility for material security and survival, and communal belonging. The vow of poverty is meant to release and challenge any individual striving for security, in order to move toward divine union. The second vow, chastity, addresses the need for intimacy. Intimacy with universal spirit heals individual strivings, such as sexual intimacy with another person. Obedience, the third vow, releases ego striving for power and control in harmonious merging into communal hierarchy.

The Puritan analogue to these three communal vows has to do with personal spiritual attainment. Personal industry brings security. Fidelity to another person meets the need for intimacy. And order in the church and society allows for appropriate personal control and power.[32] In a secular context William Schutz, in a study for the US Navy on how sailors could get along together for months on end in the confined quarters of a nuclear submarine, found three requirements: belonging, affection, and control.[33] The three poisons in Buddhism describe ego attachments a little differently. The barriers to liberation are: greed or desire; hatred or aversion; and delusion or pride.

The drama of self-transformation is complicated by changing conceptions of self in western culture. The 1680 edition of the *Oxford English Dictionary* gave "Self is the great Anti-Christ and anti-God in the world" as a typical usage of the word. By 1870, the editions offered "respect to self

32. (Foster 1985) 5
33. (Schutz 1978)

and its ultimate good pertains to the very nobility of man's nature."[34] Roy
Baumeister in an extensive study of meanings of life found that "the self"
is becoming the central value base in our culture, with problematic results:
"Modern life offers people a wealth of some form of meaning, but it doesn't
offer clear guidance about fundamental values. This 'value gap' is the single
biggest problem for the modern Western individual. A major part of the
modern response to this value gap is to elevate selfhood and the cultivation
of identity and self-knowledge into final, compelling values. . . . [Therefore]
we make ourselves vulnerable to death in an almost unprecedented way."[35]

INTEGRATION

The full development of our brain mind capabilities "between emotional
rigidity and emotional chaos" is called "integration" in brain-mind research.[36] Siegel describes integration in the acronym FACES: flexible,
adaptable, coherent, energized, and stable.[37] Integration can include the
"awareness of awareness"—the awareness of mental events as they emerge
moment by moment.[38] The benefits of mindful awareness include the
"capacity to regulate emotion, to combat emotional dysfunction, to im-
prove patterns of thinking, and to reduce negative mindsets."[39] In mindful
awareness there is a "process of receptivity and meta-awareness that seems
quite different from the active stimulus-driven attentional processes."[40] It
allows us to "approach our here-and-now experience with curiosity, openness, acceptance and love."[41] In mindfulness meditation, integration moves
toward unlimited awareness and unconditional love.

Integration marks the full development of meditation and of the
brain mind. There are eight domains of brain mind integration operating
in combination with each other which also describe wholeness in spiritual
knowing.[42]

34. (Baumeister 1991)112
35. (Baumeister 1991)6
36. (Siegel 2007)67
37. (Siegel 2007)76
38. (Siegel 2007)48
39. (Siegel 2007)6
40. (Siegel 2007)110
41. (Siegel 2007)15
42. (Siegel 2007)72–76

The first domain is stabilizing attention, which opens us to the full range of our perceptions and is the basis for all the other domains. It leads to the experience of a self "deep in the ocean" of our psyche, experiencing, but not being taken over by, all storms and stresses of internal and external stimuli. At its most profound, in "choiceless awareness" the usual sense of self melts away, is "unimportant, nonpresent." Siegel reports, "I observed this sensation of no 'I' . . . this sense was that things happening were just present participles, sounding, sitting, breathing awareness."[43]

The second domain is the integration of the right- and left-brain hemispheres with their somewhat different and complementary capabilities. Meditation involves shifting awareness to a focus on the body away from left hemisphere linguistic concepts toward the nonverbal imagery and somatic sensations of the right hemisphere. The shift is a function of the left hemisphere and involves an ongoing narration, even without words.[44] That is why experienced meditators show left-hemisphere activation with more positive emotions, and more equanimity.

The right brain involves those experiences we think of as spiritual, which neuroanatomist Jill Bolte Taylor has described in her book *My Stroke of Insight*—bliss, empathy, sense of the whole or oneness with all that is, and pure awareness. For her, the implications for spirituality and religion are in her aphorism: "[A]ll religions are the left hemisphere story that helps us get into the right hemisphere experience." At the age of 37, Dr. Taylor awoke one morning feeling increasingly sluggish, and soon unable to speak or read. Being a brain scientist, she realized that she had suffered a massive stroke in the left hemisphere of her brain. She quickly became locked up inside herself, unable to respond to her professional and anxious caregivers. But through the entire trauma, except for a blinding pain behind her left eye in the beginning, she was at peace within herself. She came to recognize she was living out of her right brain instead of the left brain previously favored by her as a scientist. She writes about her experience after her recovery:

> My right hemisphere is all about right here, right now . . . all the richness of this present moment. It is filled with gratitude for my life and everyone and everything in it. It is content, compassionate, nurturing and eternally optimistic. To my right mind character, there is no judgment of good/bad or right/wrong, so everything exists on a continuum of relativity. It takes things as they are and

43. (Siegel 2007)80–81
44. (Siegel 2007)47

acknowledges what is in the present . . . my right mind is open to the eternal flow whereby I exist at one with the universe. It is the seat of my divine mind, the knower, the wise woman, and the observer. It is my intuition and higher consciousness. . . . It is tuned into the subtle messages my cells communicate via gut feelings as it learns through touch and experience.[45]

She also recognizes the critical thinking, analytical capabilities, and penchant for story telling of her left brain and its necessary place in her life, as well as its negative and judgmental traits. But she is clear that she primarily and essentially lives her life out of her right/"right" mind.

The third domain of brain-mind integration is the vertical integration of the higher brain or cortex with the midbrain or limbic emotional area and with the brainstem's life support functions, linking them into a functional and integrated whole. These include the information from our five senses, a "sixth" sense of bodily sensations, and a "seventh" sense of mental events themselves. Mindfulness meditation facilitates this vertical integration.

The fourth domain is the integration of our explicit memories in the narratives of factual and autobiographical information (largely the task of the left brain) with our implicit memories which begin in the womb and predominate in our early years (largely the task of the right brain). From our implicit memories we create mental models of how the world works. The hippocampus in the midbrain has the function of integrating all these memories into a coherent whole. It links together "widely separated areas of the brain—from our perceptual regions to our repository for facts to our language center. . . . [It] converts our moment-to-moment experiences into memories."[46] In times of trauma and extreme stress, as in post-traumatic stress disorder and childhood sexual abuse, the experiences can be so wounding that the person has to dissociate and bypass the integrating function of the hippocampus in order to survive. Powerful implicit memories, especially fearful ones, are laid down in the amygdala, also in the midbrain. When they are not integrated into and leave gaps in the conscious narrative of the left brain, special attention and care are needed to reintegrate them into the narrative. In centering prayer, the mind can spontaneously unload the damage.

45. (Taylor 2006)139–141
46. (Siegel 2010)19

The fifth domain is the ability to accept and embrace all the different states of being we embody at different times in meeting fundamental needs: closeness and solitude; autonomy and dependence; caregiving and mastery; and others. When these different states are integrated, we move past shame and denial to become open to our needs and to meeting them in different ways at different times. Unlimited awareness and unconditional love mark the full integration of states of being.

The sixth domain is integrating the "me," "you," and "we" maps in the resonance circuits in our brain, discovered by Italian researchers in the mid1990s who "implanted electrodes in the premotor area of a monkey's cortex. . . . When the monkey ate a peanut, a certain electrode fired. . . . What was astonishing was that when the monkey watched one of the researchers eat a peanut, the same motor electrode fired. What was even most astonishing was that the 'mirror neurons' as they came to be called, fired only when the act of another animal or person was intentional and fitted into a recognizable pattern."[47] These internal maps created by mirror neurons are hardwired in our brain, do not require conscious thought or effort, and are the root of empathy in us. At their best they enable us to feel the internal worlds of others while also remaining in tune with our own internal world, resulting in true and lasting intimacy.

The middle prefrontal cortex also creates "we maps" that enable us to think about and behave for the good of the larger group or community.[48] These maps enable us to come to terms with our own felt experiences of abandonment or betrayal, and allow us to love and be loved without giving up our own self. Intimate relationships can be integrated with our own sense of identity and freedom. Meditation practices such as *metta* and *tonglen* (described in the next chapter) aim at developing this capacity to love.

The seventh domain is the integration first achieved at the height of the Axial Age of our sense of time and anticipation of our own death and the death of our loved ones. Religions focus on this integration which is the task of the prefrontal cortex and essential to all of the integrative tasks together.

The eighth and final domain of integration is the profound sense of interconnectedness with all there is—the great achievement of the religions of the Axial Age. Siegel claims, "Science has shown that well-being and true happiness come from defining our 'selves' as part of an interconnected

47. (Siegel 2007)166
48. (Siegel 2010)8

whole—connecting with others and with ourselves in authentic ways that break down the isolative boundaries of a separate self."[49]

Integration with the senses takes place in a tiny column of six cells deep in the brain, says Siegel, and "That's it. Our powerful perceiving-and-planning cortex is organized by stacking six neurons on top of one another and clustering these piles—or 'cortical columns'—like an interconnected honey comb"[50] This is true of vision in the occipital lobe in the back of the brain, hearing in columns in the parietal lobe on the side of the brain, touch higher in the same lobe, motor action in the frontal lobe, and images of our own mind or the mind of others in the middle prefrontal area.

The flow through these six cell deep columns goes both ways. Sensory data comes in through the brainstem and goes upward—"bottom-up" information flow. But what we have learned before comes top-down and shapes what comes in through the senses. Our present state of mind, our memories, our emotions, and external environment come down from layers one to three. The sensations come up from layers six to four. These two streams of information meet or "crash" in layers three and four.[51]

When top-down information flow overwhelms bottom-up flow, awareness of the present moment disappears as "automatic" mental patterns take over. In automatic thinking, life becomes "repetitive and dull" mindlessly reacting to situations in repetitive applications of past mental models.[52] Mindfulness meditation melts away top-down thinking to recover and enhance the awareness of the present moment.

Repeated practice of mindfulness meditation can actually change the physical structure of the brain through producing certain proteins that strengthen or actually create new synaptic linkages and new neurons in the brain. It also stimulates "the production of myelin, the fatty sheath around axons, resulting in as much as a hundred-fold increase in the speed of conduction down the neuron's length."[53] As Siegel writes, "The mind uses the brain to create itself." Scientific studies of experienced meditators have demonstrated that two portions of the brain develop and grow thicker with meditative practice. They are the insula, which connects or integrates the emotional centers of the midbrain and life support functions of the

49. (Siegel 2010)259
50. (Siegel 2007)104–105
51. (Siegel 2007)105
52. (Siegel 2007)14
53. (Siegel 2007)120

brainstem with the higher brain or cortex; and the medial prefrontal cortex, which integrates functions of the whole brain.

The eight levels or domains of the brain-mind correspond to the full development of mindfulness meditation. Mindfulness meditation, therefore, has the capability to integrate sensory input and the creative resources of the mind, and it can even change the physical structure of the brain.

SUMMARY

Scientific knowing in brain-mind research and clinical experience informs and supports spiritual knowing in meditation. *Vipassana* in the Buddhist tradition, also called mindful awareness or mindfulness meditation, is a central example of meditation. Awareness of bodily rhythms, personal experiences, and personal growth modalities further help describe meditation. Eight levels of integration constitute the full development and interaction of scientific and spiritual knowing in inner experience.

The next chapter describes three great dimensions of spiritual knowing. These dimensions—silence, ritual and vision—are practiced in many different ways.

CHAPTER SIX

DIMENSIONS OF PRACTICE

SILENCE, RITUAL, VISION

Silence is God's first language.

—THOMAS KEATING[1]

The last chapter described the integration which marks the full develop-ment of mindfulness meditation and brain-mind function. What does that look like in actual practice? Karen Armstrong writes that the essence of world religions is not descriptions of reality but prescriptions of how to live intentionally, realized in practice. "Religion is a practical discipline . . . not primarily something that people thought but something they did."[2] The three primary dimensions of practice are silence, ritual, and vision. These dimensions are not discrete and separate activities, nor can they be reduced to a single technique. Each implies the other, and they are expressed in many specific ways in which persons and communities have practiced spiritual knowing through the ages.

---

1. (Keating 1994)55 Thomas Keating cites St. John of the Cross, "The Father spoke one word from all eternity and he spoke it in silence, and it is in silence that we hear it." He comments, "This suggests that silence is God's first language and that all other languages are poor translations."

2. (Armstrong 2008)xii-xiii

DIMENSIONS OF PRACTICE

SILENCE

Silence can be defined as: practicing spiritual knowing beyond spoken words or language. A friend took me to Green Gulch, a Soto Zen Buddhist communal farm in Marin County, north of San Francisco and close to the ocean. It was one of the communities founded by Shunryu Suzuki Roshi (roshi meaning "teacher"), who came to San Francisco in 1950 and worked as a dishwasher in a restaurant until he founded the Tassajara and other communities in California. Every morning at 4:30 a.m., I could hear the sound of wooden blocks clapped together. In the dark I fumbled to put on my clothes, and found my way to the *zendo* (meditation hall) down the hill. The zendo had no glass on its open windows, and in the cold December pre-dawn, soft flakes of snow drifted in. There was a good deal of rustling of robes, coughing and cracking of joints as we found our favored positions on the *zafus,* or meditation cushions, and gradually a profound silence settled over the zendo. We all faced a plain wall, lit very dimly by a minimal number of candles on the altar. We sat there. That's all we did. We just sat there in silence, finding our way into our natural way of being as the roshi put it. It was dark and cold; sometimes drowsiness, dream images, or perhaps actual sleep would creep over us, and certainly over a neophyte like me. At those times we would watch for the shadow of the tanto, or head of practice, silently walking behind us. When the shadow was behind me, I would *gassho*— bow. He would take his *kyosaku,* a long thin slat of wood, and hit me sharply and precisely on the erector spinae muscles on either side of the spine, just inside the shoulder blades. You have to be quite skilled to do this task. Warmth and energy would rush through me and I would return in the silence to the goalless goal of realizing our true nature.

Silent meditation and prayer was one of the great discoveries of the Axial Age. The first mention of silent prayer in the Hebrew Scripture is in 1 Samuel:

> Hannah rose and presented herself before the Lord. Now Eli the priest was sitting on the seat beside the doorpost of the temple of the Lord. She was deeply distressed and prayed to the Lord, and wept bitterly . . . As she continued praying before the Lord, Eli observed her mouth. Hannah was praying silently: only her lips moved, but her voice was not heard; therefore Eli thought she was drunk. So Eli said to her, "How long will you make a drunken spectacle of yourself? Put away your wine." But Hannah answered, "No, my Lord, I am a woman deeply troubled; I have drunk neither

wine nor strong drink, but I have been pouring out my soul before
the Lord (1 Samuel 1:9–15).

The passage describes something new in history. Eli, the priest and the
mentor of the prophet Samuel, had never witnessed anything like it before,
and concludes that Hannah has been drinking too much. But she explains
to him that instead she is deeply troubled and shamed and has been pouring out her heart before the Lord. In the patriarchal culture of the time she
is valued for her ability to bring forth a son, and of course because she is
unable to do so, it is clearly her fault. So she vows that if God grants her
desperate plea, she will consecrate her son to God.

Praying—or for that matter, reading Scripture silently without saying
the words aloud—is a fairly recent development in history. In 305 CE, Augustine was astonished to see that Ambrose could read Scripture without
moving his lips or saying the words aloud. It seemed a remarkable thing
to him, and he decided to master the art himself.[3] About that time in
history, silent meditation and prayer became widespread among the Abbas
and Ammas, the desert fathers and mothers who went out into the desert
to perfect their walk in Christ.

Paul, in his letter to the Romans, also mentions this radical development: "Likewise the Spirit helps us in our weakness; for we do not know
how to pray as we ought, but that very Spirit intercedes with sighs too deep
for words. And the One who searches the heart knows what is the mind of
the Spirit, because the Spirit intercedes for the saints according to the will
of God" (Romans 8:26). In silence we intend ongoing self-surrender and
love for others like God's love for us and all beings.

Silence opens up a depth of presence invoking radical awareness and
unconditional love. We may tend to think of silence as negative—as the *absence* of language, talking, and noise, either outwardly or in our own inner
experience. Some instructions on meditation and prayer perpetuate this
limited understanding by encouraging us to *stop* our thoughts, make our
minds *blank*, or some other exhortation that we cannot possibly achieve.
Stephen Mitchell's insightful paraphrase of Psalm 131, however, describes
it more accurately:

> My mind is not noisy with desires, Lord, and my heart has satisfied
> its longing.
>   I do not care about religion or anything that is not you.

3. (Maitland 2008)148

> I have soothed and quieted my soul, like a child at its mother's
> breast.
> My soul is as peaceful as a child sleeping in its mother's arms.[4]

D.W. Winnicott, the psychoanalytic pioneer in child psychiatry, compares our experience to that of an infant satisfied at our mother's breast. Our heart has satisfied its longing for physical and emotional nurturing, and we are at peace and at one in our mother's arms. I understand that it is, perhaps especially at a nighttime feeding, equally a time of mutual oneness, silence, peace, and love for her as well. For Winnicott, in the beginning, "There is no such thing as a baby. . . . The centre of gravity of the being" is the total set-up "of mother-baby which gradually differentiates into the individual infant and 'good-enough' caring mother."[5]

Much can be said about silence, even though at its center there is nothing to be said. Silence is ineffable by definition; it is beyond words. But precisely because of that, it reaches beyond the limitations and traps of the words of our personal story, including the assumptions, fears, fantasies and hopes we carry from the past and project onto our future. It is the realm of freedom as well as the realm of love. We are no longer caught and imprisoned in the brain chatter inward and the noise and stimulation outward, repeating the narrow prison of the past into the future.

Silence is the realm of creative integration. We let go of the barriers and limitations of language to which we are accustomed and obsessed with using and repeating.

Sensory experience is often intensified in long periods of silence. Colors become more vivid. Sights, sounds, body sensations, touch, smell, and tastes become sharper, clearer, and sometimes astonishingly pleasurable and beautiful.

Silence reaches to the limits of human experience, enthralling and dangerous. In silence, great joy can come at times. Continuing bliss and equanimity have been recorded through the ages by mystics in all tradition. But we also need to say that the rapture and bliss that can come from extended silence can also be a deadly temptation to slip the last barrier to freedom.

In 1968, the *London Sunday Times* announced the first Golden Globe race, sailing single-handedly non-stop around the world. Nine persons entered the race; only one finished. Bernard Moitessier had the best-designed

---

4. (Mitchell 1993)72

5. (Winnicott 1958)99

boat and was the most experienced sailor. He started the race enthusiasti-cally and was still in the lead by the time he entered the Pacific. But some-where south of Tahiti he simply "lost interest" in the race, so enthralled was he by the simple experience of boat, sea, and silence. In fact he didn't even go home to England; he just kept sailing around the world until he finally ended up again in Tahiti.

Frank Mulville wrote about a comparable experience, sailing alone in the Caribbean. He decided to tie one end of a long rope to himself and the other end to his boat, and float away in the sea:

> It made me feel quite dizzy to look at her [the boat]. She seemed the most lovely thing dipping in and out of sight as she mounted the long Atlantic swell and then slipped into the hollows. This it struck me, was the supreme moment of my life; I had never achieved anything to equal it and I was never likely to again . . . it was my dream and I had it. Why not let go of the rope? To melt into the sea at this apex of experience was the only thing left. Nothing that could happen in the future could better this. Why not trump the ace and walk out?

> I stayed at the end of the rope for a while and I began to get fright-ened—not so much of what might happen to me but at what I might do to myself. . . . I glanced deeply into the womb of the sea, watched the shafts of sunlight as they spent their energy uselessly in its density. . . . I slipped the bowline off my shoulders and hung for an instant on the very end of the rope—my fingers grasping the bare end of life itself—then I hauled myself back hand over hand. When I stood on the firm familiar deck I swore I would never do this thing again. I was running with sweat and shaking all over.[6]

The risks of disorientation lead monastic communities, in their wis-dom, to create inflexible rituals of bells, chanting all 150 psalms every week, stated times for corporate worship, eating, work, and study—in or-der to create anchors in conventional reality, acting as safe containers for the adventure in silence. This is also why gurus and teachers are strongly recommended for anyone embarking on the path of extended silence and spiritual growth. Warnings are given that one may become disoriented, lose contact with their accustomed sense of self, and experience existential dread and fear when going further and further within and beyond ordinary experience.

6. (Maitland 2008)78–79

There is one other caution that needs to be noted. Silence needs to be something I choose, not something that is forced upon me by the violence of others—terrorists confining people for indefinite periods, or solitary confinement for prisoners. When that happens, when I am forced into silence, I have to invent rituals for myself in order to keep my sanity, to keep even the barest shreds of voluntary choice and control over my environment.

Joe Simpson and his friend and climbing partner Simon Yates got to the top of a previously unscaled mountain in the Peruvian Andes in 1985. On the way down Simpson fell over an edge of rock and broke his pelvis. Yates roped the two of them together and laboriously and repeatedly let Simpson down a ways on the rope and then followed him down. After hours of this exhausting labor, at one point Simpson slipped over a cliff and dangled in midair. Yates' emotional resources and physical strength were altogether gone. He could not pull Simpson back up over the edge. He took out his knife and simply cut the rope, leaving Simpson to fall to his death, and found his own way down to the safety of base camp. We have no record of how Yates handled his own silence during this time.

As it turned out, Simpson fell quite a ways through the air, and was further injured, but was not killed. Incredibly, he kept on crawling, since he could not stand or walk, over sharp boulders for four days and four nights, until he finally crawled into base camp just before it was dismantled and any hope of survival gone.

During his ordeal, as occasionally happens in extended silence, he heard a voice. He described it later, "The voice was clean and sharp and commanding. It was always right and I listened to it when it spoke and acted on its decisions. . . . The voice has banished the mad thoughts from my mind. An urgency was creeping over me and the voice said, 'Go on, keep going . . . faster.'" Joe Simpson had found his own ritual, heard as an external voice, which anchored him to reality and literally saved his life.[7]

Silence is the realm of our creativity. Most of us will never experience such extreme conditions, and our short twenty or thirty minutes of silence at a time will not occasion such dramatic events, but our times of silence will contain moments of surprising and cherished joy. Even more, over time, we will begin to experience an equanimity that spills over into everyday life. It is as if we have been to the mountaintop, and known ultimate reality. With

7. (Maitland 2008)100–101

that vision, the rest of our lives can increasingly be experienced in the calm and peace of the true nature of reality we have glimpsed in the silence.

In the Spirit, in the Presence, we glimpse freedom and love and truth that open new possibilities for us. Silence can lead us into new insights beyond the language and the metaphors of our accustomed ways of living and doing things. In the gospels of Mark and Luke especially, again and again Jesus frames his life and his ministry in silence and solitude: "In the morning, while it was still very dark, he got up and went out to a deserted place, and there he prayed. And Simon and his companions hunted for him. When they found him, they said to him, 'Everyone is searching for you'" (Mark 1:35–36). He goes apart, apparently without telling anyone, and in that silence finds the truth, energy, power and love he then gives to the world.

Tenth-century BCE Hindu rituals brought one into the presence of Brahman in ultimate silence. One of them, called *Brahmodya*, was a model for authentic spiritual discourse. The participants would go on retreat and do spiritual exercises, including fasting and *pranayama* or breath control. In the process they would concentrate their minds and enter a deeper level of consciousness. Then a contest would begin in which each in turn would attempt to describe this ultimate reality. After each attempt, the opponent would attempt to offer a more subtle, nuanced image or sound or description. The process would continue until the limitations of language and the impotence of speech became manifest. And the only possible response was silence, a direct glimpse of ultimate transcendence, reality, and mystery.[8]

One of the great stories in Buddhism concerns Sariputra, Buddha's most brilliant disciple, as he was struggling to achieve this realization. A flag would be raised to the top of a pole at the entrance of the monastery to announce occasions of dharma debate or combat. During Sariputra's agony and struggle to reach liberation, Buddha appeared, gave him an axe, and told him to cut down the dharma combat pole. Instantly, it was said, Sariputra attained liberation as he realized the futility of words to describe it.

RITUAL

I once had the opportunity to walk the labyrinth in the cathedral at Chartres, an hour's train ride southwest of Paris. If you have been there, you know you need to first go to a corner of the nave. There you will find a

8. (Armstrong 2009)13

wonderful old Englishman named Malcolm Miller, who has been there for-ever. He gives English-language tours of the church, interspersed with witty comments. He also writes books, available in the gift shop, which you also will buy after hearing his lecture. He points out that at the end of the twelfth century, when the present structure was built, the only Bibles were pains-takingly handwritten copies; most people had never seen a copy of it and could not read it if they had. Therefore, the cathedral itself was text, and meant to be. Each rose window told some part of the story of Jesus' life: the incarnation, the passion, and the resurrection. The statues in the porticos were of the great figures of the Hebrew Scriptures and the New Testament.

The labyrinth at Chartres is thirty-six feet in diameter with eleven con-centric circuits into the center, which is ringed with six rose petal shapes. It amounts to about one-third of a mile to walk in and out. I mentioned that Mr. Miller wrote the books in the gift shop on Chartres, except one: the book on the labyrinth. Sometime late in his talk, he noted dismissively that you could walk the labyrinth also, if you wanted to, "Although I don't know why anyone would," which I thought was curious. At one time there were labyrinths in a number of churches in France, but they were all destroyed in the seventeenth and eighteenth centuries, except this one. Even here, the priests tried unsuccessfully to tear it out, on the grounds that it was just a children's game with no Christian meaning; indeed, the center originally had a brass plaque depicting Theseus slaying the Minotaur in the maze on Crete. It was torn up to make cannonballs during the Napoleonic era and only the ugly studs that held it in place remain.

My wife and I were there by chance on a Friday, and it is only on Fridays that the chairs in the nave are cleared away and stacked to uncover the labyrinth so it can be seen and walked. It was crowded on this particular Friday; a high-school choir from Traverse City, Michigan was there to give a concert later in the day. Most people simply walked over the labyrinth as if it did not exist. Some walked it as if they were late for work, to be done in time for the concert. Little kids joyfully ran it; one girl ducked around me with a big smile on her face. One young woman stood meditating in the center from before I entered the labyrinth until after I left. When I finally arrived in the center and turned and looked up at the rose window, the most astonishing and surprising rush overflowed my heart. As I walked out, I thought of the pilgrims who had walked those scarred and pitted stones for more than a thousand years. It wasn't part of the official teaching of the church, and the explanations for its existence are a little dubious, but it had been the peoples' sacrament. They had walked it all those centuries, perhaps so often that the priests in their jealousy had tried to do away with it. It was one of the rituals by which they had enacted the great symbols of their faith, as I was enacting mine.

In ritual we act out our spiritual knowing physically, literally and symbolically. In the Christian tradition, sacraments are "outward and visible signs of inward and spiritual grace, given by Christ as sure and certain means by which we receive that grace."[9] The word "sacrament" was first used in the western (Roman Catholic) church by Tertullian; in Roman culture, it was "a sum of money put in a sacred place as a guarantee by a litigant in a legal case. The *sacramentum* of the person who lost went to the gods (priests). A *sacramentum* was also a consecratory act, or something consecrated. Its most popular use was to designate the military oath of allegiance to the emperor."[10]

The Orthodox Church uses the word *mysterion*. For Paul the *mysterion* is in Christ, the wisdom decreed before the ages, and now revealed and present to human beings (1 Cor. 2:7,; Eph. 3:9; Col. 1:26). *Mysterion*, Spirit ultimately beyond definition, is embedded in specific acts, and even material substance in the liturgy of the church. For Eduard Schillebeeckx, the Dutch Roman Catholic theologian, *mysterion-sacramentum* establishes a new meaning, a *transignification*, not as an abstract idea, but as Spirit action in the community.[11] Different Christian traditions list different numbers of sacraments: two for most Protestants, none for Quakers, seven for Roman Catholics, more for Orthodox. But new meanings can be discerned and refined in specific communal and personal acts far beyond specific liturgical definitions. If one needs to, one may call them *sacramentals*—in work, in play, in farming, in intimacy—wherever and whenever specific actions take on spiritual meaning and larger context.

Sacramentals may happen for children of all ages. I grew up on a farm in the high desert near the Bitterroot Mountains in eastern Washington State. The winters were cold, hard, and clean, the summers scorching hot, and we were all expected to get an angry red sunburn the first day the sun was really hot. Being the youngest of the work crew, I would get to drive the old pony, dragging the wooden sled up to the hay field. We would pitch the hay into shocks and load the sled. Back at the barn, we would pull the load

9. (Book of Common Prayer 1979)857

10. (Browning 1985)33

11. (Browning 1985)7

up to the rafters on ropes, release it, and the indescribably rich smell and dust of fresh alfalfa hay would drift over us all. Much later I imagined that if there is a heaven, it must contain a great hay loft where, on summer afternoons late into the dusk, sweaty and grimy little boys, muscles exhausted beyond imagining, scratchy hay between their clothes and their skin everywhere, can jump and launch themselves from rafter to empty space to welcoming hay just one more time before they have to go into supper, and then, just once more . . . and once more as long as they could possibly want.

Mary Oliver wrote a poem about *mysterion-sacramentum* in "The Vast Ocean Begins Just Outside Our Church: The Eucharist"

> Something has happened
> to the bread
> and the wine.
> They have been blessed.
> What now?
> The body leans forward
> to receive the gift
> from the priest's hand,
> then the chalice.
> They are something else now
> from what they were
> before this began.
> I want
> to see Jesus,
> maybe in the clouds
> or on the shore,
> just walking,
> beautiful man
> And clearly
> someone else
> besides.
> On the hard days
> I ask myself
> if I ever will.
> Also there are times
> my body whispers to me
> That I have.[12]

12. (Oliver 2006)24–25

VISION

Vision is the transformation of our sensory experience. Spiritual knowing in visions can be described in terms of line, shape, color, texture, materials, mental states, even numerical ratios, but they are not defined by those terms. They are presentations of the numinous—uncontrollable, unpredictable, indefinable spiritual power.[13] God resides in beauty as well as in truth and goodness. Visions may be as minimalist as the proportions of the white clapboard building, spare pulpit and leaded glass windows of a New England meeting house, or as elaborate as the ceiling of the Sistine Chapel; as improvisational as the "hooping" of a black preacher or as specific and controlled by tradition as the writing of an Eastern Orthodox icon.

It may be as eternal and evanescent as creating a Tibetan Buddhist mandala. A lama sits in the corner of the room quietly chanting a mantra and blessing those who come to him . . . *Om Mani Padme Hum.* This phrase is perhaps rendered as: *Om*—infinite, omnipresent, ultimate reality; *Mani*—manifested, incarnated bright, clear, imperturbable as diamond; *Padme*—human beings like lotus flowers born in mud, transformed and gleaming white and pink on the surface of a pond; *Hum*—spirit breathing out into the world. Monks are gathered around a large table or circle on the floor bent over to their exacting task: gently, precisely, patiently tapping out grains of colored sand to create a large mandala, a brilliant multi-colored presentation of the path to liberation with symbolic fortress. It can be thought of as a mesocosm, uniting the microcosm (us) with the macrocosm (ultimate reality). After many hours, as soon as it is completed, they sweep it up and dump it into the nearest river, accompanied by appropriate chanting, acting out *anicca* (impermanence) and *sunyata* (emptiness).

Carl Jung found recurring images in dreams, art, and the human psyche across cultures and history, which he called archetypes. He and the theoretical physicist Wolfgang Pauli, who discovered the exclusion principle describing the spin of subatomic particles, shared Pauli's dreams and interpretations over years of collaboration. They were particularly interested in the archetypes of the smallest whole numbers which they thought might hold the key to integrating spirit and matter. They are expressed in the Axiom of Maria, from medieval alchemy: "One becomes two, two becomes three, and three becomes four which becomes one."[14]

13. (Otto 1923)25ff

14. (Lindorff 2004)95

Vision perceives in a new way: revealing and hiding. Here is a classic account in the New Testament:

> Now about eight days after these sayings Jesus took with him Peter and John and James, and went up on the mountain to pray. And while he was praying, the appearance of his face changed, and his clothes became dazzling white. Suddenly they saw two men, Moses and Elijah, talking to him. They appeared in glory and were speaking of his departure, which he was about to accomplish at Jerusalem. Now Peter and his companions were weighed down with sleep; but since they had stayed awake, they saw his glory and the two men who stood with him. Just as they were leaving him, Peter said to Jesus, "Master it is good for us to be here; let us make three dwellings, one for you, one for Moses, and one for Elijah"—not knowing what he said. While he was saying this, a cloud came and overshadowed them; and they were terrified as they entered the cloud. Then from the cloud came a voice that said, "This is my Son, my Chosen; listen to him!" When the voice had spoken, Jesus was found alone. And they kept silent and in those days told no one any of the things they had seen (Luke 9:28–36)

A colleague, who did his doctoral studies at Yale Divinity School in church history, often told this story about his experience of Luke's account of the Transfiguration while he was in graduate school. In the stacks deep in the Yale library one day, while working as a graduate assistant to the church historian Roland Bainton, he came across a handwritten copy of Luke from the fourth century. The unknown monk who copied the gospel had also added his own understanding of the meaning of the story of the Transfiguration in the margins. The monk had written that the true meaning of the passage was not that Jesus somehow miraculously changed his appearance into the blindingly white figure the disciples saw. Not at all. The true meaning of the passage was that the disciples for the first time saw Jesus as he really was, had always been and would be. The miracle was that the disciples saw him as he really was for the first time. Jesus had been that Spirit-filled person all along. Now the disciples could see the light, and carry the gospel to the world. They had, as the gospel wrote, stayed awake, even though they were weighed down with sleep, perhaps because the event took place at night. And because they were awake, and had stayed awake, they were able to see Jesus clearly. That was the miracle.

Jesus was talking to Moses and Elijah about his departure. The Hebrew word here is *exodus*, referring to the whole witness of Jesus Christ: his healing, his teaching, his whole ministry, his death and resurrection. That's when the disciples were able to see Jesus clearly, as he is. But even though they could see Jesus clearly, they still didn't know what to do about it. They were sort of in the position of the blind man, healed by Jesus, who at first saw people looking like trees walking. The disciples were healed, but only part-way. Therefore Peter, the organizer, wants to create an institution, a building, something they could see externally and physically.

We all do this. When life-changing events happen to us, we want to remember them; we turn them over again and again in our minds. We want to make sure that not only do we not forget them, but that they remain permanent and unchanging, so that we can go back again and again, as if nothing has changed and never will change. We want to do that; the church as an institution often wants to do that. We all want to create our own religious hall of fame, as it were.

It can't happen, of course. So that's where the cloud comes in. In the Hebrew Scriptures, "cloud" and "blinding light" go together in epiphanies. We catch glimpses of the blinding light of God in signs and experiences, but we still only see partly and in moments. God is both hidden and revealed together, in cloud and blinding light. A cloud covered Sinai when Moses went up on the mountain to speak with the blinding light of God and receive the Ten Commandments (Exodus 24:15–18). When he comes down from the mountain, his face is shining and he has to put a veil over his face like a cloud to protect the Israelites.

It's no wonder the disciples didn't say anything to anyone after the Transfiguration. How could they possibly put all this into words? What could they say that others could possibly believe? What could they say that would not be the same old confusion, the same old attempt to control and hold on to the past?

Paul writes that the veil or cloud is removed in Christ. "Now the Lord is the Spirit, and where the Spirit of the Lord is, there is freedom. And all of us, with unveiled faces, seeing the glory of the Lord as though reflected in a mirror, are being transformed into the same image from one degree of glory to another; for this comes from the Lord, the Spirit" (2 Corinthians 3:17–18).

An anonymous fourteenth-century English mystic tries to explain all this in the classic treatise *The Cloud of Unknowing*:

> When you find inner and outer distractions pressing in upon you
> when you would direct yourself to God alone . . . behave as though

you are not aware that those thoughts are pressing so strongly upon you between you and your God. Try to look, as it were, over their shoulders, as though you were looking for something else; and this other thing is God enclosed in a cloud of unknowing. . . . Whenever you feel your memory to be occupied with nothing physical and with nothing spiritual but only with the very substance of God . . . then you are above yourself and beneath your God. . . . You will always find that it is a cloud of unknowing between you and your God. One thing I tell you—there has never been a creature pure enough, nor ever shall be, so deeply lost in ecstasy and love of God that there is not always a high and marvelous Cloud of Unknowing between them and their God.[15]

Vision unexpectedly reframes what we perceive with our senses, puts it into a new context of spirit availability previously hidden or closed, now open and inviting us.

The Hebrew and Christian Scriptures have a number of different words and examples of visions and dreams. Joseph interprets Pharaoh's dreams to explain current events in Egypt. Peter, waiting for lunch, goes up on the roof on a hot sunny afternoon and falls asleep. In his nap he has a dream/vision in which he is hungry. He is waiting for lunch, after all. All sorts of meat appear before him. But it is food forbidden to him by Jewish law. He recoils and protests that he never eats anything that is unclean. Three times the vision appears; he protests, and an accompanying voice speaks: "What God has made clean, you must not call profane" (Acts 10:15). He awakes, is told that a Gentile centurion named Cornelius wants to see him. Peter gets it. As unclean food can be reframed into a sacred substance, so the gospel reframes who is deemed worthy of salvation.

I have seen Michelangelo's magnificent statue of David in Florence, Italy. It is seventeen feet high, and the stone seems to almost glow with the energy and determination of young David, about to go out and risk everything in the life and death struggle with Goliath and the Philistines. Michelangelo was twenty-two or twenty-three years old when he completed the enormous statue. He had worked on it for three or four years, and it was a work of such astonishing beauty and maturity that the critics of the time simply did not believe that such a young artist could have done it. So Michelangelo carved his name in it to establish that, in fact, it was his.

It is often said that the way a sculptor works is to somehow envision or see the completed image within the block of marble. In this case, David is

15. (Progoff 1973)59, 68

somehow hidden within the stone, and all the artist has to do is to carefully cut away the outside of the block until David emerges. There is this block of marble and there is the vision in the mind and heart of the artist, who then patiently and with great skill cuts away until the inspired and immaterial vision is revealed in solid marble.

In this metaphor of the sculptor, God is the artist who releases our true self in the cutting away of the hard stone of our unconscious and conscious barriers so that love and freedom and our true self-image in Christ can emerge.

How does this actually work? I have a close friend, a minister with lifelong interests in architecture, theater, and stone carving. He suffers from arthritis, and can no longer follow his vocation of sculpting in stone, which involves using power tools and hand chisels. Now he must work in softer materials, like alabaster or wood. In one of our conversations I asked him a question which might also have occurred in thinking about Michelangelo carving the statue of David. No matter how skilled the sculptor is, doesn't she or he occasionally make a mistake and cut too deep? Perhaps his chisel unwittingly cuts away what the artist meant to be a finger on David's right hand—a key and necessary detail as he holds the smooth stone that will ultimately prevail over Goliath.

What does my friend the stone cutter do when he cuts too deep? Well, he says, it's only a mistake if you insist on your previous expectations, because you decided you wanted the piece to come out a certain way. Actually, my friend says, it's an opportunity; it's a whole new ball game. It's an opportunity to reimagine, to rethink, to recreate the whole thing again.

The metaphor of stone carving has some limitations here. We are not just like David, inert, lifeless, until God the artist brings us to life. We have something to say about it. Even when we are helpless, powerless to affect the outcome, we can at least lament, protest, tell God it shouldn't have been like this.

Nonetheless revisioning, cutting, is also a continuing process. It never ends for God, nor for us. Michelangelo may have cut David's hand too deeply. That didn't ruin the statue; it actually made a different David, perhaps a grander David, like the one that took my breath away in Florence.

The same thing is true for us. Visioning is an interactive process. It takes two to play: God and me. We create together. We cut too deep together. We reframe a new and different and grander image and reality together. Visioning co-creates with God.

Visioning or imaging happens in all sense modalities, even though the term seems only to suggest seeing. The most intimate modality is within our body in proprioceptive sensors, sometimes incorrectly called the kinesthetic sense (which refers to sensing the body's position in space). Eastern traditions describe a number of methods for proprioceptive visioning: yoga, tantra, kundalini, chakras and Qigong, in the Chinese tradition. In the west, yoga and various ways of energy healing have become widely known and used. The sense of smell powerfully affects us, sometimes triggering important early memories deep in the brain, accessed by incense in Catholic and Orthodox Christian traditions. There is taste in a sacred meal.

Touch overlaps these modalities and is so important, from the laying on of hands in blessing and ordination, to receiving bread and wine or acceptable substitutes in the Eucharist.

Hearing, both in the intimate and distant senses, is central to Hebrew religion. *Dabar* is the creating word that brings the world into being. Sanskrit and Hebrew letters are sacred sounds with esoteric meanings. Gregorian chant and plainsong, Jewish *nigun*, the western tradition of sacred music, and Tibetan Buddhist chanters able to sing two tones at the same time are all examples of auditory vision and sacred sound.

Seeing is perhaps the most universally practiced modality. It trades the immediate intimacy of proprioceptors and touch for panoramic distance vision. The forty-eight peaceful and fifty-two wrathful deities in Tibetan Buddhism are not separate gods. Constructed according to precise instructions, they are so carefully memorized that they can be visualized in complete detail in meditation. In doing so, they facilitate "the process of imaging and then realizing the stages of dissolution of consciousness" that occurs at death and "lies at the heart of higher Tibetan Buddhist meditation practice"—the "resonance of pure awareness, the natural purity of mental consciousness."[16]

Icons are venerated in the Christian Eastern Orthodox tradition. Icons, as holy images, refer to art forms as diverse as fresco paintings, illuminations, mosaics, stained glass, and embroidery. According to the Second Council of Nicaea (the Seventh Ecumenical Council in 787) which restored them to accepted Christian practice, they are not to be adored (*latreia*) which "is proper only to the one divine nature," but venerated (*proskynesis*) "in the same way" as the "cross, the holy Gospel and other sacred objects." Icons are "written," not painted—hence the term iconography, since they

16. (Tibetan Book of the Dead 2005)xxx-xxxi

have to do with Scripture. The iconographer should fast, pray, and concentrate all thoughts on the sacred object and follow the conventions in the manual.

In Orthodox theology it is forbidden to make an image of God the creator, so the passage from Genesis 18: 1–15 is reframed. Three *enowah pro enoshe* visit Abraham and Sarah at the Oaks of Mamre. The Hebrew term means "mortal" from the root meaning "frail." Welcomed with Bedouin hospitality, they announce to a disbelieving Abraham and his ninety-year-old wife Sarah, sitting just inside the tent, that she will become pregnant and have a baby. It becomes a proverb among the Hebrews: "Sarah laughed." In 1425, Rubiev "wrote" a famous Orthodox icon showing the three visitors as the Old Testament Trinity: Creator, Christ, Spirit.[17]

Vision transforms our sensory experience. It is an interactive process. Spirit and we now sense the mystery of reality as it truly is. Vision can happen in all senses, in ancient practice, and in personal experience.

SUMMARY

Spiritual knowing does not essentially describe reality, but prescribes how to live, approaching the infinite limit of unlimited awareness and unconditional love. Three dimensions of spiritual knowing are silence, ritual, and vision.

Silence was discovered in the Axial Age, accessing a spiritual experience and integration beyond words, analogous to an infant nurtured and at rest in its mother's arms. Silence can dangerously test the limits of conventional reality, and needs to be a voluntary choice, not extremely coerced. In silence we may know clarity, joy, and creativity.

In rituals we act out spiritual knowing in mystery, embodied in specific sensory action. Sacraments and sacramentals can range from central, traditional, liturgical acts to ordinary activities transformed in spirit.

Visions are manifestations of spiritual power in beauty, in all sensory modalities. In vision we see, hear, touch, smell, or taste in a new way, revealing reality, in blinding light and cloud, displayed and hidden. Like sculptors, we and God co-create together, both following ancient instructions and improvising.

---

17. (Nouwen 1987)20

CHAPTER SEVEN

COSMOLOGY

THE SELF-ORGANIZING UNIVERSE

To study the dharma is to study the self
To study the self is to forget the self
To forget the self is to be entranced by
The myriad things of the universe

—Dogen, *Genjo Koan*[1]

The last two chapters explored spirituality in a scientific world in relation to inner experience, describing mindfulness meditation in the context of brain-mind research. Now we explore spirituality in the context of what the physical sciences have discovered about the extended world around us. We choose the context of the physical sciences because they give the most inclusive and general descriptions of the world that science knows. They have been able to tell us the age of the universe, how it began and evolved, and its fundamental laws and constituent parts. But we don't need to know subatomic physics in order to know how to start our car, change the oil, or communicate with our loved ones. Every level of our lived reality, from universe down to specific aspects, has its own structure and laws for how it works. They include both "rules of thumb" and well-tested scientific explanations. It is also true, however, that understanding the smaller specific

---

1. (Dogen 1233) "Actualizing the Fundamental Point," Robert Aitken and Kazuaki Tanahashi, trans. http://www.thezensite.com/ZenTeachings/Dogen_Teachings/GenjoKoan_Aitken.htm (last accessed 2/15/14)

parts of the universe ultimately depends on scientific explanatory powers applied to the universe as a whole. That brings us to cosmology.

Cosmology is the province of scientific knowing in physics and astronomy, as well as the near-universal interest of religions from earliest times until now. Almost every religious tradition also has a cosmology, a story of origins—the beginning of everything. Symbols and rituals present and act out activities and concerns of ordinary life, such as initiation into adult roles and responsibilities. The symbols and rituals manifest a transcendent, usually eternal realm that gives meaning, coherence and purpose to this world, and the human beings in it.[2] Humans sing and dance into being the transcendent realm, and its relationship to this world.[3] Cosmologies can be as beautiful and profound as the creation drama in the first chapter of Genesis and the wisdom texts in Hebrew Scripture. At the other extreme they can be as banal as the famous protest by a lady to Bertrand Russell's lecture on cosmology. "The world," she exclaimed, "is actually flat, and it's supported by a giant elephant that is standing on the back of a turtle." A bemused Russell asked her what might be supporting the turtle. She explained, "It's turtles all the way down."[4] There is even a joke about science and cosmology, contrasting traditional Christian and contemporary scientific explanations of reality. A group of scientists goes to see God. They tell him, "We have discovered how to create life." God, interested, says, "Show me how you do that." One of the scientists picks up a handful of soil. God says, "Wait a minute. Get your own dirt."

What can science say with confidence about cosmology? There are two grand themes of the physical sciences. The first theme is that the universe and its parts are simple—radically simple. The second theme is evolution—that the universe changes over time. First, what does it mean that the universe is simple? There are a few foundational blocks for the whole universe and they are the same everywhere in the universe, "The mass of the known universe is roughly 75 percent hydrogen, 24 percent helium, and 1 percent minor impurities."[5] Further, those "impurities," those other elements, can be detected by the color spectra of the light they emit; and those color signals are the same everywhere, from the light from the furthest star billions of years ago to right here and now on earth. The Nobel

2. (Eliade C. 1958, 1975 ed.)3; (Bellah 2011)8–9

3. (Bellah 2011)140–141

4. (Holt 2012)131

5. (Wilczek c.1987, 1989 ed.)83

Prize-winning physicist Frank Wilczek invites us to "marvel and rejoice at the wealth of meaning and structure that can emerge from arrangements of vast numbers of utterly simple stereotyped units."[6]

It is important to note that those identical interchangeable units behave unpredictably. If you fire an electron directly at an atom, it may deflect to the left today. But tomorrow in exactly the same situation, it may deflect to the right. There is no way to tell or predict which way it will go. What quantum mechanics can do, as will be described later, is to give some probabilities about what may happen. But that's all.[7]

These "arrangements" are more permanent and fundamental than the "units" they arrange. Aristotle and medieval scholastics insisted on permanent unchanging perfection in certain physical objects in the universe: the sun, planets, and stars. Tycho Brahe, Galileo and other astronomers demonstrated that to be simply untrue empirically. The moon was not a perfect sphere; it had mountains and valleys just like earth. If the earth changed over time, so must the moon and other celestial objects. Hence came the two major themes of modern physics: 1) There is no fundamental difference between "star things" and "earth things," and 2) the universe is evolving. The laws of transformation, working out over time, by which things are arranged and rearranged,[8] seem to be permanent, not even bound by time and space.[9] They are the same everywhere and at all times, for all observers.

LARGE VERSUS SMALL

We have been talking so far of large and enormous things in the universe—stars, galaxies. When scientists studied very small things, smaller even than atoms, they discovered that the laws of transformation were very different and could not be reconciled with the laws of transformation that governed large things. It was not that these new laws about tiny things were inexact or only partially known. The Standard Model of subatomic particles is quite complete and verified. There are fermions and bosons. Two fermions cannot be in the same place, while bosons are, much of the time. Subatomic particles act like they are spinning, and numbers and fractions are assigned

6. (Wilczek c.1987, 1989 ed.)22
7. (Davies 2007)64
8. (Wilczek c.1987, 1989 ed.)60
9. (Wilczek c.1987, 1989 ed.)39

to the spin. Bosons spin in whole numbers like 1, 2, and so on. Fermions spin in half numbers, like 1/2, 3/2, and so on. Gauge bosons, which mediate the strong force, are gluons; those mediating the weak force are weak bosons; and those with electromagnetic force are photons (light particles). There is also the Higgs boson so recently discovered, and the yet undiscovered graviton.[10]

The Standard Model is not a matter of debate. Its predictions have been proven time and time again. It "works extraordinarily well"—so well in fact that it doesn't give sufficient clues about the further nature of reality that may lie beyond or beneath it.[11] The problem is not that it doesn't work; the problem is that the laws of transformation in subatomic quantum physics cannot be reconciled with the laws of transformation in larger objects. The word "quantum" refers to the fact that an electron may be in one orbit around an atomic nucleus indicated by a whole number or quantum, then may be in another orbit designated by a different number or quantum. It doesn't go from one orbit to the other. No time passes. There is no route from one to the other. It simply is in one orbit, and then in another. It jumps, if you will, to the other ring. But the word "jumps" doesn't explain or refer to any process. It's just in one place, then in another. In the larger world, distance and reality are continuous; we move from here to there in time and space. In the quantum world distance and reality are discrete: the particle is simply here or there. There is no way to put these two realities together in some common understanding or framework.

Niels Bohr addressed the problem by what he called the "correspondence principle." Every quantum system has only discrete different values, whether "its energy, or its momentum, or its angular momentum (a measure of the strength of rotation) or its electric charge."[12] But in classical physics, the laws of larger, slower objects that Newton discovered, everything is continuous. The correspondence principle says that there is a gradual boundary between the two. The smaller the quantum change, the more you can use the laws of classical physics. But where large changes of energy are involved, as when an electron close to its atomic nucleus changes to a

10. (Randall 2011)335 Fermions include quarks with strange names: up, charm and top are up-type quarks; down, strange and bottom are down-type quarks. Leptons are also fermions; neutral leptons go from light to heavy and charged leptons include electrons, muons and tau.

11. (Randall 2011)106

12. (Wheeler 1998)289

further orbit, a classical law "has practically no validity at all."[13] You have to use the "clouds" or probability waves of quantum mechanics that cannot tell exactly where the electron is or how fast it is going.

The smaller one goes, the greater the quantum fluctuations, and the more enormous the energy needed to explore those domains. From the size of a single proton "we would have to go twenty powers of 10 further [smaller] to reach the Planck length." In this "roiling chaos" there "would literally be no left or right, no before and after. Ordinary ideas of length would disappear. Ordinary ideas of time would evaporate." Wheeler named it "quantum foam."[14]

String theorists create possible mathematical models in this realm. Particles are a mathematical problem here, so perhaps instead there are flexible strings or loops "so tiny that it would take a chain of a hundred billion billion of them to stretch across a single atomic nucleus."[15] The energy required to investigate this domain is so enormously far beyond our current capabilities, needing a "particle accelerator trillions of times more powerful than anything" we have,[16] that there is no way to investigate it empirically.

According to Wheeler, the "most compelling idea in all of physics"[17] is the gravitational collapse that happens in a black hole, according to general relativity. If a star is massive enough, at its death it will finally "collapse to a point of infinite or near infinite density from which neither light nor anything else can escape. Only its gravitational aura will remain."[18] In that extremity "space can be crumpled like a piece of paper into an infinitesimal dot . . . time can be extinguished like a blown out flame" and laws of physics no longer hold. Even baryons (protons, neutrons and other particles) can be crushed out of existence.[19]

In the macro world, objects can be located in time and space. A thing is either here or there, an event happens in this moment or that moment. In the quantum world that is not possible: To the extent that you know *where* a particle is (its location) to that extent you cannot know *when* it is (its

13. (Wheeler 1998)290
14. (Wheeler 1998)248
15. (Davies 2007)111
16. (Davies 2007)111–112
17. (Wheeler 1998)298
18. (Wheeler 1998)294
19. (Wheeler 1998)298

velocity). Werner Heisenberg's mathematical uncertainty principle states in words that "it is impossible simultaneously to make accurate measurements of both a particle's position and its velocity. The more accurate you make your measurement of position, the more you disrupt the particle's velocity—and vice versa."[20]

Then we come to an impasse, to mystery, or at least to the end of our current scientific knowing. There is no way to fit gravity into the picture. There are four forces in the universe, two discovered in the last century. In addition to gravity and the electromagnetic field there is the strong nuclear force which binds atomic nuclei together even against the mutual repulsion of two or more positively charged protons. It is extremely strong but acts only at a very short distance, dropping off to zero at a range of one ten-trillionth of a centimeter. And finally the weak nuclear force is responsible for some nuclear particles decaying into others, as happens in radioactivity.[21] Scientists know how to integrate the electromagnetic force, the strong force and the weak force into a common understanding. But gravity cannot be fit into the picture. Therefore there is no common understanding of the forces in the universe, no theory of everything or "T.O.E."

FIELDS

What is the best way to understand the radically simple nature of the universe? It seems to be fields, illustrated by subatomic particles, such as photons that emit light. They seem to resemble both waves and particles. Wilcsek writes: "Light comes in lumps but interferes like waves." He invents a name for them which may or may not be of any help here: photons are "laves." Laves are mathematical waves that describe the probability for manifesting particles. "A mathematical wave emerges from the atom and expands at the speed of light . . . it is a table of odds. It specifies the probability for finding a lump of light." Electrons, neutrons, indeed all particles act the same way according to the "central doctrine of quantum physics, which is simply that everything in laves."[22]

Here is a more familiar term for waves or laves: fields. Fields are information-rich, non-material environments within which material interactions pass in and out of existence. For many centuries, forces that can

20. (Wilczek c.1987, 1989 ed.)131

21. (Davies 2007)94

22. (Wilczek c.1987, 1989 ed.)116–118

act on objects from a distance have been known. Gravity is the obvious example, but not the only one. According to the physicist Richard Feynman, the most important event of the nineteenth century was the discovery that electrical and magnetic fields acted the same way.[23] In fact, you can see such a field by putting iron filings around a bar magnet. You can see a field, the lines of the invisible force field or medium, made visible in the filings. Further, you can create electric fields by moving the magnet around. That's what an electrical motor does. The rotating magnets produce electricity and vice-versa: changing electrical fields produce magnetic fields.

When you change or disturb an electro-magnetic field, the change travels at the speed of light. In fact, that's what light is. James Clark Maxwell wrote with great excitement in 1860 of his discovery: "light itself, (including radiant heat and other radiations if any) is an electro-magnetic disturbance in the form of waves propagated through the electro-magnetic field according to electro-magnetic laws."[24] Subatomic particles are fields that, when activated, give birth to particles. Fields are everywhere. Fields permeate space, contain energy and affect the size of the universe. Scalar fields, like the inflation of the newly born universe, can make it expand. The Higgs field, so recently demonstrated, is another example of a Scalar field.[25] It manifests a particle called the Higgs boson. Subatomic particles moving through the Higgs field acquire mass, which accounts for their mass.[26] Gravitation and electromagnetism can be described as fields. Quantum mechanical equations describe the possibilities of fields manifesting and annihilating subatomic particles.[27] More satisfactory than just a particle bouncing around in empty space, a field describes a much richer environment in which change and action are possible at every point, not just where there happen to be things.[28] These invisible media or fields are more fundamental and important than particles or things. The fundamental

23. (Wilczek c.1987, 1989 ed.)155–156

24. (Wilczek c.1987, 1989 ed.)159–160 The word "field" comes from the heraldic background of figures on a knight's or king's shield.

25. (Davies 2007)57

26. (Davies 2007)156

27. (Davies 2007)95–97

28. (Einstein 1973)368 Einstein writes "The emancipation of the field concept from the assumption of its association with a mechanical carrier finds a place among the psychologically most interesting events in the development of physical thought."

ingredients we need to describe the world are fields that fill all space like an invisible ocean.[29]

Even hunting-gathering people may describe their lived reality as something like fields. Bradford Keeney is an ethnographer who has spent years studying and actually dancing with !Kung bushman doctors, or shamans, in the Kalahari Desert. He remarks on the "slippery and amorphous ways" these hunting-gathering people describe their spiritual reality. He suggests their spiritual knowing "derives from the constantly changing forms they see in nature as well as the transformational personal experiences that arise in their healing dance and in a doctor's special dreams. For a Bushman, change and transformation are the most constant aspects of life." His description resembles fields within which material forms spontaneously manifest and change. When spiritual power transforms a doctor, she or he "can become indistinguishable from an ancestor or even God"— an echo of fractals in human "I"s and "Thou"s, to be further described in the next chapter. These insights are not rational ideas. They come in their healing dance or trance. "The Bushman way is more polymorphic, improvisational, performative, playful and biological than the texturally ruled world that anthropologists inhabit."[30]

In fields, particles connect non-locally; nothing crosses the space between them. An Irish physicist, John Stewart Bell, in 1964 demonstrated non-locality mathematically. The connection is not affected by the distance between them, and the effects of the connection happen simultaneously. "A non-local interaction is, in short, unmediated, unmitigated and immediate." And permanent; once connected, always connected. Bell's theorem has been proven true experimentally a number of times with subatomic particles such as photons. When the particles are separated from each other, no matter how far apart, they continue to simultaneously coordinate their spin.[31]

Fields were also discovered scientifically in the macro world in chaos theory. Newton's linear laws, powerful and universal as they are, quickly reach their limit in accounting for complex real-world situations. In 1960 Edward Lorenz, a scientist at MIT, was trying to develop a method for forecasting weather by inventing a computer simulation that was deterministic and non-periodic. We are not talking about chance or randomness here.

29. (Wilczek c.1987, 1989 ed.)159, 161
30. (Keeney 2003)143–144, 194, 155
31. (Dossey 1989)180, 186

Besides being determined, the simulation had to be non-periodic; that is to say, it could never exactly repeat itself. What he discovered about such a complex system, later called "chaotic,, was how extraordinarily sensitive it is to the tiniest changes in its initial condition. When he rounded off a number by one ten-thousandth, the difference grew exponentially until it completely overwhelmed the solution. He gave a lecture in 1972 entitled, "Predictability: Does the Flap of a Butterfly's Wings in Brazil Set off a Tornado in Texas?" Hence the term "butterfly effect" (his original title had to do with a seagull's wings) which is a hallmark of chaotic systems.[32]

So there you have two characteristics of chaotic systems. They are determined and unpredictable at the same time. Again, we are not talking about chance or randomness here. You can specify the laws that govern them; they are determined. But you can never predict the consequences—what will actually happen over time and repetitions—because you can never specify the initial conditions exactly.

Chaos is a fascinating combination of order and disorder. Over a long period of time, a chaotic system settles into a normal long-term mode of behavior called a strange attractor—called such because it seemed so weird or strange to Lorenz and others who first discovered them. Lorenz's strange attractor looked like the two wings of a butterfly (there's the butterfly again). The particle would zip around one of the wings, for a while, and then jump to the other wing, chaotically, never repeating its path exactly, like thin layers of mica stacked together.

Chaos theory is not statistics as usually understood, which map the behaviors of events or particles in a constrained system by a Gaussian distribution or bell-shaped curve. We may be familiar with that curve, in which two-thirds of the data occurs within one standard deviation around its center. Chaotic systems, because they lack constraints, have what is called a long tail or a fat tail toward the end of the curve in which one event can significantly change the whole system. For example, if you wish to measure the average height of 100 persons in a room, and the tallest person in the world walks into the room, the average will not change much because biology severely constrains height. That's statistics. But with the same 100 persons, if you wish to measure their average wealth, and Bill

32. (Strogatz 2008)27

Gates walks into the room, the average will be very different by that one addition because there are few constraints on how wealthy one can be. That's chaos theory.[33]

Chaotic systems are non-linear. Instead of there being a smooth curve, as in calculus, the line divides into two, the two divide into four, the four into eight, and so on, until very soon it reaches what is called the accumulation point in which the dots are all over the place in a truly chaotic mess. A so-called orbit diagram is a picture of the whole path.[34]

Both chaotic systems in the macro world and quantum physics in the micro world are fields, information-rich non-material environments within which material interactions arise and pass away. These interactions evolve over the history of the universe. That brings us to evolution, the second theme of modern physics.

EVOLUTION

The first of the two major themes of modern physics describes arrangements of simple units that are uniform throughout the universe from stars to earth. The second theme is that the universe is constantly evolving, changing. Evolution is widely accepted scientifically and has been extraordinarily fruitful in producing other scientific discoveries.

Science has been able to trace the origins of the universe back to its first moments. The process is called postdiction. It uses the same unchanging physical laws as prediction, but reverses time. It searches for relics of an earlier time in the universe to see if those same laws can predict later stages, and explain earlier stages if the passage of time were reversed.[35]

In both science and the Christian tradition, as noted earlier, the universe has a beginning. For Augustine, "the world was made with time and not in time."[36] Einstein's general theory of relativity combines space and time into a space-time continuum. The big bang emerges from a singularity of infinite density and infinite space time curvature. Hartle and Hawking

33. (Strogatz 2008)73

34. (Strogatz 2008)46–47 At certain points the orbit diagram, after being white with dots all over, will suddenly collapse into periods of six dots, then after some chaos, periods of five, then after some more chaos, an especially prominent period of three dots. Then the diagram will again explode into chaos for a while, and so on.

35. (Wilczek c.1987, 1989 ed.) 42–43

36. (Davies 2007)69

created a complex mathematical model in which, one Planck length before the singularity, the space-time continuum began simply as space. The Planck length is about -10^{33} centimeters, or 10–20 times smaller than an atomic nucleus.[37] There is no "before" prior to the big bang singularity. In Buddhism, in contrast, the universe has no beginning, has always been there.

In the beginning the universe was perfectly uniform or symmetrical. The evolution of the universe consecutively breaks symmetries until we get to the differentiated universe we know. An example of symmetry breaking is the cooling of an iron bar. Above 770° centigrade iron atoms are magnetized in all directions uniformly, there is symmetry and the bar itself has no magnetic properties. As the bar cools, the atoms start to line up, their symmetry is broken and a magnetic field emerges in the whole bar itself.[38] High energy creates high symmetry. And energy manifests as heat. At the very beginning, both the density and the temperature of the universe rose without limit. All the energy was concentrated and uniform. As the universe expanded and cooled, energy was dissipated and symmetries were broken one after another as the early uniformity into evolved into the rich complexity we know.

We know pretty much what happened between a millionth of a second and several minutes after the big bang. A split second after the big bang the universe exploded in size at least 10^{25} (ten trillion trillion) times.[39] That's why the early universe was so uniform—all the irregularities were stretched smooth. Then the inflation dramatically slowed as the universe continued to expand much more slowly until more recent times.

One second after the big bang the temperature was 10 billion degrees, so that even atomic nuclei could not stick together. Protons, neutrons and electrons swam uniformly, symmetrically in the primal soup, called plasma.

From about 100 seconds to a few minutes on, protons and neutrons were unable to get together to form the nuclei of atoms. After the universe had cooled enough, protons, which have a positive electrical charge, couldn't overcome their mutual repulsion and nuclei were formed. But electrons couldn't be captured in atoms until the cosmic microwave background 380,000 years later. Until then, if you could have been there, you

37. (Davies 2007)73
38. (Davies 2007)160
39. (Davies 2007)55–56

couldn't have seen anything because the free electrons kept getting in the way of the photons trying to fly around.[40]

The cosmic microwave background is still detectable in the static background of your television set. It is a key relic of an earlier stage of the universe. The tiny differences in temperature in the mostly uniform cosmic microwave background later differentiated into the gas giants, stars, galaxies and planets in the universe.

We live on a small planet in a solar system around a medium sized star we call the sun, which is at the edge of what we call the Milky Way galaxy, which contains more than a hundred billion stars, in a universe with several hundred billion such galaxies, some much larger than our own. And this universe we call ours is expanding at an increasing rate, due to the increasing dominance of dark energy mentioned earlier.

THE EVOLUTION OF HUMAN LIFE

Four billion years ago this planet cohered from particles in space, perhaps even getting water from crashing asteroids. Rocks, volcanoes, water vapor and changing atmosphere became the volatile, changing, nurturing environment for the first one-celled life forms, perhaps spontaneously emerging from certain clays; we really don't know.

In the history of the universe, we know that if the chemical and energetic relationships in it were just the tiniest bit different, we would not be here; life and we would not exist.

One of the stubborn facts of the universe is how it is designed to support life. Certain chemical elements are needed: carbon, oxygen, hydrogen, nitrogen, sulfur, phosphorus. Liquid water, energy source (from the sun) are also needed in a stable, benign environment which is old and cool enough for complex chemistry. Paul Davies writes, "If almost any of the basic features of the universe—from the properties of atom to the distribution

---

40. (Davies 2007)50, 23 Photons causing light have no mass, no weight, so they can zip to the ends of the universe over billions of light years, moving at 186,000 miles per second, the speed of light. They are the only subatomic particles we can sense with unaided eyes. Some of us have experienced something like that when we visited one of the great caves in Virginia or Kentucky. When we were in the deepest part of the cave, the guide would extinguish all lights, and we stood helpless and blind in total darkness, unable literally to see our hand in front of our face. Then, after our eyes had accommodated to the darkness, the guide would light one match, and we could see the entire interior of the cave by that single light.

of the galaxies—were different, life would very probably be impossible."[41] One example is the formation of carbon atoms. Three helium nuclei have to come together at the same moment to form a carbon nucleus, and the chances of that happening are impossibly small. In 1951, physicists discovered something called carbon nuclear resonance that made it possible; if the strong nuclear force were different by as little as one percent, it couldn't happen.[42]

Speculation and interpretations as to how and why this is true abound. Perhaps there are uncounted numbers of alternative universes—a multiverse. In most or almost all of them, conditions are such that life is impossible. By chance or random selection, we just happen to live in the one in which we *could* live. That's the weak anthropic principle. In the strong anthropic principle, as Aristotle taught, purpose and teleology are built into the very structure of the universe. Something or somebody designed it so life could evolve.[43] But as empirically established as the age of the universe or the onset of the cosmic microwave background, the ineluctable fact is this: the universe was created and fine-tuned precisely and exquisitely with the emergence of life, consciousness, us.[44]

Approximately 1.6 to two billion years ago some one-celled creatures, called eukaryotes, learned to gather more energy by merging with, invading, or eating other cells. And from that great evolutionary advance all multi-cellular life evolved.

In the course of evolution, more complex systems came into being. Complex systems can be characterized by the preservation of identity amid changes, organized complexity, and are goal- directed. The first two characteristics can be understood as "autopoiesis" or "self-construction," "a self-maintaining process by which a system (*e.g.* a biological cell) functions as

41. (Davies 2007)2

42. (Davies 2007)125, 128

43. (Davies 2007)222

44. (Fields 2010)50–51 Mineralogist Bob Hazen has explored the origins of life by imitating hydrothermal vents, or cracks off the bottom of the ocean, where molten lava or rocks heat water to hundreds of degrees Fahrenheit. He created a pressure cooker with temperatures over 1800 degrees Fahrenheit and pressures up to 10,000 times the atmosphere at sea level. In various experiments he put in nitrogen, ammonia and other molecules that may have existed early on in the earth. In doing so he and his coworkers created different organic molecules, amino acids and sugars—basic ingredients of life. Later researchers are exploring whether minerals might form a rough surface where amino acids could gather together to form a protein. The definition of life used here is self-replication and passing information on from generation to generation.

a whole to continually produce the components (*e.g.* parts of a cell) which themselves make up the system that produces them."[45] An example is the dissipative structures in chemistry, for which Ilya Prigogine won the Nobel Prize in 1970. When certain chemical open-ended systems encounter new information from their environment that threatens their identity and structure, they dissipate or lose energy to their environment. If the system cannot deal with the disturbance in its present form, it may simply fall apart and cease to exist. But there is another possibility. If the system is able to maintain its identity "it can self-organize to a higher level of complexity, a new form of itself that can deal better with the present."[46]

This dynamic disequilibrium is built into evolution. The myriad forms of life on the planet through time illustrate the possibilities. Incredibly successful "eusocial" insects constitute only two percent of insect species but eighty percent of the mass of insects on the planet.[47] These insects and "eusocial" humans communicate across generations, and members of the community perform simple acts for the benefit of the complex community as a whole. The biologist E.O. Wilson writes that specialized and rudimentary leaf cutter ants, for example "cut fragments from leaves, flower and twigs, carry them to their nests and chew the material into a mulch, which they fertilize with their own feces. On this rich material they grow their principal food, a fungus belonging to a species found nowhere else in nature. Their gardening is organized as an assembly line, with the material passed from one specialized caste to the next."[48]

There is, of course, no head ant who creates or controls all this. There is just the complex, self-organizing, evolving community or organism operating far beyond the capability of its simple rudimentary parts. And then there are the autopoietic systems of most interest to us, ourselves. In time, some organisms encephalized—gathered a bunch of specialized cells called neurons at one end of their body, called the head, as a primitive command and control center called a brain.

At first the brain was capable of coordinating basic life support functions. We can call it the reptilian brain, and it still exists in each one of us, in what we call our brainstem. And when a new embryo is formed in the womb, it develops a reptilian brain first. In a rough way, each one of us

45. (Mitchell 2009)297–298

46. (Wheatley 2006)21

47. (Lehrer 2012)38

48. (Bloom 2012)30

repeats or recapitulates the history of life on the planet as we emerge and grow into who we are.

After the reptilian brain appeared on earth, millions of years later, little creatures called mammals developed a further brain stacked on top of it, appropriately called the mammalian brain. We each have one of those also, which we grew in the womb, stacked on top of the reptilian brain. The mammalian brain is the center of feelings and emotions and the vitality and energy of life.

Our cats are pure mammalian brain. They make irritating noises when they are hungry and want you to feed them. They play with the end of a rope you hold, or make mock attacks on each other. They stare out the window twitching their tails and making delicate high mewing noises, which their instincts tell them will attract birds. And they purr, rub against your hand, and wag the last two inches of their tails when they want you to show them affection.

And finally, stacked on top of the reptilian brain and the mammalian brain, is the cortex. In our human arrogance, we call it the higher brain. Although there are more connections between humans and other animals than we might like to think, our cortex does pretty much what no other animal can: it can create mental representations and search for meaning in all of this drama of creation and life. It can observe itself. It can observe itself observing itself. It can find patterns of meaning in all of this for our personal lives, our common lives together, the world around us and the largest context we know: the universe and the context of ultimate reality beyond that.

It can even figure out and tell the story of the whole drama of creation and life just briefly summarized.

HOW HUMANS SHAPE EVOLUTION

At this point, the creation enters a whole new dimension. For the first time in the history of the universe, creatures appear who in awareness, self-awareness, and awareness of self-awareness can, in a very real sense, choose and decide who they are and want to be.

It's an extraordinary achievement. There have been self-organizing, open living systems around for a long time. But, in fact, as far as we know, there is nothing else like us anywhere else in the universe. There are those who search for and perhaps hope to find life something like ours elsewhere in the universe. But for now, that hasn't happened.

In a fundamental sense, we human beings create ourselves. We create who we want to be in the future, we create our past out of our memories as we retell them, and we have an enormous and frightening present impact on the rest of creation on this planet.

These choices we make give us a measure of awareness, freedom, and power that was unthinkable and unimaginable before we arrived. We human beings stand before an empty canvas, with a pallet of rich colors in one hand we may call our DNA; and a set of brushes for different purposes in our other hand, which we may call the environment which nurtured us. We decide what we will choose in the present moment, in how we intend our future, and how we remember our past.

Evolution is no longer only physical. It is now also cultural, and greatly sped up because of that advance. Cultural "memes," as they are called, grow and propagate rapidly—creating and distributing new information, ideas, concepts, and possibilities at an astonishing and increasing rate. And new technologies such as social networking are well suited for facilitating this change.

This evolution is not so much a series of discrete steps as a great flow of wisdom, developing and increasing through the eons. David Brooks imagines a neuroscientist describing this in greater detail: "We inherit a great river of knowledge, a flow of patterns coming from many sources. The information that comes from deep in the evolutionary past we call genetics. The information passed along from hundreds of years ago we call culture. The information passed along from decades ago we call family, and the information offered months ago we call education. But it is all information that flows through us. The brain is adapted to the river of knowledge and exits only as a creature in that river."[49]

It may be, as Thornton Wilder wrote in his play about Julius Caesar, "the universe did not know that men were living in it."[50] But at the sub-atomic level, even the simple human observation of events actualizes or changes them. The physicist Erwin Schrödinger famously created a thought experiment to illustrate the strange nature of quantum superpositions. A cat, along with a timer activating a flask containing poison, is placed in a shielded and sealed box. The poison may or may not be released. The

49. (Brooks 2011)32
50. (Gottlieb 2013)76

mathematical equations of quantum mechanics suggest that the cat is simultaneously alive *and* dead. When we open the box, our observation actualizes one of the two possibilities—the cat is *either* alive *or* dead. As the Copenhagen interpretation puts it, the superposition of all possible states collapses to a finite state only at that exact moment of measurement.

The double-slit quantum experiment explores the influence of the observer even further. In 1907 G. I. Taylor devised a way to discover how photons (light particles) could also create an interference pattern as waves do. When two waves meet, they create alternating bands of light and dark called an interference pattern. He made the light from a gas flame go through several layers of smoked glass and then a small hole. The light was so dim the film recording it had to be exposed for three months. It was equal to a standard candle slightly over a mile away. One photon at a time passed through a set up consisting of two slits and landing on a film surface beyond it.[51] The bizarre result was that the single photons passing through caused a wave interference pattern on the film surface. "This result is weird because it seems to imply that any given photon must somehow know about both slits so that it can cooperate with the other photons in creating the collective interference pattern—despite the fact that a particle should be able to pass only through one slit."

Even more bizarre, the wave interference pattern only happens if no-body is looking. If the experimenter watches the photons passing through, they will not create the wave interference pattern but behave as particles.[52] John Archibald Wheeler designed an experiment to confirm this in the 1980s. The film surface had detectors to detect which slit each photon was going through. When watched, the photons manifest as particles; when not watched, they manifest as waves. The further astounding result is that "the experimenter can *delay the choice*—wave or particles—right up to the moment that the photon arrives" at the surface.[53]

How can this be? How can the observer in the present moment determine the choice the photon made earlier in the past when it decided to manifest as a particle or wave on passing through the slit? Paul Davies suggests this means the photon is "in some sense less than real in the absence of an observation." The present wave/particle decision made by the observer helps create the photon choice in the past. "The observation has

51. (Wilczek c.1987, 1989 ed.)113

52. (Davies 2007) 245

53. (Davies 2007) 246

a crucial relevance to the past—maybe even to the very remote past"[54]—even though no signal or information can pass from the present to determine what happened long ago.

Davies concludes, "Because of the backward-in-time aspect of quantum mechanics, the past can be shaped by observation at any stage in the cosmological future."[55] That doesn't make sense because the past determines the present. "The theory of relativity, which permits time to be warped by motion and gravitation, predicts circumstances in which physical objects, including observers, can loop back into the past."[56] One can imagine a sort of wormhole between different points in space. The observer going through the wormhole in one direction goes into the future; in the other direction into the past. "Observer participants interrogate nature for information (ultimately via quantum mechanics) and thus help shape physical reality, even in the far past."[57] This idea need not clash with the theory of evolution that reality is determined by mutations favored by natural selection, because mind in the future helps shape physical realities as they evolved in the past. Wheeler puts it this way: "Physics gives rise to observer-participancy, observer-participancy gives rise to information, information gives rise to physics."[58]

Wheeler insists that neither life nor mind nor human beings are necessary for the observation. What is necessary is the measurement or "registration." That turns the potential choice in the past into the present actuality "whether by a person or a device or a piece of mica (anything that can preserve a record)." However, rocks do not carry out double slit quantum experiments or write peer reviewed papers recording the observations or observe the marks on the mica. Only human beings do that. Wheeler admits that he is at the end of his understanding of "the quantum, leaving this unanswered query: information may not be just what we *learn* about the world. It may be what *makes* the world."[59]

Another approach to the role of the observer in quantum phenomena was created in the eighteenth century by an English clergyman named Thomas Bayes and further developed by the French physicist Pierre-Simon

54. (Davies 2007) 248
55. (Davies 2007) 249
56. (Davies 2007) 252
57. (Davies 2007) 254
58. (Davies 2007) 249
59. (Wheeler 1998) 341

LaPlace. Whether the cat is either alive or dead, or whether a proton wave or particle manifests in the double-slit experiment, is not determined by the collapse of the wave function at the moment of observation as in Niels Bohr's Copenhagen interpretation. It is determined instead by the "degree of belief" of the observer—and not just one observer, but the communication of the subjective experiences of many observers into a coherent result. The wave function is simply a mathematical resource to guide the observers, along with other information, even including their intuition and personal beliefs. The mathematics have yet to be all worked out, but the proponents of Quantum Bayesianism, as it is called, are enthusiastic about its ability to remove some of the "absurdities" of the Copenhagen interpretation, e.g., that the cat is both alive *and* dead. As Christopher A. Fuchs summarizes it, "With every measurement set by an experimenter's free will, the world is shaped just a little as it participates in a kind of moment of birth." He concludes, "In this way, we become active contributors to the ongoing creation of the universe."[60]

Wheatley remarks "We cannot know what is happening to something if we are not looking at it and, stranger yet, nothing *does* happen to it until we observe it."[61] And when we decide to look at one thing, we lose the information that would have come from looking at something else. Wheatley continues, "We each actively participate in creating our worlds. 'Whatever we call reality,' Prigogine and Stengers advise, 'it is revealed to us only through an active construction in which we participate.'"[62]

IS MATHEMATICS REAL?

Because these descriptions of fields and their effects depend upon mathematics, a side discussion is needed here about whether mathematics gives a true description of the nature of reality. Scientific cosmology depends on mathematics. Its insights are mathematical concepts and equations. The evolution of mental representations is wondrously illustrated in mathematics. The Piraha Indians in the Amazon mastered the ability to count one, two, and many. Other hunting-gathering people learned to count by mapping: touching their fingers, their toes, then, if needed, other parts of

60. (Von Baeyer 2013) 50–51
61. (Wheatley 2006) 61
62. (Wheatley 2006) 65

their bodies.[63] The Pythagoreans were enthralled by the magic and power of whole integers or numbers to explain and create reality. The Indians, or perhaps the Arabs, invented zero, and mathematics took another great jump forward. Now mathematics has progressed so far and fast that only specialists in a particular area may even understand their own inventions. And yet, these mental representations can so explain, perhaps even create things in the world that their power is a mystery. Are the mathematics themselves as real as the results of their empirical verification are?

Here we begin to cross over the boundary into various philosophical views and opinions—subject to discussion, difference, and argument, but not themselves real in the physical world, and not verified in scientific cosmology. One view is that mathematicians create imaginary wholes or complex fictions, needing only to be logically consistent and perhaps beautiful.[64] But mathematics works so extraordinarily well in explaining things in the world that it seems to be more real than that. Perhaps mathematics represents Plato's eternal transcendent ideas or forms, as his parable of the cave illustrates. Perhaps these perfect forms are the primary reality, and both the physical world and the mind are in some mysterious way connected to, shadows or by- products of them, as Sir Roger Penrose at Oxford suggests.[65] Mysterious, because we really don't know how that happens.

We don't really know whether we are making mathematics up, or discovering something about the true nature of things, or even actually changing or creating reality. Mario Livio of the Hubble Space Telescope Science Institute took it upon himself to investigate Eugene Wigner's puzzlement over the "unreasonable effectiveness of mathematics." He concludes that "Our mathematics is a combination of inventions and discoveries."[66] For example, the Greeks invented the concept of prime numbers. The Babylonians, Egyptians, and Chinese got along without that invention in their own math. So mathematics is part of human culture. But all the theorems about prime numbers are derived from that invention. They are discoveries, not inventions. Yet when invented or discovered, they are universally, eternally valid. That doesn't change, even if over time the insights may be incorporated into a larger context, as happened with Euclidean geometry, for example. Sometimes a new mathematics had to be invented to explain

63. (Diamond 2012) 273–274
64. (Holt 2012) 181
65. (Holt 2012) 171–177
66. (Livio 2009) 4, 238

new empirical findings: Newton had to invent calculus to account for his laws of motion. Sometimes the invention of a new mathematics facilitates new empirical discoveries, e.g., knot theory and DNA.

It is true that mathematics is "unreasonably effective," but then again it is unreasonably effective for those endeavors for which it *is* unreasonably effective, recalling Mark Twain's remark that "To a man with a hammer, everything looks like a nail." And scientific discoveries may not even need math; evolutionary theory is simply stated in words. Mathematics cannot describe everything in the universe; it works with the problems at hand with which it can work. Livio concludes his exploration by connecting mathematics to Bertrand Russell's comments on philosophy which themselves end on a transcendent spiritual note. "Philosophy [mathematics] is to be studied . . . for the sake of the questions themselves; because these questions enlarge our conceptions of what is possible, enrich our intellectual imaginations and diminish the dogmatic assurance which closes the mind against speculation; but above all because, through the greatness of the universe which philosophy contemplates, the mind is also rendered great, and becomes capable of that union with the universe which constitutes its highest good."[67]

THE CHALLENGE

We may be at a tipping point in the evolution of the self-organizing universe. The power wielded by this invasive species called humans may now be about to wreak irreversible damage on its ecosystem, the earth. We may have mistakenly implied that evolution is something like linear progress. Things just get better and better, life just keeps growing, more of it, and more complex forms of life in the history of the planet. Unfortunately, and ominously, the evolutionary record uncovered by science contradicts that. It is a rather new idea in recent history. We used to assume that life forms were eternal and fixed, nothing new came into being, nothing old died out. The first mastodon bones to be carefully studied were found on the east bank of the Ohio River, near Cincinnati, in 1739.[68] After much discussion and debate about the nature and origins of these and other bones, Georges Cuvier announced what became the scientific consensus: life on earth died

67. (Livio 2009) 252
68. (Kolbert 2014) 25

out and species became extinct.[69] *The Sixth Extinction* by Elizabeth Kolbert summarizes five times in the past history of this planet when life came close to being wiped out. Worst was the partial extinction of life at the end of the Permian period, 252 million years ago, when something like ninety percent of all species of life on earth were eliminated. It happened very quickly in geological terms, perhaps less than one hundred thousand to two hundred thousand years. We don't know exactly why it happened. We do know it had something to do with global warming. There was a massive release of carbon dioxide into the air, the oceans became as much as eighteen degrees hotter and turned acid. And the amount of bacteria producing poisonous hydrogen sulfide into the water exploded in number.[70]

Each past partial extinction of life has a different, often only partially understood origin. The easiest one to explain before the present happened over fifty million years ago. A huge asteroid slammed into the Yucatan Peninsula in Mexico, leaving a crater a hundred miles wide and blasting dust into the air, blocking sunlight and causing a winter lasting several years. The most famous victims were the dinosaurs, all of whom died out.[71] And there have been lesser crises, such as a series of ice ages thousands of years ago, that forced life forms to migrate south before expanding glaciers, and then north when the planet warmed up again.[72]

But the most relevant extinction, the sixth one happening right now, is the only one totally caused by human beings, by us, as we mess up the incredibly complex, subtle, and often little understood arrangements by which our planet sustains its millions and millions of life forms. It is estimated that one third to one half of all amphibians, a quarter of all mammals, a fifth of all reptiles, and a sixth of all birds are headed toward extinction.[73]

Al Gore has summarized ways in which the evolution of human power now imperils the fundamental natural resources necessary for life.[74] To pick only a few examples, ground water accounts for around thirty percent of all fresh water in the world, surface fresh water only about one percent. Ground water depletion has doubled since 1960, and is now accelerating much faster. The diversion of ground water to biofuels and energy extrac-

69. (Kolbert 2014) 30
70. (Kolbert 2014) 103–104
71. (Kolbert 2014) 80–81, 87
72. (Kolbert 2014) 60–61
73. (Kolbert 2014) 17
74. (Gore 2013) 164

tion make matters worse. Crises and conflicts for food production and safe drinking water are increasing around the world. Many of the great rivers of the world "no longer reach the sea: the Colorado, the Indus, the Nile, the Rio Grande, the Murray-Darling in Australia, the Yangtze and Yellow Rivers in China, and the Elbe in Germany."[75]

"Almost one third of the arable land on earth" suffers from topsoil and consequent productivity loss. "Without urgent action, the majority of the Earth's topsoil could be severely degraded or lost before the end of this century."[76]

Irregular atmospheric circulation around the world is creating chaotic weather patterns in temperate latitudes and "consistent drought patterns further south with expanding deserts—deserted by people." These areas are already suffering from increasing water shortages. "Higher greenhouse gas emissions are predicted to bring almost unimaginable deep and prolonged drought conditions to a wide swath of highly populated and agriculturally productive regions, including all of southern and south-central Europe, the Balkans, Turkey, the southern cone of Africa, much of Patagonia, the populated southeastern portion of Australia, the American Southwest and a large portion of the upper Midwest, most of Mexico and Central America, Venezuela and much of the northern Amazon Basin, and significant portions of Central Asia and China."[77]

"Climate experts" demonstrate clearly "that there has been up to a 100-fold increase in extreme high temperatures in recent years compared to earlier decades."[78] Oceans are now "more acidic than at any time in the last 55 million years—and the rate of acidification is faster than at any time in the last 300 million years."[79] In addition to acidification, dynamite fishing, bottom trawling, and agricultural runoffs contribute to disappearing ocean habitats like coral reefs, mango forests, and sea grass meadows. Large algae blooms and huge dead zones full of garbage without life in the oceans and mouths of rivers result because of oxygen depletion.[80]

And of course, because of the melting of polar ice, sea levels rise. Half of the world's people live within fifteen miles of the ocean. James Hansen,

75. (Gore 2013) 165–166

76. (Gore 2013) 183

77. (Gore 2013) 307, 304

78. (Gore 2013) 293

79. (Gore 2013) 300

80. (Gore 2013) 301–302

a leading expert on climate change, predicts a "multi-meter" sea-level rise in this century.[81]

We may now be entering what is called the Sixth Great Extinction, the only one caused not by natural events but, as E.O. Wilson wrote, "Precipitated entirely by man."[82] These few examples and the disappearance of forests described earlier are evidences of the evolution of human mental capabilities. Human choices may now have to make another advance from choosing from narrow self-interest to choosing for the whole earth human community—for the sake of both our invasive species and its ecosystem. We may not need another area of the brain stacked on top of what we already have to do that. Perhaps we have all the brain power and platform we need. We even have specialized parts of the brain such as mirror neurons, described earlier, which are especially suited to that advance. In addition, we developed spiritual knowing two thousand years ago that is elegantly suited to awareness of and care for the whole. Whether we will do that—for the sake of the whole earth community, and whether we will do it in time—is the central question.

SUMMARY

What does science know about the universe?

- It is incredibly vast—infinite at the largest, mystery at the smallest, and it has a beginning.

- It is an ocean of fields—information-rich, non-material environments, within which matter arises and passes away.

- It is self-organizing, giving rise to complex systems in which the whole creates simple parts which themselves create the whole.

- Simple identical parts do not behave identically, and there is no way to predict or control which part will act one way and which part will act another way.

- The universe is growing in every way, in complexity, in the complexity of its systems, in size.

- In the brain, meditation changes neurons, and neurons make meditation possible.

81. (Gore 2013) 298
82. (Gore 2013) 143, 339

- Emerging mind in the present and future may shape what happened in the past that creates the present.

We humans are able to choose how we remember the past, intend our future, and act in the present. Amazingly, our observations help shape reality, even what happened in the past. We may be now at a tipping point in evolution, given the ecological damage we have inflicted on the planet.

We know an amazing amount about the eternal and unchanging ways things work—except that maybe they are *not* unchanging and eternal. "Our knowledge is tiny, our ignorance is vast" (David Deutsch). "Not only is the universe stranger than we imagine, it is stranger than we *can* imagine."[83]

83. Attributed variously to Sir Arthur Stanley Eddington, J. B. S. Haldane, Werner Heisenberg, and Sir James Jeans

CHAPTER EIGHT

SPIRITUAL KNOWING IN OUR EVOLVING UNIVERSE

It is no longer I who lives, but Christ who lives in me.

—GALATIANS 2:19

In the self-organizing universe described in scientific cosmology, fundamental laws of transformation are the same everywhere in the universe,
and the universe evolves over time. These laws constitute fields—mathematically described, information-rich, non-material environments—within which material interactions pass in and out of existence. In the course of
evolution, complex systems come into being, most recently with the emergence of human beings capable of mental representations. The double-slit
quantum experiment demonstrates that human observer-participancy
actually helps shape physical reality, even in the far past. As physicist John
Archibald Wheeler, quoted in the last chapter, put it, "Physics gives rise
to observer-participancy, observer-participancy gives rise to information,
information gives rise to physics."[1]

In chapters five and six, we described mindfulness meditation in the
context of brain-mind research, followed by experiences of spiritual knowing in silence, ritual, and vision. Now we explore spiritual knowing in the
extended world and universe around us building on the platform of scientific cosmology.

What is the experience of spiritual knowing in the extended universe?
William James, in his classic *Varieties of Religious Experience*, reports

1. (Davies 2007) 249

personal experiences of "cosmic consciousness."[2] People sometimes report breathtaking sunsets in which the separate self momentarily melts away into a larger vision of nature or reality. I remember at an early age, perhaps five or six, outside on a summer day, immersed in an inchoate serene sense of undifferentiated presence. Since my family did not attend church regularly, and religion was assumed but not talked about in our home, I had no language for such an experience, and I was too young to try to put words to it anyway. I do remember at about the same age, although never mentioned to anyone, being terrified wondering what was outside the universe. I still do not have adequate words to describe experiencing the unbounded whole of reality, including everything, even me. Sigmund Freud explained the oceanic feeling of early infancy, but it did not adequately match what I knew. I since have had occasional experiences like that throughout my life. My parents owned cottages on various lakes in northern Idaho when I was growing up. I remember being cool from swimming and warm from the sun lying on a deck on the lake gently rocking from the waves. In the spring, the water level was two or three feet higher up around the trunks of trees along the shore, allowing me to poke my little row boat among them, searching for some unspecified origin or beginning. As a young adult I explored the sources of various rivers, and once found a little stream of water trickling out of the ground that was the source of the Susquehanna River which empties into the Chesapeake Bay. On occasion, resting on the beach, I am immersed in the late afternoon sun pouring countless tiny epiphanies of light on the still surface of the bay. Is there a sturdy scientific or mathematical platform for this undifferentiated presence or relationship between human and cosmic I-Thou, between wholeness itself and specific manifestations of wholeness in I-Thou relationships in the ultimate field of love?

Specifically, how does human observer-participancy actually participate in the physical evolution of the world? Modern physics has removed the old dichotomy that science has to do with real matter, while spirituality and religion are about immaterial or ethereal concerns. Sir Arthur Eddington dated the change to around 1927, when quantum physics saw the "final overthrow of strict causality by Heisenberg, Bohr, Born, and others."[3] Science only creates mathematical idealizations of experience. Werner

---

2. (Ehrenreich 2014) 218

3. (Eddington 1985) 204

Heisenberg wrote, it "has nothing to do with immediate experiences."[4] Eddington defined what physical science can do: "whenever we state the properties of a body in terms of physical quantities we are imparting knowledge as to the response of various material indicators to its presence, *and nothing more*."[5] (Italics in the original.) Ken Wilber comments, "Whereas classical physics was theoretically *hostile* to religion, modern physics is simply *indifferent* to it . . . Physics cannot help you in the least, but it no longer objects to your efforts . . . What more could one possibly want?"[6]

Some writers on science and religion take advantage of the new situation to draw analogies between mathematical idealizations and spiritual realities. For example, theoretical physicist and Anglican priest John Polkinghorne describes bursts of light and other subatomic phenomena that behave sometimes like waves and sometimes like particles of matter. That's just the way it is; the wave/particle duality cannot be resolved into one or the other. It is the necessary outcome of recognized experiments, and it doesn't make sense or correspond to anything else in our common human experience. In the same way, the divine/human nature of Jesus Christ is revealed in the resurrection and the empty tomb. The resurrection doesn't make sense or correspond to anything else in our common human experience. And it is the truth, the reality of God's love manifest for us and for the world.[7]

Others draw looser analogies, or even claim that physical science now supports spiritual doctrines and explanations. Eddington wrote in exasperation that, "I repudiate the idea of proving the distinctive beliefs of religion either from the data of physical science or by the methods of physical science."[8]

FRACTALS OF WHOLENESS

In Chapter One we pointed out that human discoveries, in both scientific and spiritual knowing, rest on two legs: experience or observation; and explanation or theory. Are there credible mathematical idealizations or mental representations from modern physics that offer reasonable explanations for

4. (Heisenberg 1985) 40

5. (Eddington 1984) 170

6. (Wilber 1984) 169–170

7. (Polkinghorne 2007) 24, 66–67

8. (Eddington 1984) 168

spiritual experiences such as cosmic consciousness, and the great insights of world religions from the Axial Age? The mathematical and geometric ideas of fractals present perhaps the best opportunities.

In the last chapter we described the universe as an ocean of fields. Fields are mathematically described, information-rich non-material environments within which material interactions arise and pass away. Fields in the universe manifest greater complexity over the course of evolution. Life and other complex systems come into being. Human beings emerge, who in observing physical reality, actually participate in shaping physical reality, even the past. Human beings can be understood as fractals of ultimate fields described in Axial Age insights as unlimited awareness and unconditional love. In the Judeo-Christian tradition human beings are created in the image of God, fractals of those ultimate fields. Fields of creating are called "God the Creator," fields of unconditional love are called "God the Redeemer," and fields of undifferentiated presence are called "God the Holy Spirit."

Human fractals touch or meet ultimate fields in I-Thou relationships. Experiences of I-Thou relationships are called by various names in scientific and spiritual knowing. They have been described here as observer-participancy, mindfulness meditation or *vipassana*, silence, ritual, and vision. The transpersonal psychologist Jorge Ferrer wrote that human fractal participation in ultimate fields can "invoke every aspect of human nature, from somatic transfiguration to the awakening of the heart, to erotic communion to visionary cocreation [*sic*] and from contemplative knowing to moral insight."[9]

In chaos theory, the relationship between wholes and parts of wholes is described by fractals. Fractals are the geometry or embodiment of chaos. Fractals are self-similar. The bifurcations in the orbit diagram in chaos theory look like trees in winter; each smaller branching looks like the larger branching that precedes it. They are self-similar. For another example, if I take four square blocks, each two inches wide, and put them together in a larger square, each block is a fractal, self-similar to the larger square. The two-inch width of each individual square block multiplied by itself—2x2, or 22—equals four inches, the width of the larger square. Now there is a fractal with a magnitude of two; that is, the larger square is self-similar to the smaller square, and larger by a power or magnitude of two.

9. (Ferrer 2002) 12

True fractals, as mathematical entities, are scale-free; they can exist at any number of magnitudes. But they have amazing applications in the real world at a large number of magnitudes even when they are not exactly or perfectly self-similar. For instance, the coast of Norway is filled with jagged fjords. Using a technique called box counting, we can overlay a grid on the coastline, count how many boxes in the grid touch the coastline, change the size of the boxes in a grid by some magnitude, and again see that there are fractals of the larger coastline. One nice thing about chaos theory is its indifference to details and its emphasis, literally, instead, on the larger picture.

One example of fractals as self-similar distributions or fractal dimensions at different scales is astonishing. It is about the unity of life on the earth and wonderfully symbolizes the interconnections of the great web of life. The metabolic rates or energy needs of living beings in relation to their body mass are self-similar or fractals over twenty-seven orders of magnitude, from subcellular molecules to elephants, and including humans along the way. This is one of the most comprehensive laws in all of science. It depends on the fractals at different magnitudes of scale that can most efficiently circulate nutrients to all parts of the body, such as the blood circulatory system. The self-similarities also hold for life expectancy, and the intervals between heartbeats and breaths in relation to size, and also determine the size of the smallest possible mammal. Whether we are a vole weighing a few grams, a human being, or an elephant, we can expect to live for about one and a half billion heartbeats and about 300,000 breaths. In art, even Jackson Pollock's paintings have been shown to reveal rough fractals—smaller ones in the scattering characteristics of paint, and larger ones in his technique of intentionally leaning off balance to drip or throw the paint.[10]

In spiritual knowing, "I"'s meeting "Thou"'s are fractals of wholeness. As mentioned earlier, the key insight of classical Hinduism developed in the Axial age is that Atman is Brahman—the true self is a fractal of ultimate reality. In the carefully argued insights of Mahayana Buddhism in the Diamond Sutra, there is no separate self or indeed any being, only fractals of unlimited awareness or emptiness. Ken Wilber's highest stage of spiritual growth, the causal stage, is a fractal of unlimited awareness. The ancient hermetic insight is "as above, so below"; we are fractals of the whole. Paul's version of the fractal of spiritual knowing is being "in Christ," using the terms God, Spirit, and Christ interchangeably. In Romans 8:9 he writes,

10. (Strogatz 2008) 58–83

"But you are not in the flesh: you are in the Spirit, since the Spirit of God dwells in you." In Galatians 2: 19–20 he adds, "For through the law I died to the law, so that I might live to God. I have been crucified with Christ; and it is no longer I who live, but it is Christ who lives in me. And the life I now live in the flesh I live by faith in the Son of God who loved me and gave himself for me."

Can spiritual knowing be a thing in time and space? The nineteenth-century Christian hymn sings "On this rock I stand, all else is sinking sand." The Abrahamic religions—Judaism, Christianity, Islam—are tethered to texts, sacred scriptures endlessly translated and reinterpreted, but always held as the foundation of the faith and tradition. And there are countless statues, paintings, images of the Buddha.

But essentially, the center of spiritual knowing is not a thing, cannot be a thing, cannot even be a center located in time or space or human thought. If it has to be named: It is wholeness itself, like our expanding universe, whose center is everywhere and whose circumference is nowhere. But there is a relationship between wholeness and any particular manifestation of it. Toward the ending of the first chapter of the first book in the Hebrew Scripture, Genesis points to it. "Gods (*Elohim* in Hebrew, a masculine *plural* noun) said, let us make humankind (*Adam* in Hebrew, meaning the ruddy one) in our image (the only time the Hebrew word is used in Scripture), according to our likeness." (Gen. 1:26) "I"s are fractals of the ultimate Thou of Spirit in spiritual knowing, created in the image and likeness of ultimate Thou.

In the Christian tradition, that is expressed in the Trinity. The Trinity is a central idea in the Christian tradition. It is the framework for the Nicene Creed and the Apostles Creed, disdained by Muslims, and discussed and argued over by Christian theologians over the centuries. It can be understood as describing the three major fractals of wholeness in spiritual knowing.

Fractal of Creating

In Chapter One we described the human fractal of creating. Alan Arkin taught workshops in improvisational creativity, where participants came to recognize that in relationship, perhaps even in their devotion to their craft, they create something new—a spontaneous dance, song, or other performance. It did not exist before it arose in that relationship; it was created anew in that artistic expression. Mihaly Csikszentmihaly's research discovered *flow*—"a sense of participation in determining the content of life"—creating that which was not there before. Robert Fritz taught workshops on creativity, the ability to "bring what they imagine into reality." Annie Dillard described the process of loving an inchoate vision into an actual book or painting or other art form.

Human creating is not limited only to personal experiences or even making art. It changes things in the world. The amazing advances of science and technology testify to that. The double-slit quantum experiment demonstrated in physical reality how observation in the present helps create the behavior and reality of physical subatomic particles in the past. The physicist John Archibald Wheeler uses the wonderful term "observer-participancy." Human mind observing physical reality participates in creating and bringing it into existence. Evolving mind in the emerging future draws the physical past into being. The scientifically described self-organizing universe summarized earlier creates complexity, autopoiesis, and new possibilities becoming physical reality. Human mind emerges in evolution. Emerging mind observes and so participates in bringing physical reality into existence—it draws, pulls, and reaches infinitely into a yet unknown future. Improvisation in relationship, creating a material actuality from an intangible vision, creating in the flow of devotion: all exemplify human creativity as fractals of the ultimate field of the whole creating. In the book of Job, that field of ultimate reality challenges Job to recognize his own fractal reality. When he does, he "sees God," recognizing his own fractal kinship, his I-Thou relationship with the whole. He is a fractal of the infinite changing dynamic field of the whole, which Christians call creating or creator God.

As said before, spiritual knowing is about reaching down into the centerless center before the world begins, before form and words and specific emotions and images are fixed and material. Spiritual knowing is ultimately about being there in the eternal moment of creation, when the morning stars sing together and all the heavenly beings shout for joy, as God reminds Job. Creating is the human fractal of wholeness, called the first person of the Trinity in the Christian tradition.

Fractal of Loving

The second fractal of Trinitarian spiritual knowing is love. Jesus explicitly contrasts it with the Mosaic Law in Hebrew Scripture. In Leviticus 19:1–2, "The Lord spoke to Moses, saying: 'Speak to all the congregations of the people of Israel and say to them: You shall be holy, for I the lord your God am holy,.' *Kadosh*, the Hebrew word for holy, means clean, set apart, purified in obedience to the law. In the gospel of Luke, in what seems to be an intentional contrast, Jesus says, "But love your enemies, do good and lend, expecting nothing in return. Your reward will be great, and you will be children of the Most High, for he is kind to the ungrateful and the wicked. Be merciful, just as your Father is merciful" (Luke 6:35–36). The Greek word translated as merciful here is *oiktirmon*. In the singular it means womb, in the plural compassion, with the connotations of the nurturing compassion of the womb, giving life, giving birth. Jesus illustrates the teaching with the story of the "good" Samaritan. Samaritans lived in Samaria, now the West Bank. Jews and Samaritans were cousins. They had a common lineage and fought like cousins. Jews claimed Samaritans were not descended from Abraham, Isaac, and Jacob as they were. Samaritans did not look for a Messiah in the line of David, but one like Moses. When Jews had a chance, they destroyed the Samaritan worship center at Gerizim, and when Samaritans had a chance, they wrecked the Jewish temple in Jerusalem.

A lawyer talks with Jesus. "Teacher," he asks, "what must I do to inherit eternal life"? Jesus, in response, tells the classic story of the man beaten, robbed and left by the roadside. Religious professionals pass by without stopping. They are on their way to perform their sacred duties, and touching a man who might die on their hands would render them unclean and therefore unable to do so. But a Samaritan, of the despised cousins of Jews, stops and renders heartfelt and effective aid. Jesus ends the story thus, "Who was a neighbor to the man who fell into the hands of robbers?" Not, "what groups or reasons fall into the category of neighbor," as perhaps the legal-minded attorney would have wanted, but who *was* neighborly (*plesion* in Greek), came close, acted like a neighbor, to the wounded man? The legal expert is trapped. He can only respond, "The one who acted like a neighbor." "Go and do the same," Jesus tells him (see Luke 10:25–37).

The second part of Jesus great commandment, "love your neighbor as yourself," lacks any definition of who counts as neighbor. There is only neighborliness without barriers, restrictions, or limits—unconditional love. It can be a simple heartfelt act of vulnerability to another.

Sue Monk Kidd tells about trying to fly out of Atlanta one night when the whole airport was closed and the city in the grip of an ice storm. She calls her brother-in-law out in the suburbs to find a place to stay. He tells her to take the train out to him and that he would try to get out in the storm and come pick her up. It's a long train ride. People keep getting off, and finally there are only three people left. She writes, "A middle aged woman sits across from me. I look at her for the first time and notice that she is crying. As she wipes tears with the back of her hand, her gaze lingers on my face. A look full of ache and searching. She's asking for my attention. . . . I feel sad for her, but what can I do? I look away from her, retreating into the murmur of the train. Quietly, uncomfortably unavailable."[11] But she can't get the memory of the woman's face or the shame of her own withdrawal out of her mind in the next few days. She even dreams about the woman. She wants with all her heart to be able to live the train ride over again, but of course it's past, and she cannot. Finally, she comes to realize from her dream that she couldn't, nor did the woman want her to fix the pain, all she needed to do was to be available and present to the woman with her heart—to see her with her look, her gesture, her words.

D.W. Winnicott emphasized the "mirror-role of the mother,"[12] seeing children—validating their experience—when they come to us with joy, anger, need, self-discovery. Seeing them with our eyes, our hugs, our words. Simply seeing them. But the fact of the matter is, we often are so full of undigested experiences, ideas, things to do, whatever, that there is no space in our mind and our heart for seeing another—or for that matter, seeing ourselves. That's why we so desperately need meditation to give ourselves the time to clear out, to be alone, to assimilate, to muse and reflect, to just rest and be.

For Kidd, meditation in "solitude brings me back to a simplicity of spirit, an inner poverty that I need in order to clear room inside. It allows me to empty myself out, so there is gracious space within where I can receive myself, then God, and eventually others." She writes that it will teach you everything you need to know about living the spiritual life. "It will teach you how to die to ego and the patterns that keep your heart walled up, to those things inside that prevent you from planting your heart in the world."[13]

11. (Kidd 2006) 47–49
12. (Davis 1981) 121
13. (Kidd 2006) 88, 90

Loving because we are like God has to do with the heart—our heart. There are times—we all know what they are or were for us—when we are taken out of ourselves, when we no longer care or know who we are, because we are so enthralled with another, so in love with another. This is not infatuation, or the first stages of romantic love here, but something more universal and essential. Whenever and however we love another—a child, a spouse, a dear friend, a cause for justice and making the world a better place—without regard or thought for ourselves, we are loving as God loves. And at times we may even love like the eternal unconditional love of God for everything, that is, the whole creation. In the Christian tradition, Jesus Christ is the paradigmatic fractal or incarnation of the love, who "makes [the] sun rise on the evil and on the good, and sends rain on the righteous and on the unrighteous" (Matt. 5:45) and who "though in the form of God, did not regard equality with God as something to be grasped, but self-emptied . . . even to death." (Phil 2:6–8). Paul tells us that we are to have that same mind in us. And when we do, we are a fractal of the love of God the redeemer, the second person of the Trinity: in Christ, like Christ.

Buddhists practice developing compassion through *metta*. The root meanings of the word are "gentle" and "friend." Its purpose is lovingkindness—"to reteach a thing its loveliness," embracing all parts of ourselves and embracing all parts of the world. It is meant to be an antidote to fear and separation. It involves *karuna*—compassion for the suffering of others; *mudita*—joy in the joy of others; and *uppekha*—the equanimity that results from practicing *metta* in all of its aspects. One starts by befriending oneself, discovering one's original face and wishing for oneself freedom from danger, mental well-being, physical well-being, and ease of being in daily life. Then, as one is able, one extends that same lovingkindness to a benefactor, a friend, a neutral person, and finally, as one is able, to a "difficult" person or enemy.[14]

Tonglen, another Buddhist practice, extends compassion further. On the in-breath one draws into one's own heart suffering in the world, perhaps experienced as a dark cloud or vapor. In the depths of the heart, that suffering meets one's own darkness, suffering and lack of wholeness. The two meet and cancel each other, and from the heart, light and wholeness breathe out into the world.[15]

14. (Salzberg 1995)

15. (Chodron 2001)

The human fractal of boundless depth and breadth of compassion is expressed in a poem called "Please Call Me by True Names," written by the Vietnamese Buddhist monk Thich Nhat Hahn in 1978, and first read at a retreat in Kosmos Center in Amsterdam with Daniel Berrigan.

Don't say that I will depart tomorrow—
Even today I am still arriving.
Look deeply: every second I am arriving
To be a bud on a spring branch,
To be a tiny bird, with still fragile wings,
Learning to sing in my new nest,
To be a caterpillar in the heart of a flower,
To be a jewel hiding itself in a stone.

I still arrive, in order to laugh and to cry,
To fear and to hope.
The rhythm of my heart is the birth and death
Of all that is alive.
I am a mayfly metamorphosing
On the surface of a river.
And I am the bird
That swoops down to swallow the mayfly.

I am a frog swimming happily
In the clear water of a pond.
And I am the grass snake
That silently feeds itself on the frog.

I am a child in Uganda, all skin and bones,
My legs as thin as bamboo sticks.
And I am the arms merchant,
Selling deadly weapons to Uganda.

I am the twelve year old girl,
Refugee on a small boat,
Who throws herself into the ocean
After being raped by a sea pirate.
And I am the pirate,
My heart not yet capable
Of seeing and loving.

I am a member of the politburo.
With plenty of power in my hands.
And I am the man who has to pay
His "debt of blood" to my people,

Dying slowly in a forced labor camp.

My joy is like Spring, so warm
It makes flowers bloom all over the Earth.
My pain is like a river of tears,
So vast it fills the four oceans.

Please call me by my true names,
So I can hear all my cries and laughter at once,
So I can see my joy and pain are one.

Please call me by my true names,
So I can wake up
And the door of my heart
Could be left open,
The door of compassion.[16]

The vision of compassion at the heart of spiritual knowing is very much alive in our world. Karen Armstrong proposed a contemporary version of the Golden Rule around the world, in 2009, called a "Charter for Compassion." At the time of her writing it had been launched in sixty different locations around the world, and more than 150 partners are working together to apply it in "practical realistic action." Here is the charter in full:

> The principle of compassion lies at the heart of all religious, ethical and spiritual traditions, calling us always to treat all others as we wish to be treated ourselves.
>
> Compassion impels us to work tirelessly to alleviate the suffering of our fellow creatures, to dethrone ourselves from the centre of our world and put another there, and to honour the inviolable sanctity of every single human being, treating everybody, without exception, with absolute justice, equity and respect.
>
> It is also necessary in both public and private life to refrain consistently and empathically from inflicting pain. To act or speak violently out of spite, chauvinism or self-interest, to impoverish, exploit or deny basic rights to anybody, and to incite hatred by denigrating others—even our enemies—is a denial of our common humanity. We acknowledge that we have failed to live compassionately and that some have even increased the sum of human misery in the name of religion.
>
> We therefore call upon all men and women
> To restore compassion to the centre of morality and religion;

16. (Thich Nhat Hanh 1999)72

To return to the ancient principle that any interpretation of scripture that breeds violence, hatred or disdain is illegitimate;

To ensure that youth are given accurate and respectful information about other traditions, religions and cultures;

To encourage a positive appreciation of cultural and religious diversity;

To cultivate an informed empathy with the suffering of all human beings—even those regarded as enemies.

We urgently need to make compassion a clear, luminous and dynamic force in our polarized world. Rooted in a principled determination to transcend selfishness, compassion can break down political, dogmatic, ideological and religious boundaries. Born of our deep interdependence, compassion is essential to human relationships and to a fulfilled humanity. It is the path to enlightenment, and indispensable to the creation of a just economy and a peaceful global community.[17]

Fractal of Presence

Unbounded presence is the fractal of Holy Spirit, the third dimension of spiritual knowing in the Trinity. The universal constant of deep spiritual knowing is the loss of separation between subject and object, separate self and ultimate reality. The separateness of the fractal "I" disappears into its immediate connection, immersion and identity with the ultimate "Thou" of all that is. Moses knows Yahweh simply as "I Am." Mystery—being itself, transcending definition, transcending separation—touches down in the specific reality of the Hebrew people, their ancestors, and their present crisis. Traditional ascetical Christian theology progresses through the stages of purgation and illumination to union without separation. More precise Buddhist thought replaces union or "one" with "non-dual," since even one implies a "not one"—a distinction that disappears as the fractal "I" realizes its true identity, *anatta*/no-self.

Radical unlimited awareness is no longer limited even by language. It encompasses all reality. It is awareness of everything at once. *Sunyata*— emptiness—is not different from fullness. Like the cloudless blue sky of the high Tibetan plateau, "you should look at your own mind and see if it is like that." Its twin, its inseparable partner unconditional love, is also without boundaries, without limitations, and it happens here and now. Ken

17. (Armstrong 2011) 6–8

Wilber's final causal stage of spiritual knowing describes the human fractal losing its separate definition, even as dispassionate witness, as it simply disappears into reality. He describes: "The strangest thing happens . . . the seer vanishes into everything seen, which sees itself eternally. I no longer witness the clouds, I am the clouds; I do not hear the rain, I am the rain; I can no longer touch the earth, for I am the earth . . . precisely because I am not this, not that, I am fully this, fully that. Beyond nature, I am nature; beyond God, I am God; beyond the Kosmos altogether, I am the Kosmos in its every gesture."

Thomas Keating puts it this way in the movie *One*: "There are three steps. Step one: There is an Other. Step two: I seek to become one with the Other. Step three: There is no other."

Mental representations melt away into utterly simple, undifferentiated presence, in the fractal of the Holy Spirit. There is equanimity—quiet sustaining joy—underneath specific emotions. There are no longer distinctions, separations, and divisions between subject and object, self and other, human and divine, spirit and matter, fullness and emptiness, inside and outside, this and that, or not this and not that. There is simply the ultimate reality of utterly simple, pure, undifferentiated presence.

SUMMARY

Scientific cosmology describes a self-organizing universe of fields with fractals. Fractals are self-similar embodiments of fields. In spiritual knowing, in the Christian Trinitarian tradition, we humans are fractals of ultimate reality, in creating, loving, and undifferentiated presence.

CHAPTER NINE

MYSTERY

I think I can safely say that nobody understands quantum mechanics.
—RICHARD FEYNMAN[1]

We have described differences and similarities between spiritual knowing and scientific knowing—or, as we have also referred to them, I-thou relationships and I-it transactions. We have traced their history and present manifestations. That background enabled us to describe their interactions in brain mind research and meditation; and in fields and fractals in the universe. In these descriptions and interactions we have come up against infinity and open-ended mystery time and again.

In this final chapter, we need to own up to mystery: our ultimate not-knowing in the face of death. We described earlier the collapse of collective mental representations at the beginning of the Axial Age in the realization that we are separate individuals who will die. Now we will look at various ways we try to find an answer to fend off that realization; and finally, we will look at the epiphany/mystery of ultimate reality in this present moment.

"DUNNO" MIND

Richard Feynman is the sort of quirky and idiosyncratic genius the rest of us ordinary mortals cannot even comprehend. He won the Nobel Prize in

1. (Feynman 1965) 129

1965 for his contributions to quantum physics, especially quantum elec-trodynamics. He developed the Feynman diagrams for understanding the behavior of subatomic particles, and helped develop the atom bomb. His hobbies include picking locks, decoding Mayan hieroglyphs, and playing the bongo drums.

Many years ago he taught at the California Institute of Technology, where a friend of mine also taught in such a junior position that Feynman never knew him. My friend had managed to bring the theologian Paul Til-lich to lecture at the campus. It turned out that Feynman also attended the lecture, and my friend happened to be sitting near him. After about an hour, Feynman stood up, said to the person sitting next to him, "Well, he doesn't know anything either," and left.

For many years my friend was stung by the incident and Feynman's perceived arrogance, but recently he has been re-reading some of Feyn-man's lectures at Cal Tech, and realized that he was in fact paying Tillich a compliment. He said of Tillich what he has also said of himself: I don't know anything, either. Feynman's comments about not knowing are certainly not naïve, ignorant, nor a simple inability to understand the complexities of physics. They are the wry reflections of a brilliant mind contemplating the vast, strange, even unimaginably open course and quest of science. We have called it infinite reach.

How do you recognize spiritual knowing? When you don't know anything. When you approach life and every moment as if it were the be-ginning of the world—as if nothing was known beforehand about this mo-ment, and as if curiosity, openness, and compassion simply overwhelmed any certainty and assumptions about what is before you or what will hap-pen next—then you are open to seeing life and each moment as it really is, and perhaps in a way no one else has ever quite seen it.

Some decades ago I had the opportunity to meditate under the guid-ance of a well-known Korean Rinzai Zen Buddhist teacher. The essence of his teaching, repeated many times, was the phrase "don't know mind," or as he said, "dunno mind." In meditation we were to manifest "dunno mind" not judging, anticipating the future: nor regretting, hanging on to the past; nor thinking, analyzing, controlling in the present. We were to stay in "dunno mind," open to the inexhaustible riches of the present mo-ment transcending prior expectations and even thinking. Like Feynman's comments, the Buddhist teacher's "dunno mind" does not reflect a begin-ner's ignorant inability to understand his subject, in this case the intricate complexities and life-long disciplines of meditation. It is instead an invitation to explore even more deeply the vast, strange even unimaginably open course and quest of spiritual realization. We have called it infinite reach.

Thomas Merton prays in "dunno mind":

> My Lord God, I have no idea where I am going. I do not see the road ahead of me. I cannot know for certain where it will end. Nor do I really know myself, and the fact that I think I am following your will does not mean that I am actually doing so. But I believe that the desire to please you does in fact please you. And I hope I have that desire in all that I am doing. I hope that I will never do anything apart from that desire. And I know that if I do this you will lead me by the right road though I may know nothing about it. Therefore I will trust you always though I may seem to be lost and in the shadow of death. I will not fear, for you are ever with me and you will never leave me to face my perils alone.[2]

FACING DEATH

If the pinnacle and highest achievement of spiritual and perhaps even scientific knowing, *a la* Feynman, is not to know, what is the essence of that not-knowing? Throughout history and still with us is the one constant and universal limitation of the human condition and the origin of the central Axial Age insights: the intractability of death. Beneath all the other issues of human knowing is the one fundamental frustration of the human condition: We will all die. We, and everyone we know and love, will die. According to some sociological research, when the first child in the family born after my death dies, even all personal memory of me will be gone.

It is the center and starting point of the world's great religions from the Axial Age. The Buddha's famous fire sermon to a thousand *bikkhus* or monks begins, "Monks, all is burning. And what is the all that is burning? The eye is burning, forms are burning, eye-consciousness is burning, eye-contact is burning, and whatever feeling arises via the eye—whether pleasant or painful or neither-painful-nor-pleasant—that too is burning." And so on to birth, aging and death, to ear, to nose, to body, to mind, whatever feeling—all is burning.[3]

---

2. (Cunningham 1992)243

3. (Buddha 2012)9

Jesus announces "quite openly" to his disciples that their rabbi and teacher "must undergo great suffering . . . and be killed." Peter understandably protests; Jesus rebukes him as harshly as we imagine he could, "Get behind me, Satan!" (Mark 8: 31–33).

Not just physical death but all forms of the failure of our essential identity and well-being, so severe they seem equivalent to death, are included here: tragic loss, misfortune, sickness, starvation. It is the first of Buddha's four noble truths: "There is suffering—*dukha*."

All is burning/all life is *dukha*. The word is usually translated as "suffering," but its root meaning is more like "unsatisfactory, awry." Things don't work out just right for us. They are off kilter, somehow. It's true that sometimes we really suffer, undergo terrible losses, misfortunes, tragedies, illness, and death. But often it's just that things don't work out very well, in ordinary life day by day. They don't meet our expectations. There is *dukha* all around.

For Paul, even trying to live a good and virtuous life is death. "I am of the flesh, sold into slavery under sin. I do not understand my own actions. For I don't do what I want, but I do the very thing I hate. . . . For I do not do the good that I want but the evil I do not want is what I do. . . . Wretched man that I am! Who will rescue me from the body of death?" (Romans 7:15, 19, 22).

How can you find an answer to that? How can you find something certain, something true, some security, some assurance that can be counted on, that is permanent, that will not go away? We are religious, spiritual, for practical reasons; we need something, or want something, even if that something is the freedom from wanting or needing something. The history of spiritual knowing and, even in disguised forms, of scientific knowing goes back to seeking an answer, a certainty that will defy and annihilate death.

RESPONSES

The varieties of religious experience include the varieties of seeking some reassurance or answer to fend off death. Those who study those varieties come up against a difficulty that pastors know—there are levels to spiritual knowing. Perhaps pastors especially know the futility of coaxing, persuading, or even trying to coerce persons into a higher stage than they may be capable of. That word "higher" is difficult; it smacks of elitism, spiritual

privilege, of "I know more than you do." But there it is. It won't go away
because it offends us. Essentially, it has to do with the various ways we seek
to stave off the impossible end looming before us.

These various ways of avoiding death roughly correlate with the various stages of spiritual growth described by Fowler, Wilber, and others earlier in Chapter three. They embody different approaches to the full and
complete realization of I-Thou relationships that melt away the ego attachments and death denial of lower stages.

James Fowler describes Stage one, "intuitive-projective faith," as
"characterized by fantasy and fluid thought pattern. It is egocentric and
unrestrained by logical thoughts." A simple term for it is "magic." A few
years ago, the book and DVD titled *The Secret* were very popular. The secret
was that if you affirmed and visualized what you wanted, whatever it was—
from a bicycle to a new dress to five million dollars—you would get it. It
worked like magic. This is one important way of spiritual knowing, through
which millions of people seek secure answers in the face of the pervasive
evidence of death in all of its forms and varieties, including dashing our
fondest desires.

W. H. Auden in his Christmas oratorio "For the Time Being," pictures
a weary Herod despairing over meeting the needs of the fractious people
he rules over:

> Legislation is helpless against the wild prayers of longing that rise,
> day in, day out, from all those households under my protections:
> "O God, put away justice and truth for we cannot understand them
> and do not want them. Eternity would bore us dreadfully. Leave
> thy heavens and come down to our earth. . . . Become our uncle.
> Look after Baby, amuse Grandfather, escort Madam to the Opera,
> help Willy with his homework, introduce Muriel to a handsome
> naval officer. Be interesting and weak like us and we will love you
> as we love ourselves."[4]

Stage two, "mythic-literal faith" for Fowler, has the task of sorting out
what is real from what is make-believe. "Symbols are understood literally.
Main concerns are reciprocal fairness and immanent justice and rules and
works righteousness."

Fundamentalism is an example of literalism. It was first known as an
American Protestant invention in the late nineteenth century by ordinary
church folk reacting against elites in seminaries and denominational offices

4. (Auden 1975)187 "The Massacre of the Innocents"

coming under the influence of the new historical criticism of the Bible, the acceptance of evolution, and the increased prestige of science. The Niagara Bible conference in 1877 announced the Five Points, as proven as any science, which became the fundamentals of fundamentalism: the plenary inspiration and inerrancy of Scripture as a whole and in every word, the deity of Jesus, the virgin birth of Jesus, substitutionary blood atonement, and the bodily resurrection and premillennial second coming of Christ.[5]

Fundamentalism is a worldwide phenomenon also evident among Muslims, Hindus, Buddhists, and other world religions. It is a reaction against scientific and technological advance, rooted in the distress and dislocation of rural peasants who, even into the 1990s, probably constituted the majority of the human race. As they are displaced into urban culture by economic hardship and modern mass communication, they come up against market capitalism and experience rampant selfishness and ruthless disregard for traditional values, relationships, and their common life. Instead of the so-called advantages of capitalism, they see only "wicked middlemen growing rich at the expense of honest, hardworking people like themselves." Fundamentalists selectively retrieve beliefs and practices from a sacred past. They then modify them to create certain meanings to stand against the inroads of modern life and preserve their culture. They "may even aspire to punish unrighteousness and reform society as a whole."[6]

Substitutionary blood atonement, one of the five Christian fundamentals, was developed around nine hundred years ago. A formula was derived from Roman jurisprudence: God's infinite justice requires atonement for the sin of Adam. No finite human being can satisfy that requirement. So God sentences his own son, who is both human and divine, to make adequate atonement through death on a cross.[7] By making it into a formula, the doctrine of substitutionary blood atonement has been around ever since, promising the overcoming of death in eternal life.

For Fowler, stage three, "synthetic-conventional faith," is "a conformist faith that mirrors conventional beliefs" of larger authorities of school, church, and society that offer traditional reassurances in the face of death. "Tacit beliefs and ideology hold that because others are different, they are wrong or inferior."

5. (Fundamentalism 1989)51

6. (Marty 1993)3

7. (Borg 2004)94

One example could be termed "left-out science," and its contemporary version is called "intelligent design." Religious explanations are necessary for left-out sensory phenomena that cannot yet be explained scientifically. The approach goes back at least to the seventeenth century when new scientific discoveries were understood as proof of the existence of "an Intelligent and Knowing Cause."[8] It continues to this day in the attempts of intelligent-design proponents to identify life forms so complex they couldn't possibly be explained by evolution. One candidate for this exception was the eye, which is too complex to have evolved in stages over time. Until that is, intermediate forms were discovered by archaeologists.[9]

Stage four, "individual-reflective faith," is "counter-dependent opposition to authority with keen awareness of social systems and institutions. Demythologizing prevails with personal responsibility for beliefs and commitments . . . [with] over-confidence in the intellect, and insistence on one's own world views as the only valid one." This stage is particularly fitted to the ascendency of science and technology. Ideologies of materialism as the only reality—and atheistic dismissal of any meanings of God, Creator and religious cosmology—are cloaked in enlightenment claims of reason alone. Physical death is the only end of life, and science and technology will advance in time to a complete victory over all the limitations of death. Already there are cryogenics, actual geosynchronous satellites that will continue in orbit as long as the earth does, artificial intelligence that can even now defeat the world's chess champion player and win at Jeopardy, and technological advances that promise indefinitely prolonged life if not actual immortality just yet.

Another possibility is to insist on an empirical reality beyond death and beyond the reach of science. On November 10, 2008 Dr. Eben Alexander III, a widely known and respected neurosurgeon, awoke early with a headache—a bad headache—with pain shooting down his spine and getting worse. He remembers nothing of what happened outside him for the next seven days. But to those around him, from his wife to the finest medical specialists, he was in a deep coma, sliding irrevocably toward death, in spite of everything they could do.[10]

The doctors determined that he had bacterial meningitis from an invasion of E. coli bacteria which usually resides in the gut. Bacterial meningitis

8. (Armstrong 2009)207
9. (Tippett 2010)262–263
10. (Alexander 2012)

is so rare that less than one in 10 million people contract it, usually as a result of surgery. Dr. Alexander had not had surgery. After searching the literature and contacting specialists around the country, they could find no other instance of E. coli bacterial meningitis anywhere, ever. His case was N-1, meaning it was the only one in existence. He was given massive continuous doses of antibiotics, but they made no difference. His higher brain, the neo-cortex responsible for all the functions that make us fully human, was no longer there. It was gone, fatally dead.

The fatality rate from bacterial meningitis begins at ninety percent and reaches one hundred percent after a few days. By the end of the week, the doctors and his family had to face the reality that he was near death. His wife called their older son, away at college, to come home before he died.

That's what was happening in the world outside Dr. Alexander. Inside, he remembers filaments of white-gold light, "like the richest most complex, most beautiful piece of music you've ever heard," then lush green country- side. He was flying over trees and fields; there were children and people full of joy—a beautiful, incredible dream. . . . "Except it wasn't a dream. Though I didn't know where I was or even *what* I was, I was absolutely sure of one thing: this place I'd suddenly found myself in was completely real." Then there was an "explosion of light, color, love and beauty that blew through me like a crashing wave."[11] All his questions are answered immediately— thoughts entering directly into him without language—then, an immense void, totally dark, yet brimming with light. A transparent orb he calls "Om" interpreted to him the presence of Infinite Being, infinite vastness of Cre- ator God, immediately and directly present. He feels born into the universe, a giant cosmic womb. He comes to call this place "the Core."

He learns so many things, insights directly into his being that he never forgets. After a while he begins to slip back into his earlier experience, but finds that by remembering the glorious music, he can rise again to the Gateway and the Core. After more time he begins to see faces, and one especially that is calling him back. It is the face of a boy—his younger son. At that moment, his wife is calling their older son to come home before the funeral. His eyes open, his friend in the room screams, the doctor rushes into the room, sees him thrashing around on the bed, wanting something. Understanding, he removes the breathing tube, and Dr. Alexander speaks his first words in seven days: "Thank you."

11. (Alexander 2012)46

After his recovery, Dr. Alexander came to believe strongly, as a scientist and a doctor, that he had an essential responsibility to tell his experience, to make it known. He was brain-dead, and no medical facts or theories can explain the reality and vividness of his experience without a functioning cortex. In his book *Proof of Heaven: A Neurosurgeon's Journey into the Afterlife*, he is committed, in his words, "to break the back of the last efforts of reductive science to tell the world that the material realm is all that exists, and that consciousness, or spirit—yours and mine—is not the grand and central mystery of life in the universe. I'm living proof."[12] Dr. Alexander is in Stage four—individual-reflective faith—by depending on only empirical evidence, in this case even spiritual experiences.

Stage five, "conjunctive faith," is dialogical, "multi-dimensional, relative and organically interdependent, in which symbolic power is reunited with conceptual meanings." This stage is a qualitative advance beyond the previous ones. Stage five requires reconciling and integrating two methods of knowing separated until now. One, exemplified by scientific knowing, is the use of left brain reason, I-it transactions. The other, spiritual knowing, uses symbols with layers of meaning and connotations which are more fluid and imaginative, also found in earlier stages, and in myth and intuition. Both are now needed, not separately but together.

Eckhart Tolle's books, especially *The Power of Now*, reframe our understanding of death. Our suffering happens because we confuse pain with our attachment to whatever outcomes we insist on. Our suffering is ultimately an invitation to let go of our fear of death. When we face and experience death in whatever form it may come to us—whatever we cling to and insist on as necessary for our existence and well-being—a great light of integration shines and we realize that indeed we are in God, and that there is no death. Even tragic loss can give way to a sacred sense of presence. "It is not the pain-body but identification with it that causes the suffering," Tolle says.[13]

Jack Kornfield, a teacher of Buddhist meditation, has written a book on meditation in the latter part of his career called *The Wise Heart*. He attempts to describe this level of spiritual knowing in words accessible to our left brain reason as well as right-brain wholistic awareness:

> "Your own awareness or consciousness is hard to describe. It doesn't have a color or location. This can feel frustrating and difficult to

12. (Alexander 2012)171
13. (Tolle 2005)56, 183

grasp. But the very transparent, unfixed, yet alive quality of consciousness is its nature, a bit like air around us. If you relax and allow this experience of unfixed knowing, you will discover the clear open sky of awareness. It is empty like space, but unlike space it is living: it knows experience. In its true state, consciousness is simply this knowing—clear, open, awake, without color or form, containing all things, yet not limited by them—unconditioned. Like the sky, all kinds of clouds and weather conditions can appear in it, but they have no effect on the sky itself. Storms may appear or disappear but the sky remains open, limitless unaffected by all that arises. Consciousness is unaffected by experience, just like the sky."[14]

An unlikely example is the experience of Barbara Ehrenreich, a well-known author, especially for her book "Nickel and Dimed" about the difficulties and trials of low wage earners in fast food and retail sales environments, which she experienced first-hand. She has been an atheist all her life. Her father and mother were also militant atheists, as were the rest of her family, who wore their atheism as the badge of their identity.

Her father was an alcoholic, a brilliant and handsome scientist who fought his way up from mining in Butte, Montana to an exalted corporate executive position in California, and who never exempted her from his withering contempt and judgment on who she was and what she said or did. Her mother, also an alcoholic, later became a radical social activist and also subjected Barbara to unrelenting criticism, shame and blame.

Barbara survived all of this with her formidable intellect and relentless ruthless search for what was true and real in spite of what her parents said. She called everything she possibly could into question, seriously entertained the possibility that she was truly alone, the only conscious being in the world. She did all this while she was still a teenager, and carefully kept a journal to record her thoughts.

At the age of fourteen something happened. She is outdoors with her family watching some horses, in the late summer sun. Suddenly, spontaneously, unpredictably, all the arguments, words, and mental representations with which she had tried to understand her world disappeared. In her words,

> "And then it happened. Something peeled off the visible world, taking with it all meaning, influence, associations, labels and words. I was looking at a tree, and if anyone had asked, that's what

14. (Kornfield 2008)38–39

I would have said I was doing, but the word "tree" was gone, along with all the notions of tree-ness that had accumulated in the last dozen or so years, since I had acquired language. The interesting thing, some might say alarming, was that when you take away all human attributes- the words, the names of species, the wisps of remembered tree related poetry, the fables of photosynthesis and capillary action- that when you take all this away, *there is still something left*."[15]

She struggles to understand what happened. Perhaps there was some scientifically described breakdown in mental capabilities. Perhaps she "had gained a privileged glimpse into some alternative realm or dimension."[16] She finally settles on a psychiatric diagnosis- "dissociation"- a general cognitive breakdown sometime associated with schizophrenia.

She continues to have the experience from time to time, gradually fading as she grows older. Once she tries to describe it: "The world flamed into life . . . no vision . . . just this blazing everywhere. Something poured into me and I poured out into it . . . a furious encounter with a living substance that was coming at me through all things at once, and one reason for the terrible wordlessness of the experience is that you cannot observe fire really closely without becoming part of it."[17]

She becomes a scientist, like her father and with her brilliant mind achieves pretty much whatever she wants, in molecular biology, in quantum physics, whatever. Later in life she also becomes a radical social activist, like her mother.

Even though her journal is packed away and unread for decades, she is not altogether content. She gets it that the job of the scientist is "To track down and strangle any notion of nonhuman or superhuman 'agents'- that being the general term for beings that can move or initiate actions of their own."[18] Everything must be considered dead, without any life of its own, for the scientist to study it.

But later on visiting and then living in the Florida Keys, she becomes interested in large animals, like bears, who seem to be "individuals, making minute-by-minute decisions of their own." She watches a flock of Ibises moving through the day and quotes with approval a scientist friend who

---

15. (Ehrenreich 2014) 47–48

16. (Ehrenreich 2014) 52

17. (Ehrenreich 2014) 116

18. (Ehrenreich 2014) 205

says that within certain parameters, "they do pretty much what they damn well please."[19]

Coming toward the present time, two things happen that changes her life. She gets cancer, and her house in the Keys is destroyed in a storm. All her papers, journal articles and notes are now a sodden unreadable mass. Except, that is for the old teenage journal which had been stored in the second floor of the house. She reads it, transcribes it, ponders it, and especially the question her sixteen year old younger self had addressed to her present self, "What have you learned since you wrote this?"[20]

She still occasionally has the extraordinary visions. The "Other," she experiences is something like the early Hebrew experience, not the only "others" around and certainly not the God revealed in Jesus Christ. It is like what the last century theologian Rudolph Otto named the *mysterium trememdum* "a consuming fire . . . gravely disturbing to those persons who will recognize nothing in the divine nature but goodness, gentleness, love and a sort of confidential intimacy." In her own words, "the mass inpouring and outpouring of ecstasy from heaven and back."[21]

This is her answer to her younger sixteen year old self:

> "Ah, you say, this is all in our mind. And you are right to be skeptical, I expect no less. It *is* in my mind; which I have acknowledged from the beginning is a less than perfect instrument. But this is what appears to be the purpose of my mind, and no doubt yours as well, its designated function beyond all the mundane calculations: to condense all the chaos and mystery of the world into a palpable Other or Others, not necessarily because we love it, and certainly not out of any intention to 'worship' it. But because ultimately we may have no choice in this matter. I have the impression, growing out of the experiences chronicled here, that it may be seeking us out."[22]

Finally, in Ken Wilber's highest causal stage of spiritual knowing, beyond Fowler's conjunctive faith, the separate self as knower, observer, or witness disappears into the ultimate I-Thou manifestation of the field of love. Nirvana, the final liberation in Buddhism, literally means "the blowing out of a candle." The Buddha, at the moment of his death, enters

19. (Ehrenreich 2014) 211
20. (Ehrenreich 2014) 235
21. (Ehrenreich 2014) 226
22. (Ehrenreich 2014) 237

paranirvana—beyond life and death, leaving this world and human existence for the last time, never needing to return.

What happens to death? Here is the sum of the Axial Age deconstruction of mental representations. The origin and central application of unlimited awareness and unconditional love is this: transcending the final constraint of death itself frees and liberates. There are so many ways to say this, none of them adequate.

Melodramatic:

> "Look on my works, ye mighty, and despair!"
> Nothing beside remains. Round the decay
> Of that colossal wreck, boundless and bare
> The lone and level sands stretch far away.[23]

Axial Age:

> The unnamable is the eternally real
> Naming is the origin of all particular things
> Free from desire, you realize the mystery,
> Caught in desire, you see only the manifestations.
> Yet mystery and manifestations arise from the same source.
> This source is called darkness, darkness within darkness,
> The gateway to all understanding.[24]

Simple, oh so simple:

Jesus cradles a small child in his arms to the consternation and dismay of the disciples, who have so many more important things to say and to do, to plan and to will.

Just this, just that. Not this, not that. "And a little child shall lead them." (Isaiah 11:6)

An important Dzogchen text in Tibetan Buddhism compares the mind to *Akasha*—the cloudless, empty deep blue sky in the high mountain plateaus of Tibet. Beyond the illusion of a separate self that dies, "your own mind is insubstantial like the empty sky." The text then repeats the refrain again and again, "You should look at your own mind to see whether it is like that."[25]

In the Christian tradition, Paul writes that Christ self-empties (*ekenowsin*), moving through death, and that we are to have that same mind

---

23. (Shelley 2009)298
24. (Mitchell 1989)12
25. (Reynolds 1989)14

(*nous*) in ourselves (Phil. 2:1–11). We also are to move through death in the ultimate I-Thou. Mystical teachers of the church insisted that God was not another being, but, as John of the Cross wrote, *Nada*—"nothing, nothing, nothing." Christ is present, but not as an object of meditation. Meister Eckhart, the great Rhineland mystic of the late thirteen and early fourteenth centuries, famously preached: "I pray God to rid me of God."[26] For Thomas Aquinas, and for the mainstream of Christian theology, God is not a being among other beings, but being itself, ultimately real, beyond description.

Also in the Christian tradition, the fourth-century monk Evagrius Ponticus brings together many of the strands of Axial Age insights. The goal of the first stage of spiritual practice (*praktike*) is freedom. It is known in *apatheia,* or passionlessness. "Passionlessness is a quiet state of the rational soul." This "measured calm" or passionlessness remains during waking consciousness and even during sleep and dreams. Love or *agape* is the result. "Love (*agape*) is the offspring of passionlessness."[27]

Pure prayer constitutes the second stage called *gnostike*, "the life of mystical knowledge." It includes the contemplation of created beings and nature as a whole, created in Christ. It culminates in *theologia*. "If you are a theologian, you will pray truly; and if you pray truly, you are a theologian." Such pure or true prayer transcends all images and words. "When you pray do not form images of the divine within yourself, nor allow your mind to be immersed with any form, but approach the immaterial immaterially, and you will come to understanding." Pure prayer involves "laying aside mental representations. . . . Undistracted prayer is the highest mindfulness of the mind." This mind (*nous*) is now the "place of God." "The 'place of God' therefore is the rational soul, and his dwelling is the illuminated mind." It is like the sapphire or clear blue sky, where Moses and the elders saw the God of Israel on Mount Sinai (Ex. 24:9–10). "Under his feet there was something like a pavement of sapphire stone, like the very heaven for clearness."[28]

THE KINGDOM OF GOD

In spiritual knowing the clear blue open sky of the field of love manifests two inseparable partners: unlimited awareness and unconditional love—as closely bound together as any two subatomic particles spinning

26. (Blakney 1960)218
27. (Harmless 2008)148
28. (Harmless 2008)149–153

simultaneously in opposite directions. Unconditional love is active in the world, as real as the empty blue sky of awareness. How does that happen?

In the Christian tradition, it manifests the kingdom of God. Jesus proclaims it at the beginning of his ministry. "The time has come, and the Kingdom of God has come near or close by. Turn around, change your minds and believe in the good news, the gospel" (Mark 1:15). The kingdom of God, implying a King, is a peculiar, odd phrase. We realize that field theories of modern physics were not available two thousand years ago, but still, what did he have in mind?

Jesus not only uses the term; he acts it out at the conclusion of his ministry. John Dominic Crossan and Marcus Borg describe it:[29] On Palm Sunday, from the west, Pontius Pilate entered Jerusalem at the head of a column of imperial cavalry and soldiers. The imperial procession was well known. It was standard practice for the Roman governor of Judea to be in Jerusalem at the major Jewish festivals to reinforce the permanent Roman garrison, especially at Passover, when the Jews, always a fractious lot, were especially restive. You could see the Imperial power—cavalry on horses, foot soldiers, leather armor, helmets, weapons, banners, golden eagles mounted on poles, sun glittering on metal and gold. You could hear it in the sounds of marching feet, creaking leather, beating drums. The swirling of dust would get in your eyes. Pilate represented not just the emperor as ruler of Rome, but as Son of God, descended from Augustus, son of god Apollo.

And here on the same day at the same hour comes Jesus from the east, explicitly imitating Biblical prophecy. When this obviously preplanned event on Palm Sunday happened, it was understood and staged in Biblical terms and language, and everyone who participated in it understood it in that way.

On the highest holy days of the Jewish calendar Jesus literally acted out Zechariah 9:9–10, right down to the colt: "Rejoice greatly, O daughter Zion! Shout aloud, O daughter Jerusalem! Lo, your king comes to you: triumphant and victorious is he, humble and riding on a donkey, on a colt, the foal of a donkey." The crowds shouting "Hosanna" and waving palms are not only acting out an ancient ritual for hailing a King returning triumphantly, but also a thanksgiving ritual in the temple, described in Psalm 118:26: "Hosanna to the one who comes in the name of the Lord." Jesus even enters into Jerusalem from Bethphage where, according to second-temple Judaism, the battle at the end of the age would take place. The crowds clearly got

29. (Borg 2006)2–4

the prophetic references and hailed him with great enthusiasm as their new King in the express lineage of David, come to drive out the Romans and establish again the kingdom of David.

A magnificent war horse, versus "a colt, the foal of a donkey." A grand procession of the mightiest army in the world, versus an itinerant preacher riding alone. The only superpower in the known world versus—what? What does Jesus have in mind in his performance art or, as we would have called it some time ago, guerrilla theater?

Borg and Crossan believe Jesus was presenting Walter Wink's thesis of the definitive rejection of the domination systems throughout history in favor of the ethics of love and equality. Palm Sunday was Jesus' symbolic statement of that rejection. The Kingdom of God was not a kingdom ruled by a king at all, but something very different—a spirit-filled community of love, justice, equality, and peace.[30] The Quaker Edward Hicks' early nineteenth-century paintings, sixty-one variations of the Peaceable Kingdom—animals and humans living together in harmony—are other images of that vision.

Holy Week for Christians acted out one of the great reversals of human history: that the kingdom of God Jesus proclaimed was not replacing one ruler with another, one tyrant with another, but the revelation in human history of a totally different kind of power. The *New Zealand Book of Common Prayer*[31] translates the ending of the Lord's prayer "the reign of the glory of the power that is love"—renewing the cosmos itself, overcoming the power of force and violence, of fear and greed. It was a massive reframing of what power and kingdom means in communal spiritual knowing—a planetary demonstration of the power of love, of how human beings were meant to live and be.

Pilate has a question when Jesus comes before him to be examined. "Are you a king?" Jesus responds, "Are you seeking for the sake of your own soul, or just repeating what somebody told you?" Pilate quickly backs away, "How would I know? I'm not a Jew. What did you do?" Jesus' enigmatic response: "My kingdom is not from this world, not from here." Pilate reverts to his power, his responsibility to keep order among the restless Jews on the high holidays." He pounces, "So, you are a King!"

Jesus tries to explain that this kingdom is beyond life and death itself: "You say so. For this I was born and for this I came into the world, to bear

30. (Borg 2006)7–11

31. (Zealand 1997)

witness to the truth" (John 18: 33–34). Pilate is a practical man, not a Roman philosopher or Jewish scholar. He gives up, or loses interest, "What is truth?" he mutters, and literally washes his hands of the whole deal.

What might be the largest, most wholistic image and metaphor available to Jesus for his mission in the culture of his time? The great king David embodied and represented the whole of Israel—its past imagined glories, its present reality, its hoped-for future when the anointed one, the Messiah, would come in David's lineage. Reza Aslan catalogs the long list of revolutionary leaders and messiahs before, during, and after the life of Jesus, attempting to overthrow corrupt and incompetent Roman rulers and their accomplices in the Jewish priestly aristocracy; the horrific living conditions and oppression of Jewish peasants; and the efforts of the gospel writers to authenticate Jesus as the true Messiah, fulfilling Davidic prophecies in the Hebrew Scriptures.[32]

Jesus both uses and contradicts popular apocalyptic expectations of the end of history when the Messiah would come. He tells them it will certainly come in their lifetime, but then warns them, "But about that day or hour no one knows, neither the angels in heaven, nor the Son, but only the Father. Beware, keep alert; for you do not know when the time will come" (Mark 13:32–33).

It hasn't happened yet, at least there is no compelling evidence that it has. The early church had to grapple with what seemed like a problem or a contradiction. The kingdom was close and nearby right now, but it clearly hadn't come to pass. Second Peter 3:8–9 tries to expand linear time, "But do not ignore this one fact, beloved, that with the Lord one day is like a thousand years, and a thousand years are like one day. The Lord is not slow about his promise, as some think of slowness, but is patient with you, not wanting any to perish, but all to come to repentance."

In the kingdom of God, what is time? You can think of all the different ways we use the word "time." Some are cautionary, or even despairing: Time is running out. Time's up! There isn't enough time in the day. You can't afford to lose track of the time. Don't waste time. Don't let time get away from you. Don't kill time. Some are hopeful; you can pass the time, make up time, find the time, enjoy the time, use time, and, in so many ways, spend time. And some are just the way things are: Time and time again; time passes.

32. (Aslan 2013)49ff

Christian Scriptures use two quite different words for time. The first is *kairos*, related to spiritual knowing—the decisive moment of God's action in history. When Jesus proclaims that the time has come and the kingdom of God has come near, the word for time is *kairos* (Mark 1:15). *Kairos* in spiritual knowing is rooted in our history, our natural environment, the core rhythms of our body, and the depth of our human relationships. It has the character of being present, of non-duration, of this eternal present moment. *Kairos* happens in I-Thou relationships.

The other word is *chronos*, related to scientific knowing, from which we get the English variations of chronology. It means a span of time or a period of time, the simple passing of linear time. It is not for us to know the times or periods that God has set (Acts 1:7). Since the invention of the spring-loaded clock in the twelfth century, the Industrial Revolution, and controlling the time workers spend at specific tasks, chronological linear time has become more and more central in our lives. *Chronos* happens in I-it transactions.

The kingdom of God is the manifestation of *kairos* in the field of love. It is not limited or defined by chronological time and specific space any more than a subatomic particle. Its manifestation cannot be determined any more than the path of a strange attractor in chaos theory. But like a strange attractor, it has a long-term manifestation of love in the world. As Dr. Martin Luther King Jr. preached, "the arc of the moral universe is long, but it bends toward justice."[33] Like observers shaping the outcome of quantum experiments, humans help shape reality in kingdom love and awareness. Like quantum entanglement, awareness, and love manifest directly and immediately in the world—and, like uncertainty in subatomic particles, unpredictably. The kingdom of God is not material. It is not subject to simple linear cause and effect, but its effects can be noticed in the world, like the probability equations of subatomic fields. Like chaos theory, it is a combination of order (progress in history towards greater justice and peace), disorder, and chaos. But the field of the kingdom of God is everywhere, as fields are. It is wholeness in which fractals in this world meet unconditional love known in unlimited awareness. It is the field of love, in which "I"s and "Thou"s meet—unpredictably, immediately, wholistically, even mysteriously or miraculously—in this sensory reality, here and now, in this time and space. Our "I"s meet "Thou"s in this world, fractals of the field of love, in signs of the kingdom. Jesus' proclamation "The kingdom of

33. (Mennard 2013)88

God is nearby" is not just an observation; it is an invitation to know and live in it.

Here are Albert Einstein's extended comments on what we have called the kingdom of God:

> A knowledge of the existence of something we cannot penetrate, of the manifestations of the profoundest reason and the most radiant beauty—it is this knowledge and this emotion that constitute the truly religious attitude; in this sense, and in this alone, I am a deeply religious man. I cannot conceive of a God who rewards and punishes his creatures, or has a will of the type of which we are conscious in ourselves. . . . Enough for me the mystery of the eternity of life, and the inkling of the marvelous structure of reality, together with the single-hearted endeavor to comprehend a portion, be it ever so tiny, of the reason that manifests itself in nature.[34]

For Einstein, the fractal we call

> A human being is a part of a whole, called by us the "Universe," a part limited in time and space. We experience ourselves, our thoughts and feelings as something separate from the rest—a kind of optical illusion of our consciousness. This delusion is a kind of prison for us, restricting us to our personal desires and to affection for a few persons nearest to us. Our task must be to free ourselves from the prison by widening our circle of compassion to embrace all living creatures and the whole of nature in its beauty. Nobody is able to achieve this completely, but the striving for such achievement is in itself a part of the liberation and a foundation for inner security.[35]

SIGNS OF THE KINGDOM

We can know signs and fractals of the field of love, the kingdom of God, even in ordinary Christian worship. For me, there was the Christmas eve service, celebrated together with friends who had known each other for dozens of years with the sparkling lights on the Christmas tree; the wonderful old carols sung yet another year; the reds and greens; and the lighted

---

34. (Tippett 2010)16
35. (Siegel 2007)163

candles dripping hot wax on our hands, not only signifying the light of Christ coming into the world but in that moment being that light.

There was the great vigil of Easter, going back almost two thousand years, presenting the early worship of Christians. Historically, those who had been prepared through a lengthy and arduous catechumenate were allowed and welcomed into the body of Christ through baptism and confirmation. Orthodox deacons still cry "the doors, the doors" to protect the event from outside profanation. Passages from the world history of venerable mythologized events in Scripture present what German scholars call *heilsgeschichte*—salvation history—how God indeed has been present and active in the world since the beginning. And in moments that also became true for us.

Then there was the time on an ordinary Sunday, in an ordinary church when the preacher's words took flight. The speaking of the words became the Word. The thoroughly and lovingly prepared brief dissertation on a familiar passage in the Gospels, neither original nor especially profound, became in that moment, the Gospel.

There was the small weathered, unpainted church in the woods in rural Mississippi. We walked to the service, because there were no roads. We heard the deacon line out, and the congregation sing back the moving, mournful, and joyful psalm tunes from so deep in our common human experience.

And there was our time at St. Peter's in the Vatican, the largest church in the world. The high altar is stunning; a bright gold monstrance by Bernini dominates it, containing the reserved sacrament. Flanked below it are two doctors of the western church, Augustine and Jerome, and two doctors of the eastern church, Chrysostom and Basil. We had taken the elevator to the base of the dome of the church, around two hundred feet above the altar, and were looking down at it when a cardinal and his retinue began processing up to celebrate mass. I thought what a wonderful thing it would be to attend the celebration from this great height, when a guard appeared and told us it was time to leave. I quickly took the elevator back down and found a place on the benches before the altar for most of the celebration. The mass, in its beauty going back almost two thousand years and trailing remnants of communal meals deep in our psyche from long before that, stirred those same depths in ways that neither the cardinal who celebrated it, nor the priest who offered me the host, nor I who received it could fully understand.

FINDING OUR VOICE

The ultimate Thou of radical awareness and unconditional love meet "I"s in the personal lives and testimonies of real persons who have attained the height and depth of spiritual knowing. It is true that some are legendary, like Lao Tzu, responding to the request of the border guard for some wisdom before leaving civilization for good. Others are real enough: Socrates driving his fellow Athenians to distraction with his incessant questions;[36] Buddha, having given up on all the alternatives, sitting under the Bodhi tree until the ultimate realization comes to him; Jesus disappearing from his disciples before dawn to meditate, and crying out *in extremis* on the cross.

What they and countless others demonstrated, in the fullness of their spiritual knowing, was the discovery of their own voices. Against the norms of their culture, through lifelong extreme personal doubts and struggles, sometimes punished even unto death by the society of their time, they found their own voice. Their own voice was the fruit of their spiritual knowing—their hard-earned and authentic wisdom that, because it was their personal knowledge, became universal truth, guidance, and light to so many that came after them. Their voices influenced and inspired the ways we speak our personal knowledge, our voice as well.

We discover who we truly are in this process of spiritual knowing and living. The divine in us comes forth in surprising ways. The book *The Soloist* is the true account of a reporter for the *Los Angeles Times* who happens upon a homeless man on the streets. Although he is not a musician, he recognizes the extraordinary quality of the music the man is playing on an old, beat-up violin. Over a year's friendship and struggle, the reporter, Steve Lopez, comes to know the homeless man, Nathaniel, and facilitates his move into a room of his own, meetings with principal players in the Los Angeles Philharmonic Orchestra, and gifts of new violins and a cello. It turns out that Nathaniel had been a promising student at Julliard, until the pressure and competition precipitated a psychotic break and a downward spiral that ended on the streets of LA. What so impressed the Philharmonic musicians who worked with him was not his remarkable ability to play and continue to learn after all those years, but the beautiful tone and sound he created, especially on the cello. They explained to the reporter that such a sound could not really be taught. It was the result, in some wholistic way, of

36. (Miller 2011)22–26

all and who the player is, the pouring out of a person's whole life experience and character through the bow and the strings.[37]

I have a friend who lost her husband after a terrible bout of cancer that left him gasping for breath for weeks. He was somewhat vain about his intact head of hair, and was especially distressed when it began falling out from the chemotherapy. She found herself one night weaving his sense of loss into a story, a fairy tale, about a Prince Charming losing his hair who was nevertheless loved and adored by his Princess. And so every night after that, as long as he lived, she would weave the day's pain and difficulties or small joys into another fairy tale about Prince Charming and the Princess who loved him.

While we were talking, I asked if she still played the cello. When she said that she did, I mentioned the story of the homeless street musician with the beautiful sound. She explained that when you play the cello, you rest it against your breastbone, and that the sound that comes out is from your heart, able only to express who you are on that day. If you are frustrated and cranky, that's the sound that comes out; and if you are filled with love, that also is heard in the tone.

For Gerald Manley Hopkins, the nineteenth-century Jesuit poet, we find our own voice in Christ's:

> I say more; the just one justices;
> Keeps grace; that keeps all their goings graces;
> Acts in God's eye what in God's eye we are –
> Christ—for Christ plays in ten thousand places,
> Lovely in limbs, and lovely in eyes not his
> To the Father through the features of human faces.[38]

MYSTERY

Ultimately, spiritual knowing enters into mystery. Wallace Stevens is outside on a cold, snowy winter day, white and quiet all around. He writes:

> For the listener, who listens in the snow,
> And, nothing himself, beholds
> Nothing that is not there and the nothing that is.[39]

37. (Lopez 2008)
38. (Mitchell 1989)118
39. (Stevens 2009)415

Not an answer but a longing, infinite mystery, light, life, love, more compelling than anything in heaven or on earth. It is like a dream I have had, and perhaps you have as well, in which one is endlessly falling, through the petty difficulties of daily life, through the cycling drama of personal history, through the vast landscape of the consciousness of the human race and all living beings, through the edge of the known universe and all possible alternative universes and on—never landing.

We can fall into mystery; we can jump into the mystery of the present moment. The homely word "jump" has been used and implied quite often in these reflections—the sudden emergence of the mental representations that make us human, kids leaping from rafters into empty space, moving between I-Thou and I-It, electrons instantaneously going from one orbit to another. This jump has never been better described than by Basho, in a haiku written in the seventeenth century:[40]

> Old Pond (ancient eternal wisdom, field of awareness beyond limit, love without end)
>
> Frog jumps in (sensory reality, this life situation, in time, in space)
>
> Splash (What happens. This instant, this spot. This here, this now)

Old pond
Frog jumps in
Splash

40. (Basho 2004)54

Bibliography

Abraham, Ralph H. and Christopher D. Shaw. *Dynamics: the Geometry of Behavior, Part Two: Chaotic Behavior.* Santa Cruz, CA: Aerial Press, Inc., 1982.

Adamson, Iain T. *Introduction to Field Theory, Second Edition.* Cambridge: Cambridge University Press, 1982.

Alexander, Eben M. D. *Proof of Heaven: a Neurosurgeion's Journey into the Afterlife.* New York: Simon & Schuster Paperbacks, 2012.

Allport, Gordon. *Becoming:Basic Considerations for a Psychology of Personality.* New Haven: Yale University Press, 1955.

Armstrong, Karen. *A History of God: The 4,000-Year Quest of Judaism, Christianity and Islam.* New York: Alfred A. Knopf, 1993.

————. *A Short History of Myth.* Edinburgh: Canongate, 2005.

————. *Buddha.* New York: Penguin Putnam, Inc., 2001.

————. *Islam: a Short History.* New York: Modern Library, 2002.

————. *The Battle for God.* New York: Alfred A. Knopf, 2000.

————. *The Case for God.* New York: Alfred A. Knopf, 2009.

————. *The Great Transformation: The Beginning of Our Religious Traditions.* New York: Anchor Books, 2007.

————. *Twelve Steps to a Compassionate Life.* New York: Alfred A. Knopf, 2011.

Armstrong, Thomas. *7 Kinds of Smart: Identifying and Developing Your Multiple Intelligences—Rev. ed. .* New York: New American Library, 1999.

Arnold, Matthew. "Dover Beach." In *Essential Pleasures, edited by Robert Pinsky,* by Matthew Arnold, 171. New York: W. W. Norton and Company, 2009.

Aslan, Reza. *Zealot: The Life and Times of Jesus of Nazareth.* New York: Random House, 2013.

Auden, W. H. *Collected Longer Poems.* New York: Vintage Books, 1975.

Augustine, Saint, Bishop of Hippo. *City of God, edited and abridged by Vernon J. Bourke.* New York: Doubleday Religion, 1958.

Barks, Coleman, translator for Maulana Jalal al-Din Rumi. *The Essential Rumi: New Expanded Edition.* New York: HarperSanFrancisco (HarperCollins), 2004.

Basho, Matsuo. *Basho's Haiku: Selected Poems by Matsuo Basho, translated by David Landis Barnhill.* Albany: State University of New York Press, 2004.

Bass, Diane Butler. *Christianity After Religion: The End of Church and The Birth of a New Spiritual Awakening.* New York: Harper One, 2012.

Bauby, Jean-Dominique. *The Diving Bell and the Butterfly: A Memoir of Life in Death, translated from the French by Jeremy Leggatt.* New York: Vintage International, 1998.

BIBLIOGRAPHY

Baumeister, Roy F. *Meanings of Life*. New York: Guilford Press, 1991.

Bellah, Robert N. *Religion in Human Evolution: From the Paleolithic to the Axial Age*. Cambridge, Mass.: Belknap Press of Harvard University Press, 2011.

Berman, Morris. *Coming to Our Senses: Body and Spirit in the Hidden History of the West*. New York: Simon & Schuster, 1989.

Blakney, Ramond Bernard, translator. *Meister Eckhart: A Modern Translation*. New York: Harper and Brothers, 1941.

Blakney, Raymond, ed. *An Immanuel Kant Reader; edited and translated with commentary*. New York: Harper & Brothers, 1960.

Bloom, Paul. "The Original Colonists." *The New York Times Book Review*, May 13, 2012: 30–31.

Bodhi, Bhikkhu, ed. *In the Buddha's Words: An Anthology of Discourses from the Pali Canon*. Boston: Wisdom Publications, 2005.

Bohm, David. *Wholeness and the Implicate Order*. London, UK: ARK Paperbacks, 1983.

Book of Common Prayer and Administration of the Sacraments and Other Rites and Ceremonies of the Church: Together with the Psalter or Psalms of David, The. New York: The Church Hymnal Corporation and The Seabury Press, 1979.

Borg, Marcus J. and John Dominic Crossan. *The Last Week: A Day-by-Day Account of Jesus's Final Week in Jerusalem*. New York: HarperCollins Publishers, 2006.

Borg, Marcus J. *The Heart of Christianity: Rediscovering a Life of Faith, reprint edition*. New York: HarperCollins, 2003.

Borg, Marcus. "Lecture at First Presbyterian Church, Birmingham, Michigan." n.d.

Borg, Marcus, ed. *Jesus and Buddha: the Parallel Sayings*. Berkeley, CA: Ulysses Press, 1999.

Bourgeault, Cynthia. *The Wisdom Jesus: Transforming Heart and Mind — a New Perspective on Christ and His Message*. Boston: Shambhala, 2008.

Bouyer, Louis. *Orthodox Spirituality and Protestant and Anglican Spirituality (A History of Christian Spirituality; III)*. Minneapolis, MN: The Seabury Press, 1982.

Boyce, Barry, ed. and editors of th Shambhala Sun. *The Mindfulness Revolution: Leading Psychologists, Scientist, Artists, and Meditation Teachers on the Power of Mindfulness in Daily Life*. Boston: Shambhala, 2011.

Brooks, David. "Social Animal." *The New Yorker*, January 17, 2011: 26–32.

Browning, Robert L. and Roy A. Reed. *The Sacraments in Religious Education and Liturgy*. Birmingham, AL: Religious Education Press, 1985.

Buber, Martin, translated by Ronald Gregor Smith. *I and Thou*. New York: Scribner Classics, 2000.

Buddha, The, and Ven. Bhikkhu, translator Bodhi. "The Fire Sermon (Samyutta Nikaya, Chapter 35, sutta 28)." *Parabola*, Spring 2012: 9.

Burger, Edward B. and Michael Starbird. *The Heart of Mathematics: An invitation to effective thinking; second edition*. Emeryville, CA: Key College Publishing, 2005.

Burgess, E. Clayton, Jr. *To Ring Like a Bell That Has No Flaw: A Celebration of Faith*. College Station, TX: Virtualbookworm.com Publishing Inc., 2010.

Byrom, Thomas. *The Dhammapada: The Sayings of the Buddha: A New Rendering by Thomas Byrom with a preface by Ram Dass*. New York: Vintage Books, 1976.

Cannato, Judy. *Fields of Compassion: How the New Cosmology Is Transforming Spiritual Life*. Notre Dame, IN: Sorin Books, 2010.

Capra, Fritjof. *The Tao of Physics: An Exploration of the Parallels Between Modern Physics and Eastern Mysticism*. Berkeley, CA: Shambhala, 1975.

BIBLIOGRAPHY

Carrington, Patricia, Ph.D. *Freedom in Meditation*. Garden City, NY: Anchor Press/ Doubleday, 1977.

Carroll, Sean, Ph.D. *Dark Matter, Dark Energy: The Dark Side of the Universe, Parts 1 & 2 (The Great Courses: Science & Mathematics)*. Chantilly, VA: The Teaching Company, 2007.

Carse, James P. *The Silence of God: Meditations on Prayer*. New York: Macmillan, 1985.

Chodron, Pema. *Tonglen: The Path of Transformation*. Halifax, Nova Scotia: Vajradhatu Publications, 2001.

Chopra, Deepak. *Jesus: A Story of Enlightenment*. New York: HarperCollins, 2008.

Cloud of Unknowing, The : A Version in Modern English of a Fourteenth Century Classic. New York: Harper & Brothers, 1948.

Cohen, Bonnie Bainbridge. *Sensing, Feeling, and Action: The Experiential Anatomy of Body-Mind Centering*. Northampton, MA: Contact Editions, 1993.

Collins, Francis S. *The Language of God: a Scientist Presents Evidence for Belief*. New York: Simon & Schuster, Free Press, 2006.

Crossan, John Dominic. *Jesus: A Revolutionary Biography*. New York: HarperCollins, 1994.

Csikszentmihalyi, Mihaly. *Flow: The Psychology of Optimal Experience*. New York: HarperCollins, 1990.

Cunningham, Lawrence S., ed. *Thomas Merton: Spiritual Master: The Essential Writings*. New York: Paulist Press, 1992.

Curry, Andrew. "The World's First Temple?" *Smithsonian*, November 2008: 54–60.

Damasio, Antonio R. *The Feeling of What Happens: Body and Emotion in the Making of Consciousness*. New York: Harcourt Brace & Company, 1999.

Davies, Paul. *Cosmic Jackpot: Why Our Universe Is Just Right for Life*. Boston: Houghton Mifflin, 2007.

———. *The Mind of God: The Scientific Basis for a Rational World*. New York: Simon & Schuster Paperbacks, c.1992, 2005 pbk ed.

Davies, Robertson. *Manticore*. New York: Penguin Books, 1972.

Davis, Madeleine and David Wallbridge. *Boundary & Space: An Introduction to eh Work of D. W. Winnicott*. New York: Brunner/Mazel, Inc., 1981.

de Broglie, Louis. "The Aspiration Towards Spirit." In *Quantum Questions: Mystical Writings of the World's Greatest Physicists*, by Ken, ed. Wilber, 115–121. Boston: Shambala, 1984.

Deutsch, David. *The Beginning of Infinity: Explanations that Transform the World*. New York: Viking, 2011.

Diamond, Jared. *Collapse: How Societies Choose to Fail or Succeed*. New York: Viking, 2005.

———. *The World Until Yesterday: What Can We Learn from Traditional Societies?* New York: Viking, 2012.

Dillard, Annie. *The Writing Life*. New York: Harper & Row, 1989.

Dossey, Larry, M. D. *Recovering the Soul: A Scientific and Spiritual Search*. New York: Bantam Books, 1989.

Dossey, M. D., Larry. *Healing Words: the Power of Prayer and the Practice of Medecine*. San Francisco: HarperSanFrancisco, 1993.

Douglas-Klotz, Neil. *The Hidden Gospel: Decoding the Spiritual Message of the Aramic Jesus*. Wheaton, IL: Quest Books (Theosophical Publishing House), 1999.

BIBLIOGRAPHY

Dowd, Michael. *Thank God for Evolution: How the Marriage of Science and Religion Will Transform Your Life and Our World*. New York: Penguin Group, c. 2007.

Dwoskin, Hale. *The Sedona Method: Your Key to Lasting Happiness, Success, Peace and Emotional Well-Being, Second ed*. Sedona, AZ: Sedona Press, 2003–2010.

Eck, Diane L. *A New Religious America*. New York: HarperCollins, 2001.

Eckel, Malcolm David, Ph.D. *Buddhism, Parts 1 & 2 (The Great Courses: Religion)*. Chantilly, VA: The Teaching Company, 1999.

Eddington, Sir Arthur. "Beyond the Veil of Physics." In *Quantum Questions: Mystical Writings of the World's Great Physicists*, by Ken, ed. Wilber, 167–183. Boston: Shambala, 1984.

Eddington, Sir Arthur. "Defense of Mysticism." In *Quantum Questions: Mystical Writings of the World's Great Physicists*, by Ken Wilber, ed., 194–208. Boston: Shambala, 1984.

Ehrenreich, Barbara. *Living With a Wild God: a Nonbeliever's Search for the Truth About Everything*. New York: Twelve, 2014.

Einstein, Albert. *Ideas and Opinions*. New York: Dell, 1973.

Eliade, Mircea. *Rites and Symbols of Initiation: The Mysteries of Birth and Rebirth*. New York: Harper Torchbooks, c.1958, 1975 ed.

Evagrius, Ponticus, and translated by John Eudes Bamberger. *Evagrius Ponticus: The Praktikos. Chapters on Prayer (Cistercian Studies)*. Spencer, MA: Cistercian Publications, 1970.

Ferrer, Jorge N. *Revisioning Transpersonal Theory: A Participatory Vision of Human Spirituality*. Albany, NY: State University of New York Press, 2002.

Ferris, Timothy. "Weirdness Makes Sense." *The New York Times Magazine*, September 29, 1996: 143–146.

Feuerstein, Georg, Ph.D. *The Yoga Tradition: Its History, Literature, Philosophy and Practice*. Prescott, AZ: Hohm Press, 1998.

Feynman, Richard P. *The Meaning of It All: Thoughts of a Citizen-Scientist*. Reading, MA: Addison-Wesley, 1998.

Feynman, Richard P. with Robert B. Leighton and Matthew Sands. *Six Easy Pieces: Essentials of Physics Explained by Its Most Brilliant Teacher*. New York: Basic Books, 2011.

Feynman, Richard. "Probability and Uncertainty—the Quantum Mechanical View of Nature." In *The Character of Physical Law (transcript of the Messenger Lectures at Cornell University, presented in November 1964*, by Richard Feynman, Chapter 6. Boston, MA: MIT Press, 1965.

Fields, Helen. "Before There Was Life." *Smithsonian*, October 2010: 48–54.

Finley, James. *The Awakening Call: Fostering Intimacy with God*. Notre Dame, IN: Ave Maria Press, 1984.

Foster, Richard J. *Celebration of Discipline: The Path to Spiritual Growth*. San Francisco: Harper & Row, Publishers, 1978.

———. *Freedom of Simplicity*. San Francisco: HarperSanFrancisco, (c)1981, 1989 pbk. ed.

———. *Money, Sex & Power: The Challenge of the Disciplined Life*. New York: HarperCollins, 1985.

Fowler, James W. *Stages of Faith: The Psychology of Human Development and the Quest for Meaning*. San Francisco: Harper & Row, 1981.

Fox, Matthew. *Breakthrough: Meister Eckhart's Creation Spirituality in New Translation; Introduction and Commentaries by Matthew Fox*. Garden City, NY: Doubleday Image, 1980.

BIBLIOGRAPHY

Freedman, David H. "Lies, Damned Lies, and Medical Science." *The Atlantic*, November 2010: 76–86.

Fritz, Robert. *The Path of Least Resistance: Learning to Become the Creative Force in Your Own Life, rev. ed.* New York: Fawcett Columbine, 1989.

Fronsdal, Egil. *The Dhammapada: a New Translation of the Buddhist Classic, with Annotations.* Boston: Shambhala, 2005.

"Fundamentalism." In *Encyclopaedia Britannica, 15th edition, Volume 9*, 51–52. Chicago: Encyclopaedia Brittanica, Inc., 1989.

Garber, Marjorie. *Shakespeare After All.* New York: Pantheon Books, 2004.

Gendlin, Eugene. *Focusing.* New York: Bantam Books, 1981.

Gerber, Richard, M.D. *Vibrational Medicine: New Choices for Healing Ourselves, updated ed.* Santa Fe, NM: Bear & Company, 1988.

Gilligan, Carol. *In a Different Voice: Psychological Theory and Women's Development.* Cambridge, MA: Harvard University Press, 1982.

Glorious Qur'an, The; 1st English edition; translation by Mohammed Marmaduke Pickthall. Elmhurst, NY: Tahrike Tarsile Qur'an, Inc., 2000.

Goldstein, Joseph. *One Dharma: The Emerging Western Buddhism.* New York: HarperCollins, c. 2002; paperback ed. 2003.

Goldstein, Rebecca. *Incompleteness: The Proof and Paradox of Kurt Godel.* New York: W. W. Norton, 2005.

Goleman, Daniel. *The Varieties of the Meditative Experience.* New York: Irvington Publishers, 1977.

Gopnik, Adam. "Life Studies: What I learned when I learned to draw." *The New Yorker*, June 27, 2011: 56–63.

Gore, Albert Jr. *The Future: Six Drivers of Global Change.* New York: Random House, 2013.

Gottlieb, Robert. "Man of Letters." *The New Yorker*, January 7, 2013: 71–77.

Govinda, Lama Anagarika. *Foundations of Tibetan Mysticism.* New York: Samuel Weiser, Inc., 1974.

Greene, Brian. *The Elegant Universe: Superstrings, Hidden Demensions, and the Quest for the Ultimate Theory.* New York: Vintage Books, 1999.

Grippando, James. *Born to Run.* New York: HarperCollins, 2008.

Gyatso, Tenzin (Dalai Lama XIV). *Essence of the Heart Sutra: The Dalai Lama's Heart of Wisdom Teachings.* Somerville, MA: Wisdom Publications, 2005.

Habito, Ruben L. F. *Living Zen, Loving God.* Boston: Wisdom Publications, 2004.

Hafiz, and translated by Daniel Ladinsky. *The Gift: Poems by Hafiz, the Great Sufi Master.* New York: Penguin/Arkana, 1999.

Hafiz, and translated by Jeffrey Einboden and John Slater. *The Tangled Braid: Ninety-nine poems by Hafiz of Shiraz.* Louisville, KY: Fons Vitae, 2009.

Harmless, William, S.J. *Mystics.* New York: Oxford University Press, 2008.

Hayward, Jeremy W. *Perceiving Ordinary Magic: Science and Intuitive Wisdom.* Boulder, CO: New Science Library (Shambhala), 1984.

Heinberg, Richard and Daniel Lerch, eds. *The Post Carbon Reader: Managing the 21st Century's Sustainability Crises.* Healdsburg, CA: Watershed Media, 2010.

Heisenberg, Werner. "Scientific and Religious Truths." In *Quantum Physics: Mystical Writings of the World's Great Physicists*, by Ken Wilber, ed., 39–44. Boston: Shambala, 1984.

Holt, Jim. *Why Does the World Exist?: An Existential Detective Story.* New York: Liveright Publishing Corporation, 2012.

BIBLIOGRAPHY

Jaspers, Karl, translated from the German by William Earle. *Reason and Existenz: Five Lectures*. New York: The Noonday Press, 1955.

Jung, C. G. and W. Pauli. *The Interpretation of Nature and the Psyche: C. G. Jung "Synchronicity: An Acausal Connecting Principle; W. Pauli "The Influence of Archetypal Ideas on the Scientific Theories of Kepler."* New York: Bollingen Foundation, Inc., 1955.

Jung, C. G., translated by R. F. C. Hull. *Synchronicity: An Acausal Connecting Principle, second ed.* Princeton, NJ: Princeton University Press, 1969.

Keating, Thomas. *Foundations for Centering Prayer and the Christian Contemplative Life: Open Mind, Open Heart; Invitation to Love; The Mystery of Christ.* New York: Continuum, 2002.

————. *Intimacy with God: An Introduction to Centering Prayer.* New York: The Crossroad Publishing Company, 1994.

Keen, Sam. *The Passionate Life: Stages of Loving.* San Francisco: Harper & Row, 1983.

Keeney, Bradford. *Ropes to God.* Philadelphia, PA: Ringing Rocks Press, 2003.

Kelly, Thomas R. *A Testament of Devotion.* New York: Harper & Brothers, 1941.

Kidd, Sue Monk. *Firstlight: The Early Inspirational Writings of Sue Monk Kidd.* New York: Penguin, 2006.

Kluger, Jeffrey. "The Cathedral of Science." *Time*, July 23, 2012: 32–35.

Kolbert, Elizabeth. *The Sixth Extinction: An Unnatural History.* New York: Henry Holt and Company, 2014.

Kornfield, Jack. *The Wise Heart: A guide to the Universal Teachings of Buddhist Psychology.* New York: Bantam Books, 2008.

Korten, David C. *The Great Turning: From Empire to Earth Community.* San Francisco, CA: Berrett-Koehler Publishers, Inc., 2006.

Kuhn, Thomas S. *The Structure of Scientific Revolutions.* Chicago: University of Chicago Press, 1970.

Lao-tzu. *Lao Tsu: Tao Te Ching: A New Translation by Gia-Fu Feng and Jane English.* New York: Vintage Books (Random House), 1972.

Latura, George Beke. "To Read God's Mind: Pythagoreans and the Birth of Science." *Parabola*, Winter 2012–13: 62–67.

Lawlor, Robert. *Sacred Geometry: Philosophy and Practice.* New York: Thames and Hudson, c.1982; paperback ed. 1989.

Lawrence, Brother, and Hugh, ed. Martin. *The Practice of the Presence of God and Selections from the Little Flowers of St Francis.* London: SCM Press, 1956.

LeFevre, Perry. *Understandings of Prayer.* Philadelphia: The Westminster Press, 1981.

Lehrer, Johan. "Kin and Kind." *The New Yorker*, March 5, 2012: 36–42.

Levine, Peter, Ph.D. "Trauma and Spirituality?" In *Measuring the Immeasurable: The Scientific Case for Spirituality*, 85–100. Boulder, CO: Sounds True, 2008.

Lindorff, David, Ph.D., and Markus Fierz. *Pauli and Jung: The Meeting of Two Great Minds.* Wheaton, IL: Quest Books, 2004.

Livio, Mario. *Is God a Mathematician?* New York: Simon & Schuster, 2009.

Lopez, Steve. *The Soloist: A Lost Dream, an Unlikely Friendship, and the Redemptive Power of Music.* New York: G. G. Putnam's Sons, 2008.

MacCulloch, Diarmid. *Christianity: The First Three Thousand Years.* New York: Viking (Penguin Group), 2009.

Magill, Frank N., ed. and Ian P. McGreal, ed. *Christian Spirituality: the Essential Guide to the Most Influential Spiritual Writings of the Christian Tradition.* San Francisco: Harper & Row, 1988.

BIBLIOGRAPHY

Maitland, Sara. *A Book of Silence*. Berkeley, CA: Counterpoint, 2008.

Marion, Jim. *Putting On the Mind of Christ: the Inner Work of Christian Spirituality*. Charlottesville, VA: Hampton Roads Publishing Company, Inc., 2000.

———. *The Death of the Mythic God: The Rise of Evolutionary Spirituality*. Charlottesvile, VA: Hampton Roads Publishing Company, Inc., 2004.

Marty, Martin and R. Scott Appleby, eds. *Fundamentalisms and Society: Reclaiming the Sciences, the Family, and Education*. Chicago: The University of Chicago Press, 1993.

May, Gerald G., M.D. *The Dark Night of the Soul:A Psychiatrist Explores the Connection Between Darkness and Spiritual Growth*. New York: HarperSanFrancisco (HarperCollins), 2004.

McWhorter, John. *Understanding Linguistics: The Science of Language (The Great Courses)*. Chantilly, VA: The Teaching Company, 2008.

Mead, Margaret. *People and Places*. New York: Bantam Pathfinder Editions, 1959.

Measuring the Immeasurable: The Scientific Case for Spirituality. Boulder, CO: Sounds True, Inc., 2008.

Menand, Louis. "The Color of Law." *The New Yorker*, July 8, 2013: 80–89.

Merton, Thomas. *Contemplative Prayer*. Garden City, NY: Doubleday Image, 1969.

———. *Mystics and Zen Masters*. New York: The Noonday Press, 1967.

———. *Seeds of Contemplation*. New York: Dell Publishing Co., 1949.

Meyendorff, John. *St. Gregory Palamas and Orthodox Spirituality; authorized translation by Adele Fiske*. Crestwood, NY: St. Vladimir's Seminary Press, 1974.

Meyerhoff, Hans, ed. *The Philosophy of History in Our Time: An Anthology*. Garden City, NY: Doubleday Anchor, 1959.

Miller, James. *Examined Lives: from Socrates to Nietzsche*. New York: Farrar, Straus and Giroux, 2011.

Mindell, Arnold and Amy Mindell. *Riding the Horse Backwards: Process Work in Theory and Practice*. London, England UK: Arkana (Penguin Group), 1992.

Mindell, Arnold. *River's Way: The Process Science of the Dreambody*. London, England UK: Arkana (Penguin Group), 1985.

Mitchell, Mark T. *Michael Polyani: The Art of Knowing*. Wilmington, DE: ISI Books, 2006.

Mitchell, Melanie. *Complexity: A Guided Tour*. Oxford, England UK: Oxford University Press, 2009.

Mitchell, Stephen A. *A Book of Psalms: Selected and Adapted from the Hebrew*. New York: HarperCollins, 1993.

Mitchell, Stephen, ed. *The Enlightened Heart: An Anthology of Sacred Poetry*. New York: HarperCollins, 1989.

Muto, Susan. *John of the Cross for Today: The Ascent*. Notre Dame, IN: Ave Maria Press, 1991.

Nasar, Sylvia. *A Beautiful Mind*. New York: Touchstone (Simon & Schuster), 1998.

Needleman, Jacob. *The Heart of Philosophy*. New York: Alfred A. Knopf, (c)1982, 1984 Bantam edition.

Neufelder, Jerome M., ed. and Mary C. Coelho, ed. *Writings on Spiritual Direction by Great Christian Masters*. New York: The Seabury Press, 1982.

Newberg, Andrew, M.D. *Why God Won't Go Away: Brain Science and the Biology of Belief*. New York: Ballantine Books, 2001.

Nhat Hanh, Thich. *Call Me by My True Names: The Collected Poems of Thich Nhat Hanh*. Berkeley, CA: Prallax Press, 1999.

Nouwen, Henri J. M. *Behold the Beauty of the Lord: Praying with Icons*. Notre Dame, IN: Ave Maria Press, 1987.

Oliver, Mary. *Thirst: Poems*. Boston: Beacon Press, 2006.

O'Murcho, Diarmuid. *Quantum Theology*. New York: Crossroad Publishing Company, 1997.

Ornstein, Robert E. *The Psychology of Consciousness*. San Francisco, CA: W. H Freeman and Company, 1972.

Orr, Leonard and Sondra Ray. *Rebirthing in the New Age*. Millbrae, CA: Celestial Arts, 1977.

Otto, Rudolf, and translated by Bertha Bracey and Richenda C. Payne. *Mysticism East and West: A Comparative Analysis of the Nature of Mysticism*. New York: Living Age Books (Meridian Books), 1957.

Otto, Rudoph. *The Idea of the Holy*. Oxford: Oxford University Press, 1923.

Pagels, Elaine. *Beyond Belief: The Secret Gospel of Thomas*. New York: Random House, 2003.

Palmer, Martin. *The Jesus Sutras: Rediscovering the Lost Scrolls of Taoist Christianity*. New York: Ballantine Wellspring, 2001.

Pennington, M. Basil, O.C.S.O. *Centering Prayer: Renewing an Ancient Christian Prayer Form*. Garden City, NY: Doubleday & Company, Inc., 1980.

Pine, Red (translator). *Lao-tsu's Taoteching / translated by Red Pine, with selected commentaries of the past 2000 years, 2nd ed*. San Francisco, CA: Mercury House, 1996.

Pine, Red. *The Diamond Sutra: The Perfection of Wisdom*. New York: Counterpoint, 2002.

———. *The Heart Sutra: the Womb of Buddhas; translation and commentary by Red Pine*. Washington, D.C.: Shoemake & Hoard, 2004.

———. *The Platform Sutra: The Zen Teaching of Hui-Neng; translation and Commentary by Red Pine*. Emeryville, CA: Shoemaker & Hoard, 2006.

Pinker, Steven. *The Better Angels of Our Nature: Why Violence Has Declined*. New York: Penguin Group, 2011.

Pinsky, Robert, editor. *Essential Pleasures: A New Anthology of Poems to Read Aloud*. New York: W. W. Norton & Company, 2009.

Pitcher, George. *The Philosophy of Wittgenstein*. Englewood Cliffs, NJ: Prentice-Hall, Inc., c. 1964.

Polkinghorne, John. *Quantum Physics and Theology: An Unexpected Kinship*. New Haven, CT: Yale University Press, 2007.

Pollan, Michael. "The Intelligent Plant." *The New Yorker*, December 23 & 30, 2013: 92–105.

Principe, Lawrence M. *Science and Religion*. Chantilly, VA: The Great Courses (The Teaching Company), 2006.

Progoff, Ira. *The Cloud of Unknowing: A New Translation of the Classic 14th-Century Guide to the Spiritual Experience*. New York: Delta, 1973.

Purce, Jill. *The Mystic Spiral: Journey of the Soul*. New York: Thames and Hudson, Inc., 1974.

Rahner, Karl. *A World of Grace: An Introduction to the Themes and Foundations of Karl Rahner's Theology, edited by Leo J. O'Donovan*. New York: The Crossroad Publishing Company, 1989.

Randall, Lisa. *Knocking on Heaven's Door: How Physics and Scientific Thinking Illuminate the Universe and the Modern World*. New York: HarperCollins, 2011.

Rasmussen, Larry L. *Earth Community Earth Ethics*. Maryknoll, NY: Orbis Books, 1996.

BIBLIOGRAPHY

Reynolds, John Myrdhin, translator for Karma Gling-pa. *Self-Liberation Through Seeing with Naked Awareness: an Introduction to the Nature of One's Own Mind in the Tibetan Dzoghen Tradition/ translated by John Myrdhin Reynolds; foreword by Namkhai Norbu.* Barrytown, NY: Station Hill Press, Inc., c. 1989 John Myrdhin Reynolds.

Richards, Mary Caroline. *Centering in Pottery, Poetry, and the Person.* Middletown, CT: Wesleyan University Press, 1964.

Roberts, Bernadette. *The Experience of No-Self: A Contemplative Journey.* Boston, MA: Shambhala Publications, Inc., 1982.

Rohr, Richard. *Everything Belongs: The Gift of Contemplative Prayer, rev. ed.* New York: The Crossroads Publishing Company, 2003.

Rosenbaum, Ron. "Burning Man." *Smithsonian,* April 2013: 26–33.

Sachdov, Subir. "'"Strange and Stringy."'" *Scientific American,* January 2013: 46.

Saint John of the Cross, Doctor of the Church. *Dark Night of the Soul, 3rd rev. ed.; translated and edited by E. Allison Peers from the critical edition of P. Silverio De Santa Teresa, C.D.* Garden City, NY: Image Books (Doubleday & Company), 1959.

Salzberg, Sharon. *Lovingkindness: The Revolutionary Art of Happiness.* Boston, MA: Shambhala, 1995.

Schiffmann, Erich. *Yoga: The Spirit and Practice of Moving Into Stilness.* New York: Pocket Books (Simon & Schuster, Inc.), 1996.

Schrödinger, Erwin. "The Oneness of Mind." In *Quantum Questions: Mystical Writings of the World's Great Physicists,* by Ken, ed. Wilber, 84–89. Boston: Shambala, 1984.

Schutz, William C. *FIRO Awareness Scales Manual .* Mountain View, CA: Consulting Psychologists Press, 1978.

Shakespeare, William. "Cymbeline." In *The Riverside Shakespeare, Second Ed.,* 1565–1611. Boston, MA: Houghton Mifflin, 1997.

Shakespeare, William. "The Life of Henry the Fifth." In *The Riverside Shakespeare, Second Edition,* 974–1020. Boston: Houghton Mifflin, 1997.

Shakespeare, William. "The Tempest." In *The Riverside Shakespeare, Second Edition,* 1661–1686. Boston: Houghton Mifflin, 1997.

Shakespeare, William. "The Tragedy of King Richard the Second." In *The Riverside Shakespeare,* 842–883. Boston, MA: Houghton Mifflin, 1997.

Shakespeare, Williams. "The First Part of Henry the Fourth." In *The Riverside Shakespeare, Second Edition,* 884–927. Boston: Houghton Mifflin, 1997.

Shapiro, Jr, Deane H. *Meditation: Self-regulation Strategy and Altered State of Consiousness.* New York: Aldine Publishing Company, 1980.

Shelley, Percy Bysshe. "Ozymandias." In *Essential Pleasures: A New Anthology of Poems to Read Aloud,* by Robert, ed. Pinsky, 298. New York: W. W. Norton & Company, 2009.

Siderits, Mark and Shoryu Katsura (translators). *Nagarjuna's Middle Way: the Mulamadhyamakakarika.* Boston: Wisdom Publications, 2013.

Siegel, Daniel J. *Mindsight: The New Science of Personal Transformation.* New York: Bantam Books, 2010.

———. *The Mindful Brain: Reflection and Attunement in the Cultivation of Well-Being.* New York: W. W. Norton & Company, Inc., 2007.

Smith, Huston. *Beyond the Post-Modern Mind, updated and rev.* Wheaton, IL: Quest Books (Theosophical Publishing House), 1989.

———. *Forgotten Truth: The Primordial Tradition.* New York: Harper Colophon, (c)1976; 1977 ed.

———. *The Soul of Christianity: Restoring the Great Tradition*. New York: HarperSanFrancisco (HarperCollins), 2005.

———. *The World's Religions: Our Great Wisdom Traditions, rev. and updated ed. of The Religions of Man (1958)*. New York: HarperSanFrancisco (HarperCollins), 1991.

Spong, John Shelby. *Why Christianity Must Change or Die: A Bishop Speaks to Believers in Exile*. New York: HarperSanFrancisco (HarperCollins), 1998.

Stace, Walter T. *The Teachings of the Mystics: Selections from the Great Mystics and Mystical Writings of the World Edited, with Introduction, Interpretive Commentaries, and explanations, by Walter T. Stace*. New York: Mentor Books (The New American Library of World Literature, Inc.), 1960.

Starbird, Michael, Ph.D. *Change and Motion: Calculus Made Clear, 2nd Ed. (Science & Mathematics, The Great Courses)*. Chantilly, VA: The Teaching Company, 2006.

Stevens, Wallace. "The Snow Man." In *Essential Pleasures: An Anthology of Poems to Read Aloud*, by Robert, editor Pinsky, 415. New York: W. W. Norton & Company, 2009.

Strand, Mark. "My Name." In *Man and Camel: Poems*, by Strand, 39. New York: Alfred A. Knopf, 2006.

Strogatz, Steven, Ph.D. *Chaos, Parts 1 & 2 (Science & Mathematics; The Great Courses)*. Chantilly, VA: The Teaching Company, 2008.

Strong, Emory. *Stone Age on the Columbia River, 2nd, ed.* Portland, OR: Binfords & Mort, Publishers, 1982.

Suzuki, D. T. *Zen Buddhism: Selected Writings of D. T. Suzuki, edited by William Barrett*. Garden City, NY: Doubleday Anchor Books, c.1956 by William Barrett.

Suzuki, Shunryu. *Zen Mind, Beginner's Mind, rev. ed.* New York: Weatherhill, Inc., 1999.

Swimme, Brian and Thomas Barry. *The Universe Story: From the Priordial Glaring Forth to the Ecozoic Era — A Aelebration of the Unfolding of the Cosmos*. New York: HarperSanFrancisco (HarperCollins), 1992.

Talbot, Michael. *Beyond the Quantum*. New York: Bantam Books, c.1986 (Bantam edition, 1988).

Tattersall, Ian. *Masters of the Planet: The Search for our Human Origins*. New York: Palgrave Macmillan, 2012.

Taylor, Jill Bolte, Ph.D. *My Stroke of Insight: A Brain Scientist's Personal Journey*. New York: Viking (Penguin Group), 2006.

The New Oxford Annotated Bible, 3rd Edition (NRSV). Oxford: Oxford University press, 2001.

Thurman, Robert A. F. *Essential Tibetan Buddhism*. New York: HarperSanFrancisco (HarperCollins), c. 1995.

Thurman, Robert. *Inner Revolution: Life Liberty, and the Pursuit of Real Happiness*. New York: Riverhead Books (Penguin Putnam, Inc.), 1998.

Tibetan Book of the Dead, The / composed by Padmasambhava; revealed by Terton Karma Lingpa; translated by Gyurme Dorje; edited by Graham Coleman with Thupten Jinpa; introductory commentary by His Holiness the Dalai Lama. New York: Viking (The Penguin Group), 2005.

Tippett, Krista. *Einstein's God: Conversations About Science and the Human Spirit*. New York: Penguin, 2010.

Tolle, Eckhart. *A New Earth: Awakening to Your Life's Purpose*. New York: Plume (Penguin Group), c. 2005.

Twelve Steps: A Way Out. San Diego, CA: Recovery Publications, 1987.

BIBLIOGRAPHY

Ulrich, David. "Broadening the Arc of Devotion: A Conversation with Alan Arkin." *Parabola*, Spring 2012: 14–23.

Underhill, Evelyn. *Mysticism: The Preeminent Study in the Nature and Development of Spiritual Consciousness*. New York: Doubleday, 1990.

Vaccariello, Carol P. "Journey to the Heart of God: A Study of Dreamwork Used in Spiritual Direction (a dissertation submitted to the faculty in cadidacy for the degree of Doctor of Ministry from Ecumenical Theological Seminary)." Detroit, MI, January 1993.

Von Baeyer, Hans Christian. "Quantum Wierdness?: It's All in Your Mind." *Scientific American*, June 2013: 47–51.

Ware, Timothy. *The Orthodox Church, new edition*. London, England UK: Penguin Group, 1997.

Weiner, Jonah. "Prying Eyes." *The New Yorker*, October 22, 2012: 54–61.

Wheatley, Margaret J. *Leadership and the New Science: Discovering Order in a Chaotic World, 3rd ed.* San Francisco, CA: Berret-Koehler Publishers, Inc., 2006.

Wheeler, John Archibald with Kenneth Ford. *Geons, Black Holes & Quantum Foam: A Life in Physics*. New York: W. W. Norton & Company, Inc., 1998.

Whitehead, Alfred North. *Science and the Modern World: Lowell Lectures, 1925*. New York: Mentor Books (The New American Library of World literature, Inc.), 1925 .

Whitney, Joel. "The Garden and the Sword: Joel Whitney Interviews the new U. S. Poet Laureate, W. S. Merwin." *Tricycle*, Winter 2010: 64–71.

Wilber, Ken . . . [et. al.]. *Integral Life Practice: A 21st-Century Blueprint for Physical Health, Emotional Balance, Mental Clarity, and Spiritual Awakening*. Boston, MA: Integral Books (Shambhala), 2008.

Wilber, Ken. *Integral Psychology: Consiousness, Spirit, Psychology, Therapy*. Boston, MA: Shambhala Publications, Inc., 2000.

———. *Sex, Ecology, Spirituality: The Spirit of Evolution, 2nd ed., rev.* Boston, MA: Shambhala Publications, Inc., 2000.

———. *The Essential Ken Wilber: An Introductory Reader*. Boston, MA: Shambhala Publications, Inc., 1998.

———. *The Marriage of Sense and Soul: Integrating Science and Religion*. New York: Random House, 1998.

———. *The Simple Feeling of Being: Embracing Your True Nature*. Boston, MA: Shambhala Publications, 2004.

———. *Up From Eden: A Transpersonal View of Human Evolution*. Garden City, NY: Anchor Press/Doubleday, 1981.

Wilber, Ken, and Jack Engler and Daniel P. Brown. *Transformations of Consciousness: Conventional and Contemplative Perspectives on Development*. Boston: New Science Library, 1986.

Wilber, Ken, ed. *Quantum Questions: Mystical Writings of the World"s Great Physicists*. Boston: Shambala, 1984.

———. *The Holographic Paradigm and Other Paradoxes*. Boulder, CO: Shambhala Publications, Inc., 1982.

Wilczek, Frank and Betsy Devine. *Longing for the Harmonies*. New York: W. W. Norton & Company, c. 1987; Norton paperback ed. 1989.

Wills, Gary. *Saint Augustine*. New York: Viking Penguin, 1999.

———. *What Paul Meant*. New York: Penguin Books, 2006.

BIBLIOGRAPHY

Wilson, Edward O. *The Social Conquest of Earth*. New York: W. W. Norton & company, 2012.

Winnicott, D.W. *Collected Papers: Through Paedistrics to Psycho-Analysis*. New York: Basic Books, Inc., 1958.

Wolf, Fred Alan, Ph.D. *The Spiritual Universe: How Quantum Physics Proves the Existence of the Soul*. New York: Simon & Schuster, 1996.

Wright, Robert. *The Evolution of God*. New York: Back Bay Books/ Little, Brown and Company, 2009.

Yalom, Irvin D. *Love's Executioner and Other Tales of Psychotherapy*. New York: Basic Books, 1989.

Yancey, Philip. *What's So Amazing About Grace?* Grand Rapids, MI: ZondervanPublishingHouse, 1997.

Zaleski, Philip and Carol Zaleski. *Prayer: A History*. Boston, MA: Houghton Mifflin Company, 2005.

Zealand, Anglican Church in Aotearoa New. *New Zealand Prayer Book -Rev ed.: He Karakia Mihinare O Aotearoa*. New York: HarperOne, 1997.

Zukav, Gary. *The Dancing Wu Li Masters: An Overview of the New Physics*. New York: Bantam Books, Inc., c. 1979, Bantam edition 1980.

Index

Abrahamic religions, 47, 149, 151, 156
absence seizure, 83
affection, 95
agape (love), 171
agricultural economies, 43
agriculture, development of, 35
ahimsa (do no harm), 40, 41, 51
Akasha (the cloudless), 170
Alexander, Eben, III, 164–65
Allen, Woody, 7
Allport, Gordon, 50
anatta (no self), 48n6, 156
ancient temples, 35
anicca (impermanence), 48, 48n6
animal sacrifice, 42–44
animal-human relationships, 32
anthropic principle, 131
Aquinas, Thomas, 171
archetypes, 112
Archimedes, 76
Aristotle, 48, 60, 121, 131
Arkin, Alan, 21, 149
Armstrong, Karen, 37, 39, 52, 102, 155
Arnold, Matthew, 3
Aryan migration, 39–40
Aslan, Reza, 174
Atisha (Tibetan teacher), 54
Atman (in Hinduism), 40, 44, 52, 148
atomic scale, 69
atonement, 163
attention, stabilizing, 97
Auden, W. H., 162
Augustine (saint), 23, 61, 62, 104, 128
authority, appeal to, 3–4
autobiographical self, 81, 83–84

automatic thinking, 100
autonomic nervous system, 88
avoid all violence (*himsa*), 40
awareness
  breathing patterns and, 88–89
  mindful, 96
  shifting of, 97–98
  unlimited, 46–51, 58, 77, 79, 156
awesome whys, 16–17
Axial Age
  Christianity, 61
  faith stages, 54–58
  history of, 37–38
  mental representations, 10, 170
  silence discovered in, 103, 118
  spiritual knowing, 8
  unconditional love, 51–54, 58
  unlimited awareness, 46–51
Axiom of Maria, 112

Bainton, Roland, 113
Basho (Old Pond haiku), 180
Baumeister, Roy, 96
Bayes, Thomas, 136
A Beautiful Mind (Nasar), 2
being, states of, 99
beliefs stage, 36
Bell, John Stewart, 126
Bellah, Robert, 20
Bellarmino, Roberto, 62–63
belonging, 95
Berne, Erich, 87
Berrigan, Daniel, 154
The Best Exotic Marigold Hotel (movie),
  14

The Better Angels of Our Nature
  (Pinker), 38
Bhagavad Gita, 37
biblical interpretations, 61–62
Bierce, Ambrose, 8
Big Bang, 24, 67–68, 128–130
biomedical research accuracy, 66
black hole, 67, 123
blinding light and clouds, 114
blood atonement, 163
Bodhisattva, 50–51, 77, 79
body, mediation and, 87–90
body shift, 93
Bohr, Niels, 69, 122, 137
Book of God (theology), 61
book of nature (Augustine doctrine), 61
Book of Nature (science), 61
book of Scripture (Augustine doctrine),
  61
Borg, Marcus, 4, 53, 172, 173
Brahe, Tycho, 121
Brahman (in Hinduism), 40, 52, 108,
  148
Brahmodya (spiritual discourse), 108
brain
  cortex, 84–85, 133
  mammalian, 133
  reptilian, 132–33
brain-mind research
  about, 80–81
  integration, 96–101
  medial prefrontal cortex, 84–85
  self, in function of, 81–84
  . *See also* mediation
breath control (*pranayama*), 108
breathing patterns and awareness,
  88–89
British Columbian Indians, 32
Broglie, Louis de, 10
Brooks, David, 134
Buber, Martin, 12, 15
Buddha and Buddhism
  Bodhi tree realization, 178
  Bodhisattva, 50–51, 77, 79
  compassion, 153–55
  ego attachments, 95
  emptiness, 58
  fire sermon, 160

founder of, 37
fundamentalism, 163
Hinayana Buddhist, 50
love, unconditional, 53–54
Mahayana Buddhism, 48, 49, 50, 148
mantra, 112
Nirvana, 169
presence, 156
Rinzai Zen Buddhism, 11, 159
Sariputra, 108
Soto Zen Buddhism, 87, 103
on teachings, 4
Tibetan Buddhism, 117, 170
on unity of truth, 63
universe beginning, 129
vispassa practice, 86
butterfly effect, 127

Cai Guo-Qiang, 23
calculus, 63, 65, 76, 79
Cantor, Georg, 26, 74–75
carbon nuclear resonance, 131
cardinality, 74–75
Catholic. *See* Roman Catholic
causal faith stage, 57–58, 157
centering prayer, 98
chaos, 66, 127–28, 128n34, 147
"Charter for Compassion" (Armstrong), 155–56
Chartres cathedral (France), 108–9
chastity, vow of, 95
chemistry, dissipative structures in, 132
Christian Century (magazine), 3
Christian Eastern Orthodox tradition,
  117
Christian tradition
  image of God, 147
  incarnation of love, 153
  kingdom of God, 171–77
  moving through death, 170–71
  mysterion, 110
  sacramentals, 110
  sense modalities, 117
  spiritual knowing, 149
  spiritual practices, 171
  Trinitarian tradition, 149, 157
  . *See also* Jesus Christ
Christianity, 47, 61

chronic illness, 90

chronos (chronology), 175

cimenti (trial by ordeal), 63

Cioran, E. M., 7

city-states, formation of, 35

civilization, early, 34–37

Clement of Alexandria, 61

climate changes, 140–42

The Cloud of Unknowing (14th-century mystic), 114–15

the cloudless (*Akasha*), 170

clouds and blinding light, 114

collective interference pattern, 135

collective knowing, 34–37

community, market capitalism and, 72–73

community authorization, 26–28

compassion, 52–53, 153–56

complexity theory, 66

Confucius, 37, 52

conjunctive faith stage, 56, 166

consciousness, 82–83, 84

a consuming fire (*mysterium tremem-dum*), 169

continuing cycle of self-correction, 17–18

control, 95

conventional beliefs and moral reasoning stage, 36

conviviality, 7

Copenhagen interpretation, 135, 137

core self, 81, 82–83

correspondence principle, 122–23

cosmic consciousness, 145

cosmic microwave background, 129–130, 131

cosmological constant, 68

cosmological scale, 67

cosmology
  about, 119–121
  challenges, 139–142
  evolution, 128–137
  fields, 124–28
  human life, evolution of, 130–33
  humans shape evolution, 133–37
  large versus small, 121–24
  mathematics, 137–39
  scientific, 9

Council of Trent, 62–63

counting, 137–38

creativity, 21–22, 149–150

Cree language, 32–33

Crossan, John Dominic, 172, 173

Csikszentmihalyi, Mihaly, 21–22, 150

Cultural memes, 134

Cuvier, Georges, 139–140

Cymbeline (Shakespeare), 3–4

Dabar (in Hebrew religion), 117

Dalai Lama, 63

Damasio, Antonio, 82

dark energy, 68

David in Florence statue, 115–16

Davies, Paul, 130, 135–36

Davies, Robertson, 24–25

death, 99, 160–61, 169–170

death experience, 164–66

declining violence phase in history, 38–41

Deptford Trilogy, *Manticore* (Davies), 24–25

desert fathers, 104

Deutsch, David, 3, 18–19, 74, 75, 143

The Devil's Dictionary (Bierce), 8

Dharma (in Buddhism), 50

diagonal method paring, 75

Diamond, Jared, 2, 33, 73

Diamond Sutra, 48n6, 50, 51n13, 86, 148

A Different Voice (Gilligan), 56

Dillard, Annie, 22, 150

discovery, 25

DNA, 19, 63, 69, 134, 139

do no harm (*ahimsa*), 40, 41, 51

Dogen translation, *Genjo Koan*, 119

double-slit quantum experiment, 135, 150

dreams, 115

Durning, Alan, 73

Dutch Roman Catholic, 110

early civilization, 34–37

Easter vigil service, 177

Eastern religions, 47

Eckhart, Meister, 171

ecosystem, 73–74

INDEX

Eddington, Sir Arthur, 145, 146
ego, transcending, 94–95
Ehrenreich, Barbara, 167–69
eight negations, famous, 50n11
Einstein, Albert
  cosmological constant, 68
  on field concept, 125n28
  general theory of relativity, 23, 128
  kingdom of God, 176
  on particles, 70
  on reality, 28n41, 49
  space-time continuum, 23, 128
  universe fractal, 176
Einstein's theory, 67–68
El Shaddai (mountain god), 46–47
Elizabeth (queen of England), 36
emotions, 83, 96
empathy, 7
emptiness, 58
energy sustainability, 71–72
environmental issues, 140–42
Episcopal Church, 4
epistemology, 27
equilibrium and equanimity, 88, 157
Euclidean geometry, 61, 138
eukaryotic cells, 42, 131
evolution
  how humans shape evolution,
    133–37
  of human life, 130–33
  predator-prey relationships, 42
  of the universe, 128–137
exclusion principle, 112
explanations
  individual discovery, 25
  scientific, 17–19
extended consciousness, 84
extinction periods, 72, 140, 142

FACES (flexible, adaptable, coherent,
    energized, and stable), 96
faith knowing, 61
faith stages, 54–58
fallibilism, 18, 75, 79
famous eight negations, 50n11
fat tail, chaotic systems, 127
feelings, 83
fermions, 122, 122n

Ferrer, Jorge, 20, 147
Feynman, Richard, 27, 71, 125, 158–59
Fibonacci (Italian mathematician),
    59–60
fidelity, 95
fiduciary relationship of knowing, 7, 8
fields, of universe, 124–28, 124n24
fire sermon, Buddha, 160
Five Points, of fundamentalism, 163
"The Flight of the Garuda" (Rangdrol),
    30
flow, as a state, 21–22
focusing, 92, 93
"For the Time Being" (Auden), 162
forest ecosystems, 74
four forces of the universe, 124
four noble truths, 50, 161
four truths of the human condition, 37
Fowler, James, 36, 54–55, 93, 162–63
fractals
  of creating, 149–150
  defined, 9
  of loving, 151–56
  of presence, 156–57
  of wholeness, 146–49
freedom, 171
Freud, Sigmund, 145
Fritz, Robert, 22, 150
Fuchs, Christopher A., 137
Fundamentalism, 162–63

Galileo, 62–63, 121
Gendlin, Eugene, 92
Genjo Koan (Dogen), 119
geometric proportions (*tetraktys*), 60
geometry, 61, 138
Gilligan, Carol, 56–57
global aphasia, 83
gluons, defined, 70
gnostike stage, of spiritual practice, 171
Gobekli Tepe ruins (Turkey), 34–35
gods
  mental representations, 46–47
  names for, 35–36, 47
Goedel, Kurt, 28n41, 63, 64, 94
Goland, Carol, 13
golden proportion, 59–60
Golden Rule, 52, 58, 77, 155

Gopnik, Adam, 50–51, 77–78
Gore, Al, 140
gravitational collapse, 67, 123
gravity, forces of the universe and, 124
Great Mother, of goddess religions, 43
Guth, Alan, 68

Hansen, James, 141
Hartle, James, 128–29
Harvey, William, 69
Hawking, Stephen, 128–29
Hazen, Bob, 131n44
hearing sense, 117
Heart Sutra mantra, 49, 87
Hebrew prophets, 37
heilsgeschichte (salvation history), 177
Heisenberg, Werner, 69, 124, 146
Henry IV (Shakespeare), 41
Hicks, Edward, 173
hierarchy problem, 70
Higgs boson or field, 70, 76, 122, 125
Hillel (Jewish rabbi), 52
himsa (avoid all violence), 40
Hinayana Buddhist, 50
Hinduism, 37, 40, 47–48, 93, 94, 108,
   163
   . *See also* Atman; Brahman
hippocampus, 98
Holt, Jim, 7, 8
homeostasis, 82
honor, 41
Hopkins, Gerald Manley, 179
Hsuan-tsang (Chinese monk), 49
human condition, four truths of, 37
human fractals, 147
human life, evolution of, 130–33
human scale, 67
humans
   animal-human relationships, 32
   causing origins of life, 131n44
   four truths of the condition of, 37
   nature-human relationships, 32
   shaping evolution, 133–37
hunter-gatherers, 42
hunter-gathering knowing, 32–34
hypostatization, 50n11

I and Thou (Buber), 12

Ice Age cave art in Europe, 30–31
icons, 117–18
identity, self-transformation, 93–96
illness, chronic, 90
imaging, 117
impermanence (*anicca*), 48, 48n6
improvisation, 21
Incompleteness Theorem (Goedel),
   64, 94
individual discovery, 25
individual-reflective faith stage, 56,
   164–66
infinite reach, 74–79, 160
information flow, 134
insight, 25, 93
instrumentalism, 28
integration, 96–101
intelligent design, 164
interconnectedness, 99
intuitive-projective faith stage, 55, 162
Islam, 38, 47, 149, 163
I-Thou, I-It (relationship/transactions),
   11–17, 44–45, 178

James, William, 38, 144–45
Jaspers, Karl, 37
Jesus Christ
   birth of, 37
   death of, 161
   divine/human nature, 146
   as incarnation of love, 153
   kingdom of God, 171–76
   resurrection, 146
   as sacrifice, 44
   transfiguration, 113–14
   unconditional love, 52–54, 58, 77,
   151, 178
   . *See also* Christian tradition
Job (biblical figure), 22–23, 150
John of the Cross, 171
Judaism, 37, 47, 117
Judeo-Christian tradition, 147
Jung, Carl, 112
justice orientation, 57

kairos (time), 175
Kant, Immanuel, 49

Keating, Thomas, 94–95, 102, 102n1, 157
Keeney, Bradford, 126
Kidd, Sue Monk, 152
kinesthetic sense, 117
King, Martin Luther, Jr., 56, 175
kingdom of God
    explanation, 171–76
    signs of, 176–77
Knocking on Heaven's Door (Randall), 75
knot theory, 63, 139
knowing
    fiduciary relationship of, 7, 8
    process of, 6–7
    scientific (*See* scientific knowing)
    spiritual (*See* spiritual knowing)
    subsidiary dimension of, 6–7
    tacit dimension of knowing, 6
Kohlberg, Lawrence, 55
Kolbert, Elizabeth, 140
Kornfield, Jack, 166–67
Kuhn, Thomas, 26

labyrinth at Chartres, 109
language, 24, 31, 32–33, 83, 102n1
Lao Tzu, 37, 178
LaPlace, Pierre-Simon, 64, 136–37
Large Hadron Collider, 70, 75–76
large versus small, in universe, 121–24
laves (mathematical waves), 124
learned behavior of plants, 31n4
left-out science, 164
Leibniz, Gottfried Wilhelm von, 7–8, 63, 76
leptons, 122n
Leslie, John, 8
Levine, Peter, 87
liar's paradox, 64, 94
liberation (*Satori*), 93
life, human-caused origins of, 131n44
    . *See also* evolution
light, 114, 130n40, 135–36, 146
Lion's Seat, 86
literalism, 162
Livio, Mario, 138, 139
Long Peace, 39
long tail, chaotic systems, 127

Lopez, Steve, 178
Lorenz, Edward, 126–27
love
    agape, 171
    Jesus as incarnation of, 153
    unconditional, 51–54, 58, 77, 79, 172
Love's Executioner and Other Tales of Psychotherapy (Yalom), 37

Mahayana Buddhism, 48, 49, 50, 148
Malpighi, Marcello, 69
mammalian brain, 133
Manticore (Davies), 24–25
market capitalism, 72–73
materialism, 4
mathematics
    calculus, 63, 65, 76, 79
    cardinality, 74–75
    counting, 137–38
    diagonal method paring, 75
    fractals as, 147–48
    geometry, 61, 138
    golden proportion, 59–60
    Incompleteness Theorem, 64, 94
    laves, 124
    reality and, 137–39
    uncertainty principle, 69, 124
    Vienna Circle, 64
Maxwell, James Clark, 125
"me," "you," and "we" maps, 99
Mead, Margaret, 1
medial prefrontal cortex, 84–85
mediation
    awareness shifting, 97–98
    body and, 87–90
    brain functioning during, 85
    experiencing, 90–92
    metta, 99
    mindfulness, 81, 98, 100–101
    personal experience, 152
    personal growth methods, 92–93
    tonglen, 99, 153
    Vipassana, 81, 85–86, 91, 92
    Zen, 11, 87, 93, 103, 159
    . *See also* brain-mind research
membership self, 35
memories, 84, 98

mental representations, 2–3, 10, 31, 46–48, 157

mercy, 151

Merton, Thomas, 77, 160

metta mediation, 99

Michelangelo, 20, 115–16

Miller, Malcolm, 109

mimosa plants, 31n4

mindful awareness, 96

mindfulness meditation. *See* mediation

Missouri Lutheran Synod, 27

Mitchell, Stephen, 104

Moitessier, Bernard, 105–6

monastic communities, 106

monotheism, 47

moral reasoning stage, 36

mountain god (El Shaddai), 46–47

Mulville, Frank, 106

Muslims. *See* Islam

My Stroke of Insight (Taylor), 97

mysterion, 110

mysterion-sacramentum, 110–11

mysterium trememdum (a consuming fire), 169

mystery

    death, 160–61

    faith stages, 161–171

    infinite reach, 74–79, 160

    kingdom of God, 171–76

    not knowing, 158–160

    signs of the kingdom, 176–77

    spiritual knowing and, 179–180

    unconditional love, 172

    voice, finding our, 178–79

mythic-literal faith stage, 55–56, 162

Nagarjuna, 46, 50n11

Nash, John, 2

nature-human relationships, 32

New Zealand Book of Common Prayer, 173

Newton, Sir Isaac, 26, 62, 67, 76, 126, 139

Newton's laws, 65

Niagara Bible conference (1877), 163

Nicea, Second Council, 117

"Nickel and Dimed" (Ehrenreich), 167

Nirvana, 169

no self (*anatta*), 48n6, 156

noble truths, 50, 161

non-dual contingent nature, 48n6

non-violence, 40, 41, 51

obedience, vow of, 95

observation, 25

observer-participancy, 136, 144, 145, 147, 150

Old Pond haiku (Basho), 180

Oliver, Mary, 111

One (movie), 157

ontology, 27

optimal experience, 21–22

optimistic philosophies, 7–8

Orthodox theology, 110, 117, 118

Otto, Rudolph, 169

pain, 90

    . *See also* suffering

Papua New Guinea culture, 33

paradigm shifts, 26

parasympathetic nervous system, 88

particles, 70, 123–24

passionlessness, 171

Pauli, Wolfgang, 112

Penrose, Sir Roger, 138

Permian extension period, 140

personal growth methods, 92–93

personal industry, 95

personal knowledge, 7

personal spiritual attainment, 95

pessimistic philosophies, 7–8

pet bots, 14–15

phenomena, I-It transactions and, 13

philosophy, defined, 8

Piaget, Jean, 54

Pinker, Steven, 38–41

Planck length, 129

plants, 31, 31n4

Plato, 37, 60, 138

play, emergence of, 20–21

"Please Call Me by True Names" (poem), 154–55

Polanyi, Michael, 6–7, 45

Polkinghorne, John, 146

Pollock, Jackson, 148

Polynesian language, 33

Ponticus, Evagrius, 171
population growth, 71
Porter, Bill, 48n6
postdiction, 128
poverty, vow of, 95
The Power of Now (Tolle), 166
practice, dimensions of
about, 102
ritual, 108–11
silence, 103–8
vision, 112–18
praktike stage, of spiritual practice, 171
pranayama (breath control), 108
prayer
centering, 98
pure prayer, 171
silent, 103–4
undistracted prayer, 171
predator prey relationships, 42
prefrontal cortex, medial, 84–85
presence, 156–57
pre-trans fallacy, 58
Prigogine, Ilya, 132, 137
Proof of Heaven: A Neurosurgeon's Journey into the Afterlife (Alexander), 166
proprioceptive sensors, 117
Protestant Reformation, 5
Protestants Christian tradition, 110, 162–63
protons, 130n40, 135–36
proto-self, 81–82
psychic faith stage, 57
pure prayer, 171
Puritan tradition, 95
Pythagoras, 60

Quakers, 110
qualia, 20
Quantum Bayesianism, 137
quantum foam, 123
Qur'an, 38

Rahner, Karl, 18
Ramana Maharshi, 94
Randall, Lisa, 15, 67, 75
Rangdrol, Tsogdruk, 30
Rasmussen, Larry, 73

realism, 28, 28n41
Red Pine (Porter), 48n6
relationships
fiduciary, 7, 8
I-Thou, I-It, 11–17, 44–45, 178
spiritual knowing, 20–25
religion
defined, 102
science and, 145–46
. *See also specific faith traditions by name*
religions councils
Council of Trent, 62–63
Second Council of Nicaea, 117
Seventh Ecumenical Council, 117
religious symbols, 24
renewable energy, 71
reptilian brain, 132–33
responsibility orientation, 57
revealed theology, 4
Richard II (Shakespeare), 36–37
Rig Veda mantra, 40
Rinzai Zen Buddhism, 11, 159
rituals, 108–11, 118, 171
Rohr, Richard, 55
Roman Catholic, 18, 95, 110, 117
Russell, Bertrand, 120, 139

Sachdev, Subir, 5
sacramentals, 110
sacraments, 110
sacrifice, 42–44
St. John of the Cross, 102n1
St. Peter's, Vatican, 177
salvation history (*heilsgeschichte*), 177
Samaritans, 151
Satori (liberation), 93
scalar fields, 125
Schiffmann, Erich, 90
Schillebeeckx, Eduard, 110
Schopenhauer, Arthur, 7
Schrödinger, Erwin, 10, 134
Schutz, William, 95
science and religion, 145–46
Science and the Modern World (Whitehead), 1
scientific cosmology, 9
scientific experiments, 63

scientific knowing
  about, 3, 17
  community authorization, 26–28
  discovery, 25
  explanation, 17–19
  history overview, 59–66
  infinite reach, 74–79
  scale of, 67–71
  tradition, 26
  unintended consequences, 71–74, 79
scientific measurements, 63
scripture interpretations, 61–62
sculptor metaphor, 116
Second Council of Nicaea, 117
The Secret (book and DVD), 162
Sedona (second method), 93
seizures, 83
self
  anatta (no self), 48n6, 156
  autobiographical, 81, 83–84
  brain-mind functioning in, 81–84
  core self, 81, 82–83
  definitions (1680, and 1870), 95–96
  membership self, 35
  perception of, 50
  proto-self, 81–82
  reflection on, 57–58
self-correction, continuing cycle of,
  17–18
self-inquiry, 94
self-portrait, 32
self-transformation, 93–96
sensory data, 100, 105
sensory experience, 49
Seventh Ecumenical Council (787),
  117
Shakespeare, William, 3–4, 36, 41, 59
Shamans, 42
Shunryu Suzuki Roshi, 103
Siegel, Daniel, 81, 96, 97, 99–100
silence, 102n1, 103–8
silence of your presence, 17
Simpson, Joe, 107
The Sixth Extinction (Kolbert), 140
Sixth Great Extinction period, 142
small versus large, in universe, 121–24
Smith, Huston, 24
Socrates, 37, 178

The Soloist (Lopez), 178–79
Soto Zen Buddhism, 87, 103
spiritual discourse (*Brahmodya*), 108
spiritual knowing
  about, 3, 17
  Axial Age, 37–38
  Buddhism experience, 11
  collective knowing, 34–37
  community authorization, 26–28
  declining violence phase, 38–41
  discovery, 25
  history overview, 30–32
  hunter-gathering knowing, 32–34
  mystery and, 179–180
  personal knowledge, 7
  relationship, 20–25
  tradition, 26
  transforming sacrifice, 42–44
spiritual practice
  gnostike stage, 171
  praktike stage, 171
  . *See also* rituals
stabilizing attention, 97
stage of conventional beliefs and conventional moral reasoning, 36
Standard Model of subatomic particles,
  121–22
states of being, 99
Stein, Gertrude, 22
Stevens, Wallace, 179
stillness, 90
Strand, Mark, 34
strange attractor, 127
string theory, 123
sub-atomic scale, 69–70
sub-galactic scale, 67
subsidiaries, dimension of knowing,
  6–7
substitutionary blood atonement, 163
subtle faith stage, 57
suffering, 90, 161, 166
Sunya (emptiness), 48, 48n6, 156
superposition, 134–35
sutras, 86
sympathetic nervous system, 88
synthetic-conventional faith stage, 56,
  163–64

INDEX

tacit dimension of knowing, 6
Tatsioni, Athina, 66
Tattersall, Ian, 2, 30
Taylor, G. I., 135
Taylor, Jill Bolte, 80, 80n1, 97–98
technical language, 24
technology, I-Thou, I-It and, 14–15
The Tempest (Shakespeare), 59
temples, ancient, 35
Tertullian, 110
Testament Sutra, 86
tetraktys (geometric proportions), 60
theologian, prayer and, 171
theories, scientific, 18
theory of everything (T.O.E.), 124
Thich Nhat Hahn, 154–55
thinking, automatic, 100
thought experiment, 134–35
Tibetan Buddhism, 117, 170
Tierra del Fuego Indians, 6–7
Tiglath-Pileser II (Assyria), 35, 60
Tillich, Paul, 159
time (*kairos*), 175
time, kingdom of God and, 174–75
T.O.E. (theory of everything), 124
Tolle, Eckhart, 166
tonglen mediation, 99, 153
touch sense, 117
tradition, 26
transactional analysis, 87
transcending ego, 94–95
transfiguration, 113–14
transforming sacrifice, 42–44
trial by ordeal (*cimenti*), 63
tribal culture, 36
Trinity, in Christian tradition, 149, 157
Trois Frères, France (human self-
    portraits), 32
truth, unity of, 61–63
Twain, Mark, 27, 139

uncertainty principle, 69, 124
unconditional love, 51–54, 58, 77, 79,
    151, 172, 178
undifferentiated faith stage, 55
undistracted prayer, 171
unintended consequences, 71–74, 79
universal explanations, 6

universalizing faith stage, 56
universe
    beginning of, 129
    evolution of, 128–137
    expansion of, 68
    fields, 124–28, 125n24
    four forces of, 124
    fractals of creating, 149–150
    fractals of loving, 151–56
    fractals of wholeness, 146–49
    large versus small, 121–24
    spiritual knowing in, 144–46
    symmetry, 129
unlimited awareness, 46–51, 58, 77,
    79, 156
    . *See also* faith stages

values, 96
Varieties of Religious Experience
    (James), 144
"The Vast Ocean Begins Just Outside
    Our Church: The Eucharist" (Oli-
    ver), 110–11
Vienna Circle of mathematicians, 63,
    64
violence, 38–41
Vipassana mediation, 81, 85–86, 91, 92
vision, 112–18
vision-logic faith stage, 57
visions and visioning, 115–18
voice, finding our, 178–79
Voltaire, 7–8
vows, of poverty, chastity, and obedi-
    ence, 95

wars, 38–40
we maps, 99
Weber, George, 15–16
Weber, Julie, 15, 17
Weinberg, Steven, 27
Wheatley, Margaret J., 137
Wheeler, John Archibald, 123, 135,
    136, 144, 150
Whitehead, Alfred North, 1, 4
Whitman, Marcus, 5
"why" questions, 16–17
Wigner, Eugene, 138

INDEX

Wilber, Ken, 35, 55, 57–58, 93, 146, 148, 157, 169
Wilczek, Frank, 121
Wilder, Thornton, 134
Wilson, E. O., 25, 132, 142
Wink, Walter, 173
Winnicott, D. W., 105, 152
Wisconsin Lutheran Synod, 27
The Wise Heart (Kornfield), 166–67

Wittgenstein, Ludwig, 10
The Writing Life (Dillard), 22

Yalom, Irvin D., 37
Yates, Simon, 107

Zen Buddhism, 11, 87, 93, 103, 159
Zoroaster (philosopher), 37

Made in the USA
Coppell, TX
17 November 2022

86582716R00125